S0-BDJ-850

The Fellowship of the No Longer Miserable

Bob Halloran

To Einar Gustafson and Dr. Sidney Farber.
The story begins with the two of you.

Also by Bob Halloran

Irish Thunder: The Hard Life and Times of Micky Ward

Breakdown: A Season of Gang Warfare, High School Football
and the Coach who Policed the Streets.

CONTENTS

PREFACE

First, let me say, "Thank you," for buying this book and thereby donating to the Jimmy Fund. You've done something good, and I hope you'll be rewarded with an entertaining and emotional read.

I thought you might be interested in the story behind the story. How did this book, an admittedly and proudly unique creation, come to be? Well, that story begins with my brother-in-law, Fred Safreed.

It was Fred's idea to write a book featuring sports talk radio. His thought was to create callers like "Ben from Franklin", "Abe from Lincoln", and "Isaac from Newton". Since those names make obvious references to real historical figures, it would be fun, Fred thought, to have Abe talk about honesty, or Isaac focus on the gravity of a situation, or to have Ben tell the show hosts to go fly a kite.

I liked the idea of writing a book that would be predominantly dialogue. In its infancy, I thought of it as the world's longest screenplay, and in essence, that's what it grew up to be.

It took some time to figure out what topic to write about, but once I settled on the best twelve months in Boston sports history, it was fun and relatively easy. All I did was sit down and argue with myself. I took both sides of issues like: Is Tom Brady better than Joe Montana, and was the Nomar Garciaparra trade why the Red Sox won the World Series? And then I wrote discussions and debates for fictional characters.

I selected the title of the book as a direct response to former Celtic coach Rick Pitino's complaint that the Boston sports talk radio culture is "the fellowship of the miserable". And in its original creation, the book was simply one sports talk show after another. It clearly needed a more developed story. My wife, Eileen Curran, suggested I add a narrative about an old man listening to the radio shows, and praying he could see the Red Sox win the World Series before he died. I turned the old man into a young boy with leukemia. I gave the boy the name "Jimmy" to represent the Jimmy Fund, and named the radio station WTED, or "The Ted" as a tip of the cap to Ted Williams. Jimmy not only listened to "The Ted", he became a regular caller. And while Jimmy celebrated the championships of the Patriots, Red Sox and Patriots again, he also battled cancer and the complications of a bone marrow transplant.

However, the few publishers I sent the book to really didn't know what to make of it. It is, after all, part fact and part fiction, part novel and part screenplay. I know it's different, but that's one of the reasons I like it so much.

The book sat in my computer for a few years, and it didn't appear likely that it would ever make it out, until I got a call from some guy in Vermont.

"My name is Alan Rubel," he began. "And I really don't know why I'm calling you. I just felt a strong need to reach out to you for some reason."

That's about the time I would normally have tried to find a polite way to hang up, but there was kindness, not craziness, in Alan's voice. So, we talked for a few minutes. I learned that Alan had read my book, Irish Thunder, about Lowell boxer Micky Ward, and that he had also written a boxing book called Gloves. But we weren't being brought together by our appreciation for boxing.

As the conversation continued, I also learned that someone close to Alan was involved in a fight with cancer, and that Alan owns a franchise of Proforma, a large national printing company. Now, the pieces were fitting together. I told Alan about The Fellowship of the No Longer Miserable, and suggested that perhaps the reason he called me was so we could print the book and raise money for cancer research. Ultimately, we chose to focus on the Jimmy Fund. It made sense given the subject matter of the book. Plus, we'd get to help kids.

You've also helped. So again, "Thank you". And enjoy!

CHAPTER ONE
All Is Not Well

It had been like this for going on two years now. Every day a new goal. Sometimes he just wanted to get out of bed. Other days he wanted to play catch for hours, because he knew it might be several days or weeks before he could play catch for hours again. On the good days, he felt like every other 14-year-old boy who never had occasion to visit the Dana Farber Cancer Institute. Those are the days he wondered what his life would be like if his parents had never marched him down to school to "find out what in the world is going on down there", only to be met by aa principal and a handful of teachers who were wondering what in the world was happening at home. It all began when Jimmy had been changing for gym class when another student noticed a large, purple bruise on his back. Kids started whispering and pointing until finally the gym teacher walked in and noticed the cause of the commotion. More bruises were noticed, one on Jimmy's calf, and another on his left triceps. A phone call was made. Accusations flew. And a meeting was scheduled.

Jimmy, of course, was well aware of the bruises. They did, after all, hurt. But since he had no real idea where they came from, he decided not to tell his parents. They'd want the story, the whole story, and Jimmy didn't have one to tell. That wouldn't go over well, and he knew he'd end up looking like he was keeping something from them. So, he just decided to keep the bruises from them instead.

The school administrators were suspicious that the bruises were in areas that are not generally visible, as if an abuser had intentionally selected easily concealable locations. They had also noticed a change in Jimmy's overall demeanor. The generally affable student had become more withdrawn. They were unaware of any issues at school, so they turned their attentions to his home.

Meanwhile, Jimmy's parents were concerned that their son was being picked on at school, and they were angry that school officials were accusing them, instead of looking toward other students.

On the day of the meeting, Jimmy just sat there trying to explain to both camps that all he could remember was that after he leaned back in a wooden chair, balancing it on two legs as he so often did, his back hurt. The next morning his back was still sore, but he didn't notice the bruise for another two days.

"How could you not notice it," they asked.

"I don't know," Jimmy responded. "How often do you look at your back?"

Jimmy's parents and school officials did agree on one thing. Normal people don't get bruises that look like Jimmy's from merely leaning against the back of a chair, or bumping into things. That's when Jimmy began to think that he probably wasn't a normal kid.

Nothing was settled that day in the principal's office, but it wasn't long after that Jimmy Macomber developed a fever high enough, and that lasted long enough it required a trip to the doctor. Jimmy's penchant for bruising was discussed along with an uncharacteristic lethargy that his parents attributed to a sudden onset of laziness. But Jimmy had never been disposed to idleness. He was, in fact, energetic to the point of being hyper, and conscientious to the point of being indefatigable. Jimmy had always seemed to be in a hurry, as if he had much to do and a short time to get it done. He couldn't stand for standing still. He had a rare enthusiasm for school, and an unbridled passion for sports, especially baseball. He took pride in doing things well, and even greater pride in doing things better the next time. He wanted to prove he could improve. He was always trying to get better, and that was certainly the goal now.

But his parents, unaware of any other explanation, finally surrendered to the notion that their highly ambitious son, had transformed into a normal, apathetic 12-year-old. They couldn't deny their previously high-powered, kinetic child had gradually become indolent. They watched helplessly as the boy who had made countless "to do" lists now appeared listless. It saddened them, but they assumed it was a phase Jimmy was going through and believed the enterprising son they knew and loved would re-emerge someday soon. But the phase Jimmy was going through had a name. It's called acute lymphoblastic leukemia, or ALL. Soon it would become all the Macombers thought about.

It happened so quickly. A bruise, a fever, some concerned looks from medical personnel and finally a bone marrow biopsy. Jimmy went from being a healthy 12-year-old to a cancer patient seemingly overnight. It was like an unstoppable tidal wave of emotions, information, and change.

"You might have cancer, Jimmy."

"This is what we need to do."

"Once we have the results of the biopsy, we'll know what we're dealing with."

The words echoed and faded, but never resonated in the minds of the Macombers. They were in shock throughout most of the process. First, Jimmy had a CBC, a complete blood count, done in his pediatrician's office. After those results were sent to DFCI, Jimmy was admitted to the hospital for a bone marrow aspirate. He was put to sleep before a needle was injected into the back of his hipbone and a small sample of bone marrow was drawn into a syringe. Jimmy felt nothing. Later that day, the Macombers learned they were officially a cancer family.

Jimmy had always known more about batting averages, ERA's and OPS's than most boys and even most adults, but now he knew more than he ever wanted to know about leukocytes, erythrocytes and thrombocytes.

He had dealt with his share of hematologists, oncologists and pathologists. He had spent forty-one days at Children's Hospital in Boston undergoing intensive chemotherapy, losing his hair, throwing up regularly, recovering from infections, and then celebrating the fact that he only had to go in for treatment once a week instead of every day. And he remembered the frightened look on his mother's face as the doctor explained what ALL is and how new treatments "really seemed to be working". Even his dad cried inconsolably that day.

But the Macombers were a determined lot. Jimmy's doggedness returned, and despite some setbacks, the family received more good news than bad. After all, it had been two years since the original diagnosis and Jimmy was still here. Plus, the New England Patriots were in the Super Bowl for the second time in three years!

That's why today's goal was to feel well enough to attend the small Super Bowl party downstairs. It was already past noon when Jimmy started to stir. He had slept well, thanks in no small part to the antibiotics he was taking to fight the latest infection that had chosen to mercilessly attack his insides. This latest infection had required a short hospital stay, but Jimmy was determined to make it back home in time for the big game, and for once his body didn't let him down.

Jimmy rose from bed carefully. His bones had betrayed him enough times to make him a bit defensive as a new day began. He felt his stomach, noting only a hint of nausea. That was a good sign. Maybe he could have a hot dog or some chips today after all.

He made his way to the bathroom, passing his older brother's room along the way. Mark had been up for hours. It was February of his senior year, and he still hadn't decided where to go to college. Jimmy knew Mark's current state of ambiguity was not due to ambivalence or a lack of aptitude. Mark was an excellent student with the kind of grades and SAT scores that would get him into just about any school he wanted to attend. But Mark wanted two conflicting things. He wanted to be near home, and he wanted to get as far away from home as possible. The family was close, brought closer by Jimmy's health problems, and the Boston area had a lot of quality schools from which to choose. But Mark wasn't sheepish about admitting that he occasionally wanted to get away from Jimmy and the persistent stress related to Jimmy's leukemia. The two brothers had had a conversation about it around Christmas time.

"Have you decided where you're going to school yet?" Jimmy had asked.

"No."

"What's the hold up?"

"You, if you want to know the truth."

"Me? What do I have to do with anything?"

"Oh shut up! Are you kidding me? You have everything to do with everything. We don't make a move around here without first consulting that huge calendar in the kitchen. Jimmy's trips to the doctor. Jimmy's radiation schedule. Jimmy's chemo schedule. Jimmy's post chemo schedule. Now, it's Jimmy's BMT. Everything revolves around you!"

"I always knew it bothered you. I just had no idea how much."

"It doesn't bother me that much – usually. But now I've got this huge decision to make, one that's going to affect my whole life, and I can't make it without thinking about that damn calendar. It's just not fair."

"Tell me about it."

"I'll tell you about it all right. I'll tell you that I'd really like to go to the University of Cincinnati, or Texas A&M, or Cal Poly. Outside of Harvard and Cornell, they're like the best architectural schools in the country. But do you think Mom and Dad want to worry about me being so far away on top of always worrying about you. They've already aged about twenty years in the last two."

"Have you said anything to them about this?"

"No. I just tell them I can't make up my mind, but that I'm leaning toward MIT. That almost makes them happy. MIT's got a great architectural program, too. And I might have even chosen it already, but I really wanted to pick somewhere to go without giving any thought to anyone but myself. I know that sounds selfish, but it's just the way I feel sometimes."

"Well, as someone who's going to be getting some of your bone marrow in the next couple of months, I don't think you're selfish at all. And I'd love it if you stayed around here, but of course, I'm only saying that for selfish reasons."

"I'd definitely miss you guys if I were in some place like San Luis Obispo. We'll see. That's all I'm saying for now. We'll see. All right?"

Jimmy recalled that conversation as he walked past Mark's room. He noticed an envelope on Mark's dresser. It was addressed to MIT.

"Wonder what that's all about," he said out loud to himself.

In the bathroom, Jimmy picked up his comb and smiled. Bed head was wonderful now that his hair had grown back. He hadn't cried when he learned he had cancer. He merely whimpered during the chemotherapy treatments that gave him painful mouth sores and crazy diarrhea. But he wept openly each day that large clumps of hair fell out. He cried when he looked in the mirror and saw only a random pattern of small tufts of hair. And he sobbed and moaned for hours the first time he ran his hand over his completely bald head. Vanity, to be sure, was one reason for the tears, but more than that, the baldness symbolized better than anything else what he was going through. It was a constant reminder that Jimmy had cancer.

He knew he'd be bald again soon, but for now, he matted his scraggly brown hair down with some water and decided he really didn't need the comb after all. He brushed his teeth slowly, gently. His continuous rounds of chemotherapy had made his mouth sensitive. His gums bled with little provocation. Jimmy didn't mind so much except that blood in his mouth made him want to brush his teeth, and that's where the vicious cycle began. So he'd decided long ago to take all the time he needed for brushing and flossing.

Once downstairs, he discovered the family was already fully immersed in preparing food items for the Super Bowl party.

"Good morning," his mother said as she arranged the cheese and cracker tray with a bunch of purple grapes in the center.

"Good afternoon is more like it," his father chided. "Glad you could make it down in time to help out."

"How are you feeling?" his mother asked.

"Great," Jimmy responded, and it was essentially the truth. "I'm excited about the game."

"Well, you can start with the six-hour pre-game show, or you can grab some silverware and set the table," Mark said as he bounded into the kitchen and dipped a large tortilla chip into the salsa.

"Or maybe you'd rather we turned on WTED, and you could listen to what those guys are saying about the big game," his father offered.

"No thanks. I like to listen to them after things happen. That's when they really go crazy."

"I think you listen to that radio station way too much," Jimmy's mother complained. "They can be awfully fresh, and I'm not sure it's something that a young boy should be exposed to. If it were television, some of their conversations wouldn't be allowed on the air until after ten o'clock. So, why are they allowed to bring barroom banter into the homes and cars of families all day long?"

"That's why they have those knobs on the radio that let you change the station, Mom," Mark said.

"Jimmy knows there have been plenty of times I've done exactly that while we've been driving around in the car. And I'll do it again whenever the language or the topic becomes unsuitable for children."

Then Eileen Macomber turned to her husband and whispered, "I know I'd forbid him to listen to it if he were healthy, but I just can't say no when it makes him so happy."

Glenn Macomber kissed his wife affectionately on the forehead, stared into her eyes for a moment, and then planted a long, wet kiss on her lips while the two boys moaned in the background and scurried out of the kitchen.

The Patriots' Adam Vinatieri kicked the ball off at precisely 6:21. Rod Smart of the Carolina Panthers returned the ball to the 23-yard-line before he was swarmed by a sea of blue jerseys. Jimmy leaped, albeit cautiously, and yelled, "Here we go!"

This was a good day for him. For the previous six hours he had helped with a few chores, tuned into some of the pre-game coverage, and even ventured outside into the cold air for a few moments to throw the football around with Mark. Now, they were ready for some football!

The first half was dominated by the Patriots defense. The first six times the Panthers had the ball they only gained a total of 27 yards, and mustered just one first down, and that was awarded on a Patriot penalty. But the Patriots didn't fare much better. Despite Tom Brady beginning the game with just 45 yards on his first 13 passes, the Patriots still had two field goal opportunities, but Adam Vinatieri missed the first one and the other was blocked.

So, the Macomber den was relatively quiet until the Patriots strong, young defensive lineman Richard Seymour recovered a fumble on the Carolina 19-yard-line. Surely, the Patriots would score this time! And they did.

After nearly 27 minutes of scoreless football, Brady scrambled for a first down on third and seven, and then found Deion Branch in the end zone for a 7-0 Patriot lead.

"Let the good times roll," Mark exclaimed. "The Patriots are going to do it again."

"Love your optimism," Glenn said. "But there's still plenty of football left."

Jimmy sat uncommonly quiet on the floor. He was nibbling on chips and dip and remembering where he was two years earlier when the Patriots were winning the first Super Bowl in franchise history. Jimmy and his family had only just learned of his leukemia two weeks earlier. No one could escape the shock and the fear long enough to get caught up in the Super Bowl hype. It was a quiet Sunday around the house until Jimmy's dad finally turned the TV on around 7:00. Normally, it would have been unthinkable to miss the start of the game, or any of the game for that matter. But on that day it almost seemed insensitive or inappropriate to think about a game when Jimmy's life was on the line. The TV stayed on for the rest of the game, and each of the family members made their way into the den intermittently to check on the score. But no one witnessed the Patriots last minute game-winning drive that beat the St. Louis Rams, the Greatest Show on Turf. No one celebrated that day, but they were prepared to celebrate today. In fact, they wanted very much to celebrate. Maybe it was because they were fraught with worry about the journey just ahead, or maybe it was because they were still reeling from the Red Sox customary collapse of a few months earlier.

Touchdown, Panthers! Carolina needed less than two minutes to respond to the Patriots touchdown with one of their own. Quarterback Jake Delhomme hooked up with his speedy wide receiver Steve Smith for a 39-yard touchdown, and several frustrated groans could be heard in the Macomber den.

"Yes sir, plenty of football left," Glenn repeated.

"Where did that come from?" Jimmy asked of no one in particular.

"Geez, the Panthers do nothing all day, and now they're gonna be tied at half-time," Mark lamented.

Touchdown, Patriots!

"Unbelievable."

"This is ridiculous."

"But I'm loving it."

Brady and the Patriots had gotten the ball back with just over a minute to go in the half, and that was enough time for Brady to find Branch for a 52-yard completion, and then deliver the ball to David Givens for his second touchdown pass in less than three minutes. The defensive battle was over. Now the teams were throwing caution to the wind and jolting each other with big plays in the passing game.

"Those plays are huge," Glenn advised. "You watch, if the Patriots win this game by less than seven points, that's the play right there that made the difference. That's the true mark of Brady's greatness. Whatever you need, he gives it to you."

"Yeah, and the Patriots needed that," Jimmy agreed. "Now instead of the Patriots going to the locker room deflated by the Panthers quick score, it's the other way around."

"Exactly."

Field goal, Panthers! With only 35-seconds left in the half, the Panthers had time to run one play, rushing for 21-yards, and setting up a 50-yard field goal attempt for Steve Kasay. The kick was good! And the game was shaping up to be great!

Unfortunately, Jimmy began to tire. He was dozing in and out of sleep when the half-time show was interrupted by Janet Jackson's ill-timed "flash" dance that exposed her right breast to an unsuspecting public. And Jimmy was sound asleep when the Patriots and Panthers combined for 37 fourth quarter points capped off by Vinatieri's 41-yard field goal with four seconds remaining to win the game. It was his second Super Bowl game winning kick, and once again, the Patriots had gotten the ball with less than two minutes to play and the score tied. Brady, Vinatieri, and the Patriots had done it again. And Jimmy had missed it again.

After Glenn had carried Jimmy up to bed, he and Eileen gazed at their son for several minutes. Neither parent spoke. They had shared many moments like this over the past two years, but only infrequently did they share with each other what consumed their thoughts in the darkened silence of Jimmy's room. At this moment, Glenn was relieved to know that Jimmy would be ecstatic in the morning. The Patriots were not only champions again, they were a perfectly welcomed distraction. Jimmy had been dealt a lot of tough blows, and unqualified moments of pleasure were to be embraced. Glenn smiled, turned, and walked from the room.

Eileen was remembering Jimmy as a baby, a toddler, and a small boy. The scenes flashed through her mind, all with a common thread. She had always been impressed by Jimmy's stubborn independence. It was frustrating when he refused help tying his shoes, and what could have taken ten seconds took ten minutes. And it was painful to watch him fall off his bike scraping his knees and elbows what seemed like a hundred times before he finally learned to ride. But Eileen had always waited patiently until Jimmy either completed the task, or surrendered in disgust and reluctantly asked for help. Tonight, as on many nights, she hoped the obstinacy her son was born with would be the gift that would get him through his illness. Then, against her better judgment, she set his radio alarm clock for WTED, so he could listen to "Sports Overtime" in the morning.

"Sports Overtime " Show Open, February 2, 2004

Announcer: Welcome to a Big Monday edition of "Sports Overtime" on WTED.

Elliot from *Scrubs*: Well, isn't that just the pickle on the giant crap sandwich that is my day?

Announcer: It's the morning after the Patriots won their second Super Bowl in three years, giving all of Patriot Nation a collective and simultaneous "happy ending". Time to cuddle.

Ray Barone from *Everybody Loves Raymond*: Men don't like to cuddle. We only like it if it leads to, you know…lower cuddling.

Announcer: And since he won't seem to take "You're fired" for an answer, we've got Bob Halloran, working the microphones and taking your calls today.

Elle from *Legally Blonde*: Did you see him? He's probably still scratching his head.
Paulette: Yeah, which must be a nice vacation for his balls.

Announcer: And co-chairing today's festivities we've got Fred "Freddie the Fredderman" Safreed.

Cliff from *Cheers*: What a pathetic display. I'm ashamed God made me a man.
Carla: I don't think God's doing a lot of bragging either.

Announcer: And we've got your phone calls at 888-555-1918.

Frasier from *Frasier*: So, how do the calls look today?

Roz: Well, we've got a couple of jilted lovers, a man who's afraid of his car, a manic depressive, and three people who feel their lives are going nowhere.

Frasier: Oh, I love a Monday.

Announcer: Bob and the Fredderman are back from the big game in Houston, and they're ready to celebrate Adam Vinatieri's second Super Bowl game winning field goal. So, put away those negative thoughts, and just enjoy this moment. Who knows when it will ever come around again?

Dr. Cox from *Scrubs*: By the by, this moment is so great that I would cheat on that other moment with it, marry it, and raise a family of tiny little moments. I love this moment so much, I want to have sex with it.

Announcer: Plus, because of a well-designed wardrobe malfunction, you got to see Janet Jackson in the flesh yesterday.

Garth Algar from *Wayne's World*: That is a babe. She makes me feel kinda funny, like when we used to climb the rope in gym class.

Announcer: So, get ready to flap your gums with Bob and Fred on "The Ted". After the Red Sox crushing defeat in the American League Championship Series and another Patriots Super Bowl victory, New England fans are experiencing more mood swings than a bi-polar pregnant woman watching the "Best of Oprah". But today, good times!

The Cat from *The Cat in the Hat*: Wow! This is just like the carnival, just without the abused animals and the drunken clowns with hepatitis.

Announcer: Oh, we've got those. Here's Bob and Fred.

Homer from *The Simpsons*: Wooo-hooo! Only in America could I get a job.

Jimmy sat up in bed and said out loud, "I love the show opens!" Eileen was in the kitchen thinking to herself, "What am I doing letting him listen to this stuff?"

Halloran: Oh, did we ever need this! I'm telling you, it's only been a few months since the Red Sox pulled the rug out from under us. And if the Patriots had somehow managed to blow that game, I mean, if Vinatieri doesn't come through with another clutch kick, and somehow the Patriots lose that game in over-time, I'm telling you, that would have been a kick in the groin that would be really hard to get up from.

Safreed: Are there groin kicks that are easy to get up from?

Halloran: Sure, some might barely miss their mark.

Safreed: And this one would have left a mark.

Halloran: A cleat mark.

Safreed: Why is my voice going up an octave or two?

Halloran: Imagery, baby. And can you imagine how New England sports fans would be feeling today if things didn't work out so beautifully last night.

Safreed: It would have validated and cemented their inferiority complex. All that "woe is me" B.S. would be rearing its ugly head on our air for months. It would never end until something good happened, and who knows how long that will take?

Halloran: You're right. Even though the Red Sox have had an incredible off-season, landing Curt Schilling in November, and Keith Foulke in December, when spring training rolls around in a couple of weeks, a Patriot loss would have reminded fans that not a whole lot goes right around here, so why should they believe this will be the year for the Red Sox?

Safreed: Yeah, but there's still going to be a lot of that anyway. It's easy to separate the Patriots' success from the Red Sox lack of it.

Halloran: Sure, I understand that. But there's enough overlap in Red Sox Nation and Patriot Nation that I think the euphoria of another Patriot championship will put a lot of fans in a better frame of mind.

Safreed: We'll see.

Halloran: Anyway, let's talk about that game yesterday. Where should we start?

Safreed: At the end. Has there ever been a team with such an incredible déjà vu moment? Think about it, Bob. Two years ago, the Patriots got the ball back with 1:21 to go, and Tom Brady moved them 53-yards in nine plays to set up a game winning field goal for Adam. Vinatieri This year, the Patriots got the ball back with 1:08 to play, and Brady moved them 37-yards in five plays, setting up another Vinatieri game winner. It's unbelievable! Same team, and twice in three years, they deliver a nearly identical game winning drive in the Super Bowl. This tells you how great a coach Bill Belichick is, and if this doesn't finally put to bed any debates about Brady being one of the best quarterbacks of all time, then I don't know what will.

Halloran: You're right. But I'll give the doubters this: they did have some valid reasons for doubting before yesterday, but that game yesterday leaves no room for any reasonable doubt. Brady is guilty of being one of the greatest clutch performers in the history of the game.

Safreed: What valid reasons are you talking about? When Brady beat the Rams who, by the way, were a 14-point favorite, that's all anybody needed to know. That should have been enough.

Halloran: Yes, Fred. I know, you're in love with Brady, and I'm not going to take your binky away. But he was having an awful Super Bowl until that game winning drive, and then he completed a handful of passes against a soft Rams defense that was playing that God awful "prevent" defense, and then Vinatieri had to kick a 48-yard field goal, not exactly a gimmee putt, if you know what I mean. Then, the Patriots didn't make the playoffs last year. So, all I'm saying is that to some people, Brady still had something to prove.

Safreed: And he proved it. And I'll tell ya, Bobby baby, we better not hear from anyone today telling me that Brady or this team is lucky. They tried to pull that crap two years ago talking about how all the breaks seemed to go their way, that the Super Bowl was a fluke. Well, two is no fluke. That's not luck. That's clutch. And that's heart. And that's talent.

Halloran: Well, we'll find out if the listeners agree. Let's begin with Ben from Franklin.

Ben: I think we've found lightning in a bottle with this Patriots team. But in a way, Fred, they are lucky.

Safreed: What's that supposed to mean?

Ben: Well, they're lucky to have Brady. They didn't take him until the sixth round a few years back, so anybody could have snatched him up.

Halloran: He's right about that.

Ben: And they're lucky to have a defense that forces so many turnovers. Remember, they had three turnovers against the Rams, including the Ty Law interception return for a touchdown. And during this playoff run, they forced the Titans, Colts and Panthers to turn the ball over six times.

Safreed: That's not luck, Ben. That's coaching and execution.

Ben: Hey, I'm not using the word luck like it's winning the lottery or something. I am a strong believer in luck and I find the harder I work the more I have of it. And the Patriots are like that, too. But they were lucky to get that "tuck rule" call against Oakland in the Snow Bowl two years ago. And they were lucky the Titans punter screwed up so badly that their game winning drive a month ago was 13-yards on eight plays before Vinatieri won it again. And they were lucky again last night when Carolina kicked the ball out of bounds giving the Patriots the ball at their own 40 on the game winning drive.

"I wish they'd tell this guy to go fly a kite," Jimmy said as he entered the kitchen and noticed his mother paying close attention to the program she purported to despise. Jimmy knew she had always been a big sports fan, and that she was just as hooked on the station as he was. His mother smiled and went to the refrigerator to retrieve a cantaloupe she had prepared for Jimmy an hour earlier. They sat together for a few moments with only the voices on the radio to break up the silence.

Safreed: Every team gets breaks like those. But the great teams know how to take advantage of those opportunities.

Ben: Agreed. And while you may have blocked it out of your mind, when Brady threw the interception in the end zone, and the Panthers responded with that 85-yard pass to Muhsin Muhammad, and took the lead in the fourth quarter, that could have cost the Patriots the game.

Halloran: But the Panthers couldn't take advantage of the momentum swing.

Safreed: And why was that? Because Brady engineered an 11-play, 68-yard scoring drive to give the Patriots the lead back. He responded to the one mistake he's made in two Super Bowl runs by doing what champions do. He refused to lose?

Halloran: No doubt about that anymore. Even the people who still criticize Brady because he doesn't put up gaudy numbers have to reconsider. True, he won the Super Bowl MVP award two years ago even though the offense only gained a total of 267 yards against a Rams defense that was decidedly less than the 46-defense of the '85 Bears. That was an MVP awarded because of one drive and a lack of candidates. But yesterday, Brady threw for three touchdowns and 354 yards. So, he can put up the numbers when that's what is required. Isaac's in Newton. You're up next with Bob and Fred?

Isaac: Hey guys! Sure looks like the Patriots have got this winning championships thing down to a science. To me it all starts with the head coach. Bill Belichick's father was a football coach, and apparently, the apple doesn't fall far from the tree.

Halloran: Certainly, Belichick has solidified himself as one of the best coaches ever. Remember, he won two Super Bowl rings as the defensive coordinator with the Giants, and now he's got two more rings as a head coach in New England.

Isaac: And you can see why when you watch the games. Look at how the Panthers blew it by going for a two-point conversion when they were down 21-16. I have no trouble computing the math on what Carolina was trying to do there. They wanted to get within 3 points, but there were still over twelve minutes in the game. They panicked. Then they had to try for another two-point conversion later, and they missed on that one, too.

Safreed: Meanwhile, the Patriots scored on their two-point conversion, the one that made it 29-22. So, that's six points total that Carolina blew on EXTRA points! That's the game right there.

Halloran: The Patriots did what the Panthers couldn't. It's that simple. For every action there is an equal and opposite reaction.

Isaac: I may have to write that down, Mr. Science Guy.

Halloran: And give Patriots' offensive coordinator, Charlie Weis, a little credit, too. First of all, for the first 29-minutes of that game, the Patriots only points came after Richard Seymour recovered a fumble at the Panthers 19-yard line. So, that feared Carolina defense we heard so much about heading into the game was causing a lot of problems. But Weis figured something out and managed to score 25 points in the final 31 minutes. That's not bad. Sam from Adams, you've been on tap for a while. Thanks for waiting.

Sam: Thanks for taking my call, guys. And let's raise a glass to the World Champion New England Patriots. They have helped us declare our independence from the reputation of being "Loserville". We're winners now.

"Winners-ville. That sounds pretty good." Mother and son agreed.

Halloran: We were winners two years ago and that didn't change anything. Folks went right back to being miserable as soon as the Red Sox let them down and the Patriots didn't make the playoffs. So, what's going to make it any different this time? People will just smile for a few days. They'll cheer at the parade tomorrow. And then it will all be over.

Sam: No way! Two years ago I think a lot of fans across the country thought the Patriots were lucky. They were like David slaying Goliath, or the colonists beating the British. But this year the Patriots went 10-and-0 against 10-win teams. Belichick proved he's a genius, and Brady was Mr. February again. They'll head into next season as the favorites to win it all again. The Patriots have earned the respect of the football world, and by association, New England has earned the respect of fans in "Loservilles" everywhere.

Safreed: When this guy talks there ought to be some patriotic fight song or something playing in the background. He's given me a lot of inspiration.

Halloran: To go along with your perspiration. Our next call is from Johnson, Vermont. Lyndon, what's on your mind today?

Lyndon: Well, I've got to tell you from my vantage point, this is no fellowship of the miserable. This is a great society. It's Patriot Nation, and Tom Brady is the president.

Safreed: He's got my vote, I can tell you that.

Lyndon: That's right, sonny boy. And the few people left who still don't think Brady is one remarkable young man, and a helluva quarterback, well, they're just banes of our existence.

Halloran: Pains in our neck.

Safreed: Boils on our butts.

Halloran: Open sores in need of a good salve.

"Bathroom humor," Eileen said as Jimmy fought back a laugh.

Safreed: Peeled back scabs on...

Lyndon: All right, guys! We get the point. Let's just go with banes of our existence for now. But let me ask you guys, is Brady now in the same pantheon of New England sports lore as Larry Bird and Bobby Orr?

Halloran: That's a good question. It's really hard to say. But I guess I'm going to have to go with 'no'. Sorry about that, Fred.

Safreed: And I'm sorry about you being wrong – again. Of course, he's in the same rarified air. They were the best of their time, Orr for sure and Bird was right there with Magic Johnson. Now, here comes Brady. And he's the best of his time, and he's delivering championships just like they did. It's Bird, Orr, Brady. B-O-B. Bob.

Halloran: Nice. But hear me out on this, because I'm in your camp as far as Brady being almost god-like. But Bird and Orr both delivered championships while putting up sensational stats. Even if they had never won a championship, they would have been recognized as among the best of their time. If Brady didn't have two Super Bowl rings, he'd be viewed as nothing more than a better than average quarterback.

Safreed: So what? If a frog had wings, he wouldn't bump his booty! If this! If that! Who cares if Brady doesn't light up the scoreboard? All he does is win, baby! And that makes him an equal to the likes of Bird and Orr. And it puts him ahead of Ted Williams, Carl Yastrzemski and anybody else who ever played for the Red Sox and couldn't deliver the goods.

Halloran: Willie up in Nelson, New Hampshire. Where do you stand on this?

Willie: This question is always on my mind. I tend to think about it whenever I'm on the road again. And here's what I've come up with. Fred, you just can't judge a quarterback the same way you judge a player in any other team sport.

Safreed: Of course you can. It's what we do. You pick a great player in any sport, and you elevate that player to a greater stature based on whether he won a title. That's why Bill Russell is better than Wilt Chamberlain. And that's why John Elway is better than Dan Marino.

Willie: Well, let's forget that I don't necessarily agree with those examples either. The fact remains that Bird was one of five guys on the floor at any given time, and he'd play just about the entire game. Orr was also one of five skaters, and he was out there on the power play and killing penalties. Both of those guys were playing offense and defense. Meanwhile, you've got a quarterback who's one of eleven guys just on offense. All a quarterback can do is try to manage the clock and score points. Brady does both of those things extremely well. But so have a lot of other quarterbacks who didn't win championships. Sometimes a quarterback is responsible for wins and losses, and sometimes he just doesn't have a defense, or a clutch kicker, or a great coach.

Safreed: He's still the most important player on the field. And the Patriots don't win these championships without Brady.

Willie: Agreed. I absolutely agree with you that the quarterback is the most important player on a football field. But he's not as important as a point guard, or a point forward, like Bird was, or an offensive defenseman like Orr. And he's certainly not as important as a goaltender or a starting pitcher. That's why I've never liked the idea of giving a quarterback a record for wins and losses.

Halloran: He's got a point, Fred. I was looking at this the other day. Go back to the AFC Championship game from two years ago. The Patriots scored three touchdowns in that game. One was on a punt return. Another was on a blocked field goal. And the third was on a touchdown pass by Drew Bledsoe. But because Brady started that game, he gets credit for the win. Do you think that's right?

Safreed: You're going to give me one game? One game in a spectacular career so far, and you pick the one that fits your argument, but you ignore all the other games that he came up huge.

Halloran: It's not just Brady. It's Trent Dilfer in the Super Bowl three years ago when the Ravens defense forced five turnovers. It's Brad Johnson last year. For crying out loud, the Buccaneers scored three touchdowns on DEFENSE! But if you follow your argument to its logical conclusion, you have to say that Dilfer and Johnson won those Super Bowls. And I don't think you're saying that.

Safreed: And what exactly is it that you're saying?

Halloran: I'm saying that Dilfer completed 12 of 25 passes for 153 yards and one touchdown last year. And that in Brady's first Super Bowl he completed 16 of 27 passes for 145 yards and one touchdown. The numbers are nearly identical. Both of their teams won the games. Ergo, and ipso facto, Dilfer is as good as Brady. If you're sticking to your guns that quarterbacks should have a won-loss record, then you have to come to that conclusion.

Safreed: You're argument would have made a lot more sense two days ago. But now Brady's got two Super Bowl wins, so he's better than Dilfer.

Halloran: You must be so proud. Your hero is better than Dilfer. High praise indeed, Fred. High praise indeed.

Safreed: You're not very tall.

Halloran: What's that got to do with anything?

Safreed: I just thought people should know. Go ahead with your little show.

"I love it when they make fun of each other," Jimmy said.
"Me, too," Eileen laughed.

Halloran: So, that's how it's gonna be today. Fine by me. We've got time for one more call before we listen to the "Mixed Messages" on our WTED answering machine. Bill's out in Russell, Mass. That's out near Springfield, isn't Bill?

Bill: It's loooong distance! I know that much. My cell phone's on roam, so I'll try to stay centered while making my points. First of all, the Patriots play as a team, and that's the most important thing. They've got a star player who only cares about winning. And the rest of the team follows his lead. So, whether Brady puts up big numbers or not, his greatness is obvious because he's the leader of a team with a capital "T". The rest of the fellas see that Brady is willing to do whatever it takes to win, regardless of how it affects his stats or his status in the league, and then they're willing to also do whatever it takes. And that's how a team wins.

Safreed: Where were you a few minutes ago, Bill, when I was getting ganged up on? I could have used you then.

Halloran: He's doing all right by you now. Don't worry about it.

Bill: Well, I just think it's because of all that, and because Belichick and his staff stuck to their plan through the hard times that this team was able to climb back to the top. After they won their first Super Bowl, they went 9-7. Then they started out this year 2-2. Seriously, man, they could have gone in either direction. But something happened. Something clicked. And they ran off twelve straight wins and three more in the playoffs.

Halloran: Nothing tells you how much better this team was by the end of the year than they were at the beginning than the two games against Buffalo. They opened the season against the Bills and lost 31-nothing. And then they played them on the final weekend of the season and reversed the score, beating the Bills 31-nothing. Forget how uncanny it is to have mirror image shutouts like that. What it does is show you the vast improvement this team made in seventeen weeks.

Safreed: They're the best team in the NFL with the best coach and the best quarterback, and we should all be talking about going back-to-back. Why not? I don't see why they won't win another Super Bowl next year.

Halloran: Let's not get ahead of ourselves just yet, though I do like the optimism, Fred. We don't always get that around here.

Safreed: The tide is turning, Bob. Fans are feeling good.

Halloran: And why shouldn't they? Their favorite team could be on the verge of a dynasty, and they witnessed the Super Bowl's first semi-nude review. That was quite a halftime show, wouldn't you say?

Safreed: It's a shame so many children had to see that, but what the heck; they've got to grow up sometime.

"What are they talking about," Jimmy asked.

Halloran: We're, of course, talking about Janet Jackson's wardrobe malfunction.

"What does that mean?" But Eileen didn't respond.

Safreed: And let's not forget the streaker who got clothes lined by Matt Chatham.

"Man, I can't believe I fell asleep. What else did I miss?"

Halloran: Can you "clothes" line a streaker? I mean, he's not wearing any clothes. That's the whole point.

Safreed: And it's not like he was really streaking either. He was just dancing in the middle of the field.

Halloran: That's the kind of craziness we love around here, and so do our valued listeners who call and leave us some "Mixed Messages" on our answering machine. And without any further ado, here are today's messages.

Recorded Voice: You have seven unheard messages. First message:

Message One: I don't get why they're calling it a wardrobe malfunction. It only happened because that Timberlake dude reached across her breast and ripped away part of her clothing. That doesn't sound like a malfunction to me. It sounds like a premeditated and disgusting way to demean women. Come to think of it, thanks Timberlake dude.

Jimmy looked down at his cantaloupe slightly embarrassed. "Oh, that's what happened."

Halloran: Here's what I think. As soon as Janet Jackson lost all that baby fat, she's been wanting to show off her body.

Safreed: Can we expect the same from you if you ever lose your baby fat?

Halloran: I don't know. If I lost a lot of weight, who knows, it might be something to consider.

Safreed: Then here, have another donut.

Message Two: Today I'm thankful for my HDTV and my TiVo. They cost an arm and a leg, but I'll give up those body parts for the honor and the privilege of seeing Janet Jackson's body part over and over again.

Halloran: Really. If God hadn't intended for Janet Jackson to be exposed like that, would he have invented HDTV? I don't think so.

Message Three: That was some Super Bowl. Let's see if I can remember all the hi-lites. There was a naked breast, a streaker getting tackled, commercials that included horses passing gas, cursing children, and spots for pills that give four hour erections. It's good to know the Super Bowl is still a family event – for the Osbournes!

"Isn't that the truth," Eileen said. "And then they analyze and dissect it for us all day long on the radio. And we'll probably see it over and over again on the television."
"I sure hope so," Jimmy thought."

Safreed: I think the families of Roseanne and Tom Arnold might consider it wholesome family viewing as well.

Halloran: They split up a long time ago, Fred.

Safreed: Really? Who got the trailer in the Hamptons?

Message Four: What's with all the moral outrage over a split second of barely visible and partial nudity? I've seen a lot more than that every day on the Internet, and the Spice channel, and in magazines, and in the backrooms of seedy video stores, and through a peep hole in the ladies room at work, and a whole lot of other places. I think the Super Bowl is going in the right direction.

Halloran: I'm sure he does.

Message Five: I'm just wondering how the streaker got past security. It must be that the police are so concerned about terrorism that they'll let anybody by as long as they don't have a weapon – even if they're naked! Some girl right behind the naked guy probably got stopped for having a hat pin, but the naked guy? Sure, let me just check this press credential hanging down here around Mr. Willy. Yup, you're good. Enjoy the game!

Safreed: That's a good point. How does a crazy guy like that make it on to the field?

Halloran: And when did the clothes come off?

Safreed: These are the tough questions that some industrious journalist should be getting the answers to.

"I think that's enough, don't you?"
"Just another minute, Mom. You know they'll be going to one of those 15 minute commercial breaks after a few more of the messages."
"Yes, but have you noticed they're gradually getting worse? This isn't sports talk anymore."

Message Six: I've always liked it when an artist is willing to bare their soul, especially if their soul has a nipple ring. Now that's art!

"Jimmy!"

Message Seven: Is this why they call television the boob tube? Just wondering.

Safreed: I was wondering when we were going to hear that one. So lame.

Halloran: Well, we saved the worst for last. We'll take a break here and come back with more of your phone calls on "Sports Overtime" on "The Ted". Your New England Patriots are champions of the football world! Enjoy it while it lasts. The baseball season is just around the corner, and we know what a downer that can be.

"Not this year," Jimmy said, concurring with a majority of hopelessly hopeful Red Sox fans who have never stopped waiting till next year. Then he returned to his room to get dressed. The day after a Patriots' Super Bowl victory or not, Jimmy had a very important appointment, one that required a suitcase, one that could change his life forever, and one that was scarier than most.

CHAPTER TWO
Jimmy Gets On The Radio

Jimmy's trepidation had nothing to do with pain or discomfort. He was accustomed to both. No, this time the fear had everything to do with the loss of hope. Believing in a cure, believing in the possibility of a return to health, and faith that things could and would get better had provided Jimmy and his family with the strength they needed when they needed it the most. They had seen miracles happen to other children. They had celebrated with other families when they learned they no longer had to carry the weight of the world on their shoulders. And they had smiled with only a hint of jealousy when those families assured them they would be celebrating their own miracle some day. Now, it seemed to Jimmy, they were about to grasp at the last straw. If the bone marrow transplant didn't work, what else was left?

"Waiting to die," Jimmy thought. "That's what'll be left."

It worried him most that his family might feel the same way. They needed hope as much as he did, and he needed to know that they would never give up. Otherwise, giving in to despair might be the last thing they ever did as a family.

Glenn joined Eileen and Jimmy in the car where soft rock replaced sports talk. Jimmy sat in the back and wondered if his parents were as nervous as he was, and if they knew how nervous he was. He knew he could ask them, and that they'd give him an honest answer. But honestly, he didn't want to hear the slight tremor in his father's voice, or see the tears welling in his mother's eyes. While the ground rules had been set a long time ago when everyone agreed that feelings would be shared and that difficult conversations would not be averted, it never really helped Jimmy to talk about things. More often than not, the dialogue merely confirmed his concerns. And today, he'd rather hope to be wrong.

So, Jimmy paid attention to the traffic on the Southeast Expressway, counted the lights leading up to where his Dad would take a left on Melnea Cass Boulevard, and tried to locate Fenway Park. The stadium itself wasn't visible from where they were, but there were parts of Huntington Avenue where Jimmy could see the Prudential Building which he knew stood some distance beyond the right field bleachers at Fenway Park. During these trips to the Dana Farber Cancer Institute, it made Jimmy feel better to pretend they were simply taking an alternate route to the home of his favorite baseball team. But reality gave him a jolt as the car turned left on to Binney Street, and into the parking garage on the right. Ah yes, his home away from home. Unbuckling his seatbelt and climbing out of the car, Jimmy hoped that his parents weren't scared, and he hoped they didn't know how scared he was.

Jimmy lifted his suitcase out of the trunk, struggling somewhat, but determined to do it himself. Glenn instinctively started to help his frail son, and then begged off. He knew that of all the difficulties Jimmy had to face over the past two years, the one that angered him most was his weakness. His brave, young son managed to cope with long bouts of diarrhea, vomiting, hair loss, painful bruising and pathetically empathetic looks from strangers, but he absolutely hated being weak or incapable. Jimmy would occasionally complain that his fastball was slower now than it was when he was twelve, or that he could no longer reach the manhole cover during the neighborhood games of stickball in the street. And there were times Jimmy couldn't even walk, Max, the family's golden retriever, because if Max saw or smelled something he needed to get to in a hurry, Jimmy couldn't hold him back.

Jimmy dragged the suitcase on its wheels through the automatic doors that led to the elevators at the main entrance. There were a few polite greetings as they passed the information desk and continued to the elevators. Jimmy pressed the number three, and the Macomber family momentarily stood in an uncommonly awkward silence.

The third floor of the Dana Farber Clinic is a contradiction unto itself. It is a place where children with a frequently fatal disease are alive with energy. If a person were blindfolded and brought to the reception area, they'd probably think they had been dropped off at a health club. The noisy, happy children making sand art in the corner could just as easily be waiting for their mothers to emerge from a spinning class, instead of waiting for more blood work to be done. But a visitor to this place would eventually notice how thin the children are, and wonder why the girl by the window has no hair poking out from underneath her hat, or why the boy sitting at the computer has only tufts of hair growing sporadically around his head. Ah yes, this bright, beautiful, modern place is a facility for cancer treatment and cancer research. The girl by the window might not see her ninth birthday, and the boy at the computer might not see his fifth.

"Hey, look who's back everyone!" Angela exclaimed. Angela was the nurse who had seen Jimmy nearly every Thursday for the past twenty months. Jimmy was what is referred to as a "Thursday child", because he came to the clinic every Thursday for his regular dose of chemotherapy. His trips in to the city usually lasted from three to five hours, and a lot of it was idle time. So, Angela and Jimmy talked a lot, and it's fair to say, they became friends. In fact, he had come to the clinic today explicitly because he wanted Angela to bring him to his room.

"It's the young, the talented, the incredibly handsome Jimmy Macomber. I didn't expect to see you today. Aren't you headed over to Children's?" Hi, Eileen. Hi, Glenn. Jimmy, did you bring Trivial Pursuit?"

Jimmy had to smile. Despite his fears, Angela's enthusiasm was contagious. It was as if she thought he was going to summer camp, instead of six weeks of intense radiation and chemotherapy, and several more weeks of isolation.

"Hi, Angela. It's good to see you again," Eileen said. Glenn nodded his hello.

"Under different circumstances. I know you'd prefer it was under different circumstances. But I feel very good about this visit. And we're going to make Jimmy as comfortable as possible."

"Will you be with him, Angela?"

"I actually brought two Trivial Pursuit games," Jimmy offered. "One is for juniors, and the other is all sports."

"I'll be over there as often as I can," Angela said. "But, as you know, most of my day is over here. All sports, huh? Oh, that hardly seems fair. How am I supposed to beat you in sports trivia? You've got way too much information stored away in that brain of yours."

"It's not really about winning and losing, Angela."

"Just so long as I beat you," the two of them said in unison. Everyone laughed at the old, inside joke. But even as they smiled and shared this moment, each of them knew that the laughter was hiding something that wasn't a laughing matter at all. Even Angela had difficulty keeping the mood positive as the elevator doors closed, and the not-so fearless foursome made their way over to Boston Children's Hospital.

Jimmy would prefer to stay at the clinic, but it was strictly an outpatient facility. Each time Jimmy had required an overnight stay, he was taken to "Six North", the regular oncology floor of Children's Hospital. It was just across the street, just as nice, and the nurses and doctors were just as friendly, but all Jimmy knew was that he always felt a lot sicker when he was at Children's. As an outpatient, Jimmy knew he had a week to recover from the chemo before he had to go back in for another treatment. Also, as an outpatient, he could attend school, hang with friends, and with the modicum of courage he received from having a full head of hair, he might summon up the nerve to talk to girls.

As an in-patient, he was impatient. He hated being cooped up in the hospital. The rooms were spacious and private, and children were allowed to bring a lot of personal items from home. But it wasn't home. Here he had a television, PlayStation Two, and a computer hooked up to the Internet, and Jimmy enjoyed all three to some degree or another. But it wasn't home. He'd rather fight with Mark about time allotments for the bathroom than have his own bathroom three steps from his bed. Because this wasn't home.

This was the place he came to get sick. In his heart, he knew this was really the place he came to get better, but he also knew he wasn't getting better. Returning to the hospital served as a reminder to him that two difficult years had passed, and he was right back where he started. Only now, he was much closer to the end than to the beginning.

Jimmy could hear Angela asking about the Super Bowl, but the words didn't completely register with him. He didn't know if she had asked him a question, or if she was talking to someone else. His mind had taken him back to the days and weeks when the family was deciding whether or not to try the bone marrow transplant. Jimmy learned that there are two types of BMT's, allogeneic and autologous. Allogeneic simply meant that Jimmy would receive bone marrow from a donor, while autologous meant that his own stem cells would be collected from the central line in his vein, treated, and put back in with the use of a pheresis machine.

Neither option left the Macombers overly optimistic. Autologous transplants, they learned to their dismay, are more effective in treating diseases other than leukemia. And approximately 15-percent of pediatric patients receiving allogeneic transplants die of transplant related causes. Factoring in relapse cases, sadly the number of transplant patients who do not survive is closer to 40 percent.

Each member of the family was tested to determine if any of them would be a suitable donor. Mark, as fate would have it and as the doctors had anticipated, was the best potential match. Siblings usually are. Both Mark and Jimmy had the same type of human lymphocyte antigens, or HLA. That's a protein found on the surface of bone marrow cells, but having the same HLA is not like having the same blood type. There are many variations within the five major HLA classes. Mark's antigens were similar, but they might not be the same, and there was a chance Jimmy's body would reject Mark's marrow.

"Basically," Dr. Fitzpatrick had told them, "If Mark's marrow doesn't match perfectly, Jimmy's immune system may look at the new cells as something foreign and try to destroy them. That would leave you, Jimmy, unable to create new blood."

"That can't be good," Jimmy said.

"No, it's not. It's called graft rejection. We also have to worry about graft versus host disease, which is when the new immune system you get from Mark sees your organs and tissues as foreign and attacks them. This creates an inflammatory process that can be mild, or even life threatening. Commonly involved organs include the skin, liver and intestines. Now, there are a lot of things we can do to treat these problems, but you'd be well-advised to know that nearly half of all BMT recipients also develop long-term complications, like hypothyroidism, cataracts, abnormal lung function, and infertility."

"Sounds great. Sign me up for one of those, please," Jimmy deadpanned.

But later, when the family had more time alone to think about the potential consequences, both good and bad, they began to focus on what kind of impact this would also have on Mark.

"We haven't even discussed the potential psychological impact this could have on him," Eileen said. "What if Jimmy rejects his marrow? That could devastate Mark. We're already building him up as this big hero who's going to save Jimmy's life. He's feeling wonderfully special, maybe for the first time in two years, but if something goes wrong, he could wind up feeling like he's responsible in some way."

"That would be ridiculous, honey."

"I know that and you know that, but would he know that?"

Mark, who was standing just outside their bedroom door, interrupted, "Yes, I'd know that. Look, whatever you guys decide to do, do it for Jimmy. Whatever he needs, and whatever you want, I'm on board. Don't worry about me."

The words surprised him a little bit, because truth be told, he was glad that they were worrying about him for a change. His parents smiled, but only for a moment. They still had what was very likely a life or death decision to make.

Finally, it was Jimmy who put it in perspective for everyone.

"Leukemia sucks," he announced at the dinner table one evening. The borderline vulgarity got everyone's attention, and served notice that there was more to be said on the subject.

"Mom, Dad, Mark," he said, pausing to look at each of them. "I know there's a chance the transplant won't work, a pretty good chance, I guess. And even if it does work, the doctors keep telling us that I could come down with pneumonia, or some other problem with my liver and lots of bleeding. And I'm not ignoring the fact that I could die, but I want to take a shot at this."

Eileen's eyes were tearing up as she spoke, "But Jimmy, this isn't something you take a shot at. This isn't a three-point shot in the backyard, make it and you win, miss it and you come in for dinner. This is your life we're talking about."

"I know it, Mom, MY life."

"I'm sorry. I just can't get out of my head what Dr. Fitzpatrick said, that up to 10 percent of all children receiving a bone marrow transplant will die within the first three months. What if we do this, and God forbid, the worst happens, and some new cure comes along four months later? How could we live with that?"

"Mom," Mark interjected. "How can we live like this?"

"Oh, don't give me that! We're living. That's all there is to it. It's the hand we've been dealt. We're a family living with leukemia."

"No, Mom. Maybe you guys are living with leukemia, but maybe I'm dying from it."

"Oh, Jimmy, I'm sorry. I didn't mean it like…"

"It's all right, Mom. I'm just trying to tell you what I'm feeling. I could be dying for years, or I could find out in a couple of months that I've got this thing beat. I feel good about my chances, and I haven't felt this good in a really long time."

"Eileen, honey," Glenn said, "It's got to be Jimmy's decision. He's old enough to know what he wants, and mature enough to understand everything that's going on. We can't tell him what to do either way."

"Oh, my God! Jimmy, is your mind made up?"

"Yes."

"And when would you want to do this?"

"Well, I've been thinking about that."

"I'm sure you have," Glenn said.

"I figure it takes about six weeks in the hospital, so I should go in during that lull between the football and baseball seasons. If the Patriots make it to the Super Bowl, that would be February 1st. So, I think we should get started on the second. All I'd miss is spring training."

"Sounds like you've got it all figured out," his Mom said. "We'll do what you want, but you can always change your mind. All right?"

"All right. But I won't."

"One thing I'm not sure you've considered, though," Glenn said. "Watching you two boys fight as much as you do, what makes you so sure your bone marrows are going to get along?"

Glenn meant it as a joke to lighten the mood, but it sorely missed its mark. Glenn knew it, and the horrified look Eileen shot him confirmed it. The boys smiled sympathetically toward their father.

As the overwrought group stepped off the elevator, they all washed their hands thoroughly before opening the airtight doors to Six West. Jimmy immediately began to look for familiar faces. He glanced into the rooms to see if anyone he knew was here, and he wondered if their absence was a good thing or a bad thing. Jimmy had been here just a few weeks earlier for the myriad of tests required before being approved for a BMT. There was a general exam, blood work, chest x-ray, CAT scan, dental exam, eye exam, an echocardiogram, and even a dietary consultation. He enjoyed the freedom to eat whatever he wanted before he came in for his transplant, especially since yesterday was Super Bowl Sunday.

He even had a psychological test that included a lengthy question and answer period with a doctor he had never met before. Dr. Adrianna Morgan asked him a lot of questions about sports and school, which he knew were only meant to make him comfortable. What she really wanted to know was how he was dealing with the stress of leukemia, and the fear of the bone marrow transplant. Truth be told, he was sometimes optimistic, sometimes scared to death, and all of the time he didn't feel much like talking about it. So, after thirty minutes had passed, Jimmy finally just looked at Dr. Morgan, and said: "Look, don't worry about it. I'm not crazy. I've got leukemia. Can I go now?"

He was granted his request, and as he opened the door to the office, he turned back to Dr. Morgan, and said: "You know, I don't think anyone could know what a normal reaction to having a deadly disease should be. So, how are you supposed to know what's abnormal?"

"I don't know. I really don't," the doctor said. "Good luck, Jimmy. It was nice meeting you."

But Jimmy didn't get to leave that day. The doctors wanted a 24-hour urine collection instead of a glomerular filtration rate test. So, rather than go home with several plastic cups, Jimmy spent the night in the hospital. Then the next day's CAT scan detected a slight infection in his abdomen, and that took another six days to treat with antibiotics. A few days later, he was back so a small amount of bone marrow could be removed for testing. And finally, a bout with the flu brought him back to the clinic for a few days during Super Bowl week, and now he was one hundred percent ready to go -- physically.

The future always had the potential of being better than right now. So, Jimmy kept his eyes on the prize – Opening Day. And he hoped the next six weeks would fly by. They didn't. They took exactly twelve weeks. And it was hard. Very, very hard.

"Sports Overtime" Show Open, April 5, 2004

Announcer: Welcome to a Monday edition of "Sports Overtime". It's the day after the Red Sox rang in the New Year with an uninspiring thud. But we love'em anyway.

Neidermeyer from *Animal House:* You're all worthless and weak! Now drop and give me twenty!

Announcer: We'll be taking your 'I'm already giving up' phone calls with the Little Big Man, Bob Halloran. He'll be sitting up on a phone book in the big chair.

The Fly from *The Fly:* Help me! Heeeeelp me!

Announcer: Fred "Freddie the Fredderman" Safreed is also here and he promises to stop puckering up to Tom Brady's backside long enough to defend the Red Sox from all you "die easy" fans who think the Sox are going to leave you face down in the gutter for the 86th year in a row.

Otter from *Animal House:* I put it to you, Greg, isn't this an indictment of our entire American society? Well, you can do whatever you want to us, but we're not going to sit here and listen to you badmouth the United States of America. Gentlemen!

Announcer: And as per usual, we've got the "Mixed Messages", so all you cry babies can cry like babies about whatever it is that has made you so miserable this time.

Jimmy Dugan from *A League of their Own:* Are you crying? Are you crying? ARE YOU CRYING? There's no crying, there's no crying in baseball. Rogers Hornsby was my manager, and he called me a talking pile of pig - BLEEP. And that was when my parents drove all the way down from Michigan to see me play the game. And did I cry? No! No! And do you know why?
Evelyn Gardner: No, no, no.
Jimmy Dugan: Because there's no crying in baseball.

Halloran: Oh, there's gonna be some crying today.

Safreed: At least some whining.

Halloran: I gotta tell you that was one tough game to watch last night. I mean, is it even possible that Terry Francona didn't watch Game 7 of last year's American League Championship Series? Could he possibly not know that the man he replaced got fired because he let Pedro Martinez throw too many pitches? How could he possibly leave teeny-tiny, fragile, little Pedro on the hill to throw 119 pitches?

Safreed: Just stupid!

Halloran: I mean it was 43 degrees at game time. And it was his first start of the season. Francona's got to understand that he's not taking this team to the World Series without a healthy and productive Pedro. And let's face it; it's the World Series or bust for this team this year. I mean, they've as much as said that they've emptied the coffers, because they're going for it all this year.

Safreed: Oh, they've said it all right. They're on the record saying it. That's why they spent the money to get Curt Schilling and Keith Foulke here.

Halloran: So, what was Francona doing? He's got to know that there's no World Series without Pedro Martinez. So, what's he pushing him so hard for in the very first game? Where's that opening day 80 pitch limit? If this guy tears that labrum or runs into arm troubles, the Red Sox are dead in the water.

Safreed: Well, I don't know about dead. They've still got a pretty good team...

Halloran: Dead, I tell you! Dead!

Safreed: Not dead. It'd be like a little flesh wound.

Halloran: You've to to be kidding me! You think the Red Sox could survivie without Pedro Martinez either for the playoffs or for a good chunk of the season?

"Of course, they could," Jimmy said in his hospital room. *"They've got Schilling now. That makes them by far the best team in baseball.*

Safreed: Of course, I do. The Red Sox are that much better than every team in baseball, especially the American League. People can talk about the Yankees all they want, but the Yankees are in trouble. They gave up three pitchers; Clemens, Pettitte, and Wells, who won something like 50 games for them last year.

Halloran: It was 53 games, but go ahead.

Safreed: Oh, you're so sure of that.

Halloran: Got it right here in my notes. I, unlike you, have done some painstaking research to get ready for this program. I don't just show up and sit around on my ample backside.

Safreed: Whatever. They also got Jon Lieber, who hasn't pitched in a year-and-a-half coming off Tommy John surgery. And Javier Vazquez, who everybody thinks can be good, but he's never pitched in a game that matters. Let's see how he fares under the bright lights of New York City.

Halloran: So, what's your point?

Safreed: The point is the Yankees can lay out their 180-million dollar payroll, and basically guarantee themselves a playoff spot. I'm just saying, the Red Sox will be there, too. This team is too good. Don't worry about the injuries to Nomar and Nixon. The Red Sox and Yankees will be 1-2 in the American League. And I think it'll finally be the Red Sox in first, and the Yankees will wind up with the Wild Card.

"What are you listening to?" Angela asked as she walked in to Jimmy's room. She'd been coming by almost every day for the past six weeks. "As if I didn't know."
"They're already jumping on the Red Sox, and they've only lost one game," Jimmy said.
"What is it with these guys? They're always getting ready for the worst to happen."
"I keep telling you, you should call them," encouraged Angela. "You know as much as they do, and I'm sure they'd appreciate the input of someone your age."
"Sometimes I want to call. I even dialed once and got put on hold."
"What happened?"
"They went to a commercial break, and I hung up."

Halloran: Do you know how many years in a row the Yankees have finished in first place with the Red Sox finishing right behind them?

"Six times."

Safreed: I don't know. Something like six or seven. I'm sure you're gonna tell me exactly what it is.

Halloran: I hope our listeners appreciate that at least one of us is bringing something to the table.

Safreed: Yeah. You bring plenty to the table. And when you get up from the table, there's nothing left ON the table.

Halloran: Now why do you have to go there?

Safreed: Just go ahead and amaze us with another table scrap? How many years have the Yankees and Red Sox finished 1-2 in the A.L. East?

Halloran: Six times.

"You should definitely call them."

Safreed: That's what I said.

Halloran: No you didn't. You said six or seven. You didn't know!

Safreed: Fine! If it makes you feel better to say I didn't know, then fine. But if I were taking a test and had to put down one answer, I would have said six. And I would have been right. So, I knew.

Halloran: You knew enough to take a lucky guess. But you didn't really know. There was a real lack of certainty on your part. Yet, you think you can be certain the Red Sox did enough during the off-season to move ahead of the Yankees for the first time in seven years?

Safreed: Nine.

Halloran: Nine what?

Safreed: I think the Red Sox are good enough to finish ahead of the Yankees for the first time in NINE years.

Halloran: I just told you, it's been six years. Have you forgotten already?

Safreed: It's been six years for the Yankees and Red Sox finishing first and second. But it's been eight straight years that the Yankees have finished ahead of the Red Sox. The last time the Sox had more wins than the Yankees was 1995. I'm surprised you didn't know that, Mr. Stat Man.

Halloran: You're feeling pretty good right about now, aren't you?

Safreed: Yeah. It feels good. How's all that research working out for you?

Halloran: Right now, not so much. But I'll recover.

"I love it when they zing each other!"
"I'm dialing the number. Here take the phone."
"Seriously? I don't know what to say."
"Just tell them…"
"Oh, hello. Yes. This is Jimmy. Where am I calling from? Boston. Yes, I'd like to talk about the Red Sox. All right."
"So, you're going to be on?"
"I don't know. They put me on hold again. Angela, can you turn down the radio. They hate it when people keep their radios turned up."
"Why?"
"I think it causes some sort of technical problem, like they hear the caller twice or something like that. Like an echo."

Halloran: Whaddaya say we take some phone calls and kind of take the pulse of the Red Sox Nation? Yesterday, we heard a fair amount of optimism. Folks were thinking that this will be the year. But that was before we got our first good look at Terry Francona. And I gotta tell you, first impressions weren't that impressive. And that was before the Red Sox bullpen turned a close game into a blow out.

Safreed: And before the Sox hitters failed time and again to come up with the big hit. Boy, was that frustrating! They left more men in scoring position than a Texas brothel.

Halloran: Did you work hard on that line?

Safreed: Nope. It just kind of came to me, like in a dream.

"This is no good. Now, I can't hear the radio myself. What are you laughing at?"
"Nothing, Angela. Nothing, really. Now, I have to listen in case they call my name."

Halloran: Let's see if we get that much cleverness from Otis. Otis from Reading, you're first on "Sports Overtime" today.

Otis: Hey, guys. You know, I'm just sitting here resting my bones, and I'm listening to the two of you talk about the Red Sox like there's something to be upset about.

Halloran: You're not upset at the way they played yesterday?!

Otis: No, man. It's only one game. Yesterday you thought the Red Sox were good enough to win the World Series this year. What's changed?

Halloran: Well, we got our first look at how Terry Francona might be as a manager. We got an inkling that Pedro might not be able to dominate like he once did, especially if he can't throw more than 100 pitches. And we were slapped in the face with a possible dose of reality. Maybe a lot of these guys on the Red Sox really did have career years last year. And maybe, they're in for a letdown.

Safreed: Yeah, c'mon Otis, my man! You have to admit the Red Sox were picked by many to win the World Series, at least in part, because they have great pitching and great hitting. Well, if Pedro becomes average, or even worse, injured. Then the pitching might not be enough. I'm still saying it is, but maybe it's not. And the Sox are starting the season without Nomar and Nixon. So, if Kevin Millar, Bill Mueller and David Ortiz can't come close to duplicating what they did last year, then the line-up definitely won't be enough. Even optimism relies on realism, and realistic expectations.

Halloran: And health.

Angela nodded at the notion that health is important. She had gone to the reception area to listen with a few of the nurses and staff. She knew how much he wanted to participate in a conversation about the Red Sox, especially on his favorite radio program. "God, I hope he gets on today," she said to the others.

Otis: Looks like nothing's gonna change. Everything still remains the same. You guys are gonna stoke the fires for 162 games. You're going to over-react to every win. And over-attack after every loss. Me? I guess I'll remain the same, too. I'll start worrying when there's really something to worry about. You guys are just wasting time!

Halloran: It's a living. Thanks for wasting some of your time.

Safreed: Sounded like Otis from Reading may have been sitting in the morning sun a little too long.

38

Halloran: Bill from Clinton, Mass, you're next on "Sports Overtime". How you doing today, Bill?

Bill: Great guys.

Halloran: Would you agree that if this team plays like it did yesterday that this team is going nowhere?

Bill: Well, that depends on what the meaning of 'is' is.

Safreed: Where have I heard that before?

Bill: Think about it guys. There's nothing wrong with the Red Sox that can't be cured with what is right with the Red Sox. Their problems yesterday were, in order: the hitting, the manager, the bullpen, and Pedro.

Halloran: I might quarrel with the order, but go ahead. Make your point.

Bill: Well, the Red Sox have good hitting. So, they'll be all right there. The manager is just getting started. He was handpicked by this ownership group that has earned a certain level of respect for making a lot of right decisions. The bullpen won't be nearly as bad as it was a year ago. And Pedro is Pedro. So, fans can get as frantic as they want to get, but this team is still headed for the playoffs. So IS this team going anywhere? Based on yesterday, the answer might be no. But I have no doubt the Red Sox WILL be going somewhere.

Halloran: I can't believe how much optimism we're hearing again today. These are the Red Sox! This is the team that routinely breaks your heart. They've been ruining your 'summ-ah' for the past 85 years! So, why wouldn't you assume that they would put together a team during the off-season that is the hands down favorite to win the World Series, and then just under-achieve like they always do and let another year slip by?

Bill: Because they've never done it before.

Halloran: What do you mean they've never done it before? They do it every year! What am I missing here?

Bill: You're missing the facts, but that's never stopped you before.

Safreed: Sick him, Bill.

Bill: Look, I may be from a little place called Hope, and yes, I am hopeful every spring. But the Red Sox are never the pre-season favorites to win it all. Sometimes they're considered a contender, but never the favorite. This time they genuinely look like the best team in baseball. And I'm not giving up on them until I absolutely have to. I'm telling you guys, save some of your anger and frustration. It's a long season. And believe me when I tell you, you don't want to get too excited prematurely.

Halloran: Sounds to me like Bill is the only Red Sox fan alive or dead who doesn't think this team has underachieved for the past 85 years.

"That's not what he just said," Jimmy thought. "In fact, he almost said the opposite. Why doesn't that guy listen?"

Safreed: I don't think that's what he was saying.

Halloran: That's exactly what he said.

Safreed: No, he didn't. That's exactly what you said. And just because the Red Sox haven't won the World Series in 85 years doesn't mean that they've underachieved in each of those 85 years.

Halloran: Uh-oh. I think I'm about to get hit with that Connecticut School of Broadcasting education of yours. Is that what they taught you there? That if you fail miserably and in heart-breaking fashion for 85 years that you haven't underachieved? Is that how they convince you graduates that you're not a bunch of losers?

Safreed: Go ahead and knock the CSB, but you're still missing Bill's point. The most common misconception about the Red Sox is that every year they don't go out and win the World Series they somehow break our hearts.

Halloran: Well, don't they?

Safreed: No! They don't routinely break our hearts. Look, in my lifetime, they've lost the World Series in 1967, 1975, and 1986. That's three broken hearts in almost 40-years. Throw in 1978 when they blew the big lead against the Yankees and lost the Bucky "bleeping" Dent playoff game, that's four. And throw in last year's Game 7 at Yankee Stadium, and we're up to 5 times the Red Sox have had a legit chance to break this dynasty of disappointment, but didn't get it done.

Halloran: Dynasty of disappointment? Nice phrase.

Safreed: Yeah, alliteration is big in broadcast schools. But all I'm saying is don't fan these mythical flames that the Red Sox are gonna do it to us again. Bill's point, and I agree with it, is that the Red Sox have never really done it to us. In 1967, they came out of nowhere and gave everybody a summer thrill ride, right on up to a Game 7 against Bob Gibson. In '75, they had to face the Big Red Machine with something like five Hall of Famers. Nobody thought they would win that series. Same in '86 when they were huge underdogs to the Mets. And don't forget they had to come back to beat the Angels that year. If anything, the years the Red Sox have broken our hearts, as you say, they actually OVER-achieved just to get into position for abject failure.

"Good job, Fred," Jimmy thought. "Right up until the abject failure part." Meanwhile, Angela looked at her watch, knowing it was time for her to get back to the clinic. She kept her fingers crossed that Jimmy would be the next caller.

Halloran: I think I'll leave it to George down in Foster, Rhode Island to set you straight, Fred.

George: Gladly. Hey, Fred what about last year? You don't think the Red Sox should have won last year? Don't tell me they weren't every bit as good as the Yankees. They lost the regular season series 10 games to 9, and then they had 'em on the ropes in that 7th game at the Stadium. Admit it, Fred. You cried like somebody just ran over your dog.

Safreed: Whaddaya say we leave my dog out of this? And yes, I admit I had a little trouble dealing with last year's loss. Sure, they should have won. But it's not like too many people picked them to beat that Yankee team. The Red Sox were fortunate to push it to a 7th game. But if you'd let me get to my point…

Halloran: Please do. We've all been waiting for you to finally get to your point.

Safreed: The point is that THIS is the year. This is the first time that the Red Sox are truly the best team in baseball.

"That's what Jimmy's been saying. Now bring him on. This would be perfect."

Safreed: So, if they don't win it this year, I'll gladly climb on board and say they under-achieved. Fans can look back at those other years and admit, you know what, the Red Sox had their chances, but they just weren't as good as those teams they lost to. But this year, they won't be able to say that. If the Sox don't win it all this year, then it'll be because they just blew it. And that will be the crushing blow, the one that tells every Red Sox fan, "Forget it. It's never going to happen." The stars are aligned this year, Bob. And if you need any more evidence, just listen to the calls we've been taking all spring. Guys are so excited out there their boxers are getting tight.

Halloran: Steve's in Lawrence. How are YOUR boxers?

Steve: I'm a brief man myself.

Halloran: Good, then keep it brief.

Steve: I think Fred's right. Sure he comes off like a raving lunatic, but that's just his style. And if what he's trying to say is that one of the reasons the Red Sox haven't been able to win in all these years is because of all the negative energy – from the fans, the players, the media, then I agree. Everyone's been sitting around every year waiting for the first opportunity to bury them. It's like a sport. Whoever kicks dirt on them first wins. And so far today, Bob, you're the clear-cut winner. You're the only one I've heard suggesting that one lousy loss, with 161 games left, that somehow we have to wonder if the Red Sox really are good enough to go all the way.

Halloran: Hey, don't tell me you liked yesterday's loss any more than I did.

Steve: But we're not trying to use it as proof that the Red Sox are over-rated. And that's essentially what you're getting at. Maybe the Red Sox aren't as good as we thought. That's what you're saying. Just look at the nine whole innings they've played. Well, it doesn't work that way.

Safreed: Right. And if the Sox go out and look great today, I promise I won't try to use it as proof tomorrow that they're the best team since the 1927 Yankees.

Halloran: I'll hold you to that promise. Tim in Conway, New Hampshire? Do you also think the Red Sox are better than this year's Yankees? You think they're better than the team that beat them last year, and then stole Alex Rodriguez right out from under their collective noses?

Tim: Yes I do, Mr. Rain on Everyone's Parade. Join the party, baby! It's just getting started. Right now, today, I think the Red Sox are better than every team out there. And that's why this year could end up being so devastating. I start every season with my fingers crossed. But this year I'm crossing my toes, my eyes, my elbows – everything. My hopes have never been as high as they are right now. And it's not about blind faith and wishful thinking anymore. The Red Sox are a bunch of stud ballplayers. It's realistic to expect the Red Sox to put an end to all the waiting. I agree, if the Sox don't do it this year, I think a lot of fans like me will be heartbroken like never before.

(The show producer plays a tape of Frank from *Old School* speaking in slow motion): "You're crazy man! I like you, but you're crazy."

Halloran: You are crazy. I don't care how good you think the Red Sox are. Nothing can be as heartbreaking or gut wrenching or puke inducing as Aaron Boone and Bill Buckner. Those are rock bottom occurrences in Red Sox history, and don't think for a moment that last year's ALCS isn't going to haunt these guys this year. The pressure to erase 85 years, and the enormous disappointment of what happened to these guys a year ago could very easily be too big a burden to bear. And I'll tell you this much, if they don't win it all this year, they may have to clean house. Get rid of a bunch of their free agents and start all over with a new group that isn't carrying around all that Grady Little baggage.

Safreed: That I agree with.

Halloran: First sensible thing you've said all day. Abe from Lincoln, you're next on "Sports Overtime", and see if you can convince me that Fred's not an idiot.

Abe: Well, I used to be a pretty fare debater…

Halloran: Were you a master debater?

Angela cringed, and she knew that somewhere Eileen was probably cringing, too.

Abe: Well, I don't know about that, but I was going to say that even with my strong debating skills, I'm not sure I could make a convincing argument that Fred's not an idiot.

Safreed: Thanks, Abe.

Abe: Just being honest. And look, the reason I called was to talk about free agency which is something that's always interested me. But first, I've been racking my brain trying to remember four scores from seven years ago.

Safreed: This shouldn't be too hard. What are we talking about, four games in the thousands of games that were played in 1997? This is a great call so far.

Halloran: I like him. He called you an idiot.

Safreed: No he didn't. He just said he couldn't prove I'm not an idiot.

Halloran: I think he could prove it now.

Abe: But guys, guys, I'm only thinking back to the 1997 World Series. Didn't the Florida Marlins win that one?

Safreed: Yeah. That was the year they beat Cleveland. Seven games from hell. Two of the worst World Series teams ever, and they didn't even have the decency to wrap it up in four or five games.

Abe: Well, that's what I'm getting at. You guys keep talking about the Red Sox and whether or not they're the best team or not. And I'm saying it doesn't matter. The best team doesn't always win. So, I don't care if the Red Sox LOOK like they're the best. I don't care if they lose to the Yankees during the regular season and only get to the playoffs as a Wild Card team. None of it matters. I just want them to win a World Series. Wouldn't that just be so liberating? And I absolutely agree with most of the other callers. This just feels like the year!

Safreed: Any idiot can see that.

Halloran: What are you teeing them up for me now? That one's too easy. I'm just gonna let it go.

Safreed: That's awfully nice of you.

Halloran: We've got time for another phone call here. This time it's Jimmy from Boston. What's on your mind there, Jimmy?

"This is it!" Angela exclaimed. "Jimmy's on the radio everyone!" Several nurses gathered around the radio to listen. "Go get'em, Jimmy!"

Jimmy: Oh, I've got a lot on my mind these days, but for now, I'd just like to talk about the Red Sox.

Halloran: Hey, wait a minute there. Just wait one gosh darn minute. We usually don't take phone calls from people who still have their baby teeth. How old are you?

Jimmy: I'm 14. But my voice is starting to change, and I'm going bald, if that helps.

Halloran: Ha-ha! But no, actually I'm not so sure a receding hairline IS enough. This isn't Radio Disney, you know. This is the big time. You've got to be able to bring something to the table, or you don't get to dine with the big boys. You understand that, Jimmy?

Jimmy: Yes. I listen to you guys all the time. And I'm pretty sure I can keep up with the level of conversation from the so-called "fellowship of the miserable".

Halloran: Are you in that fellowship? C'mon! You're 14. How miserable can you be? You're one great big raging hormone with feet. You get a pimple; you probably think it's the end of the world. Believe me, kid, you start rooting for the Red Sox, and you'll find out soon enough what miserable really is.

Safreed: Yeah, quit now while you've still got a chance. You don't want a lifetime of watching the Red Sox to set you up for one fall after another.

"These guys are idiots," Angela said.

Jimmy: Fred, you're all over the map today. First, you're saying the Red Sox don't break our hearts every year, and now it sounds like you're telling me to avoid getting my heart broken by rooting for some other set of laundry.

Halloran: Kid watches a lot of TV, and listens to a fair amount of radio.

Safreed: Well, what else is there?

Jimmy: Exactly. The Red Sox on TV, and listening to people talk about the Red Sox on the radio. What else is there?

Halloran: Homework maybe?

Jimmy: All done.

Safreed: School must be easy these days.

Halloran: That's right, Fred. It doesn't take six years to finish high school anymore. Hey Jimmy, here's a homework assignment for you. Are you ready? Give me an oral essay about why a Red Sox fan should be any more hopeful this year than in all the other years that the Red Sox have come up empty. Can you tell me that?

Jimmy: Sure. Because hope is all there is, Mr. Halloran. For me, hope is what makes tomorrow worth waiting for. It's what everybody holds on to when they don't have anything else to hold on to. I can't even imagine what my life would be like without hope. I hope the Red Sox win. I hope it doesn't rain. I hope my brother and friends all get to live their dreams someday. And I hope my parents go an entire day without feeling any sadness. I'm hoping all the time.

Halloran: You're a very hopeful kid.

"Good job, Jimmy. That was great!"

Safreed: Smartest thing anybody's said all day. And it comes from someone with a bedtime.

Jimmy: Well, my Dad always says if you're not hopeful, you're hopeless. Which would you rather be?

Halloran: I'd rather be eating a donut. Let's take a break. Anything else today, Jimmy, before we let you go back to checking out women's underwear ads?

Jimmy: Yeah, I also hope the Yankees' pitching staff falls apart by the All-Star break. I hate the Yankees. I mean, nobody knows if this is the Red Sox year, or if any year is going to be THE year. But I just don't want to see the Yankees win it ever again.

Safreed: A kid after my own heart.

Halloran: Call again, Jimmy. Take it easy.

Safreed: Bright kid.

Halloran: And think about what it's like for a 14-year-old. He probably didn't even start liking baseball until he was at least six. So, do the math. He's six in, what, 1996. And in his first five years of loving the Red Sox, he's gotta watch the Yankees win four World Series Championships. That's a tough break for the kid.

Safreed: That's right. At least when I was growing up, the Red Sox weren't winning, but neither were the Yankees. They had that horrible run from 1981 when they lost to the Dodgers up until '96. I mean, they weren't even very good most of those years.

Halloran: Good times.

Safreed: Definitely.

Halloran: All right. We'll be right back with more of your phone calls. That's next on WTED.

CHAPTER THREE
Faith, Hope and Love

Jimmy hung up the phone and smiled. His mind told his body to get out of bed and dance around the room, but his body wouldn't listen. His body just lay there incapable of making a response that would properly reflect the magnitude of the moment.

"I was just on the radio with Bob and Fred," Jimmy said in a whisper. He rolled over on to his right side, because the bucket he used to throw up in was on his left side, and he added, "It doesn't get any better than this."

He wanted to call his parents to see if they had been listening, but he used up most of his strength attempting to project himself as a confident and healthy kid for his first appearance on the radio. It seemed to go well, but he wanted confirmation from someone, anyone.

So, he closed his eyes and waited for Angela to come back into the room. He was proud and excited, and he wanted to thank Angela for making the phone call and pushing him toward his big day in the sun. But when she didn't return immediately, he realized he was lonely. Six weeks it had been. For six weeks he had been trapped in this box, a box with modern conveniences, a box that he had filled with Red Sox posters on the walls, sports magazines on the desk, and baseball cards in the photo album on the couch, but it was a box nonetheless. He wasn't allowed to leave, and Opening Day had come while he was still in isolation.

Now that Six West had an air filtration system inside the rooms as well as outside in the hallway, patients were technically allowed to leave their boxes to walk around, or spend time in the Teen Room, but the thrill of walking up and down the halls past the nurses' station wore off in a hurry. There was nowhere to go and all day to get there. Plus, Jimmy didn't have a strong desire to walk or to greet people while he was battling constant nausea and diarrhea. The diarrhea was perhaps the most embarrassing result of Jimmy's treatment. He needed to wash, not just wipe, after going to the bathroom. He soaked in the tub at least twice a day, and he applied a moisturizing cream. It was all so demoralizing to him.

While Jimmy waited for Angela, he tried to ignore the queasy feeling that haunted him almost constantly. He knew that was part of the deal. Dr. Fitzpatrick had described to him in great detail what would happen during the "conditioning" regimen and beyond. Throwing up, feeling like throwing up, and cleaning up from throwing up were high on the list of things to expect. And Dr. Fitzpatrick, who had explained to Jimmy that preparing for a bone marrow transplant required intense chemotherapy, had certainly delivered on his promise.

"Explain intense," Jimmy recalled politely demanding.

"Well, as you know, we generally administer chemotherapy in cycles," the doctor expounded. "You've received treatment for a while, then we wait to allow for a recovery period, and then we start it up again. Not this time. Intense means we're going to destroy your bone marrow and your immune system. The drugs and radiation you'll receive will come in such large doses that there will be a real concern about your body's ability to fight any kind of infection. We're going to have to watch you very closely, and you're not going to feel well for quite a while."

Dr. Fitzpatrick had been Jimmy's doctor for the entirety of the past two years, and he knew that Jimmy wanted to hear the truth, that his initial reaction would probably include a glib response, a joke in the face of fear, and that Jimmy would assimilate the information in his own time. Like so many of the cancer patients Dr. Fitzpatrick treated, Jimmy was an old soul. He had wisdom beyond his years, courage beyond realistic expectations, and an undying spirit. It was a shame that such special qualities were so often taken from this world at an early age.

"What could these children become, or be able to accomplish, if they were able to live long, full lives?" he often wondered. "They could change the world, if we could just save them."

Saving Jimmy was the goal right now. Jimmy had only given Dr. Fitzpatrick a subtle look that day that indicated he understood. Dr. Fitzpatrick hoped that look also meant Jimmy was ready to endure the intense chemo and the incredible discomfort that went along with it.

"And you also understand, Jimmy," the doctor continued. "Because of the concerns we have about infection, you'll be isolated for about six weeks, maybe longer."

"Isolated? You mean I can't have any visitors?"

"Your family can come. In fact, we encourage one parent to be here at all times, but the visits from other family members or friends will be short. We'll have them wear high filtration masks, and if they have so much as a sniffle, they can't come in. But you'll have your phone and the Internet, so you can keep in contact with the outside world. And, of course, you'll be able to listen to the radio. I know how much you love that."

It was true. Jimmy had started listening to the guys on WTED when he was first diagnosed and spent those first 27 days in the hospital tolerating chemotherapy for the first time. Still in shock by the diagnosis, stunned by the abrupt loss of hair, scared every time they took his blood work to the lab, and feeling so bad he sometimes wished he were dead, Jimmy believed it was Bob and Fred who had helped him maintain his sanity two years ago.

Already a huge baseball fan, Jimmy became a bigger fan. Already proficient on the Internet, Jimmy became more adept and spent hours researching information about his favorite teams, the Red Sox and the Patriots. Already confident and outspoken, he became his most outspoken when he was offering his approval or barking disapproval toward the hosts and callers on the radio. If he was alone in his room, and he was often alone in his room, the radio was tuned to sports talk. It was the only thing that gave him energy, and got his adrenalin going.

There was so much fear back then, so much not knowing, so much difficulty trying to wrap his brain around his new plight in life. How does a boy go from trying to find the courage to talk to a girl to trying to find the courage to bear the burden of induction?

Induction is the initial intensive treatment for leukemia. Once the doctors confirmed Jimmy had ALL, they wanted to treat it as quickly and as aggressively as possible.

"It's a matter of survival," Jimmy and his parents were told.

So lives were turned upside down. Insurance companies were called. Leaves of absences were taken. Tears were spilled. And there was plenty of Internet research being done as the Macombers tried to learn everything they could about the drugs Jimmy was given. There was daunorubicin, vincristine, methotrexate, asparaginase, and others. The drugs were administered intravenously (shots into the vein), intramuscularly (shots into the muscle), subcutaneously (shots under the skin, and intrathecally (shots into the spinal fluid). And Jimmy had them all!

But with so many IV treatments required for the chemo drugs, blood and platelet transfusions, and antibiotics, Jimmy was placed under general anesthesia and brought to the operating room where he was given a central line. A small incision was made in the skin over his chest, and a small flexible plastic tube was placed under his skin. One end of the tube went through the chest directly into a large vein in his neck that leads to his heart. The other end of the tube had a screw cap at the end and hung outside Jimmy's body. The central line served the dual purpose of lessening the number of needle pokes and reducing the possible side effects from the chemo drugs coming into contact with Jimmy's skin. The line was great for putting things IN Jimmy's body, and it could also be used to take blood OUT for testing.

The central line is susceptible to infection. So, even Eileen and Glenn had to learn how to change the dressing that covered the site. They also had to learn to flush the tubes to keep them from becoming infected, and they were always on the lookout for blood clots that could develop in the tubes and prevent the proper infusing of medication.

The only downside, as Jimmy viewed it, was that his initial central line was of the external variety. There were two tubes that hung out several inches outside his chest. It was just plain weird, he thought. He was skinny, bald, and bruised, and now he had two rubber tails. The disease that could kill him wouldn't be successful until it had stripped him of all his dignity.

This was Jimmy's new life. He was given a barrage of chemo drugs intended to knock out cancer cells as well as rapidly growing bone marrow cells. That resulted in red blood cells, so-called good white blood cells, and platelets not being formed. That resulted in a need for transfusions of red blood cells and platelets. The white blood cells were monitored closely with at least three blood tests each week.

"C-B-C now!" Jimmy had heard the phrase more times than he could count. It meant the nurse or doctor wanted a complete blood count done immediately.

There were other invasions to his body during Jimmy's initial treatment.

Jimmy also had leukemia cells in his spinal fluid, which required a lumbar puncture.

"This is spinal tap," Dr. Fitzpatrick said, not quite recognizing that his 12-year-old patient would have no frame of reference for a 20-year-old movie.

Simply put, the chemo drugs don't travel to the spine or the brain, so a small needle was placed into Jimmy's spinal cavity while he lay in a fetal position, and the drugs were delivered directly into the spinal fluid. That took care of that.

Then there was the radiation therapy. Nothing to it, Jimmy thought. Whichever area they were going to irradiate was marked with a dye. Everybody else left the room leaving Jimmy strict instructions not to move, and high levels of radiation were delivered as simply and easily as an ordinary x-ray. Of course, ordinary x-rays don't take several minutes.

The goal of the first phase of treatment was to thrust the disease into remission. It didn't happen for Jimmy, at least not very quickly. Generally, patients achieve complete remission in less than 28 days. It took Jimmy nearly six weeks. That's why there was tempered enthusiasm when Dr. Fitzpatrick announced that Jimmy's leukemia was in remission. The Macombers already knew that if it took more than four weeks to reach remission then Jimmy's prognosis wasn't especially good. While they hoped for the best, they knew remission didn't mean cured, and they were already preparing for the day Jimmy would relapse and a bone marrow transplant might be necessary. Fear was never very far away from a leukemia celebration.

So, for six weeks, Jimmy listened to men arguing about three-point shooting, penalty killing, draft choices, and starting rotations. It was some of Jimmy's best medicine. When he was immersed in the conversations of strangers, he could escape from the nagging uneasiness regarding his health. He could forget about how sick he felt, how scared he was, and how much he worried about his parents and his brother. He could laugh. He could get upset about something other than cancer. Those guys on the radio didn't know it, but they were Jimmy's best friends. He leaned on them more than anyone else, and they saved him more than anyone other than Dr. Fitzpatrick. The day he sat there listening to his doctor explain the transplant process, Jimmy knew he was going to need those faceless voices on the radio again.

Right now, he needed a visitor. He needed his parents to walk in and say they had just heard him on the radio, and that he was wonderful. He'd even settle for his brother, Mark, who would undoubtedly tease him for sounding young or foolish. He would take the razzing, because he'd know that Mark would be either jealous or proud, or both. But no one came to visit. Jimmy went from an incredible high to a devastating low in a matter of moments. He considered getting up to check to see if he had any e-mail messages. Maybe one of his friends had heard and fired off a congratulatory note. But it wasn't likely that any of his friends were listening on a Monday morning during the school year, and the way Jimmy felt right now, it wasn't likely he'd be getting out of bed to check on a longshot e-mail.

Mercifully, Jimmy had fallen asleep, and when he awoke a few hours later, Angela had returned to his room for one last visit before she left for the day. When Jimmy saw her, he found enough energy to bring back a pure, uninhibited smile to his face. Angela had missed seeing that the past few weeks. Like all the kids, Jimmy had his good days and his bad. He showed her more than he showed his parents, and she knew that. She respected that and never betrayed his confidence. But she had begun worrying as much about Jimmy's mental health as his physical health. She watched him put on a brave face when his parents came to visit, but she knew and they knew, it took more effort for him than usual.

"Did you get on the radio, or did you just hang up again?" she asked.

"You didn't listen?"

"Hey, I've got a job to do around here. So, you got on?"

"Yeah. It was pretty cool. At first, they tried to make fun of me because I sounded so young, but then we talked about the Red Sox. I really wish you had listened. I wish somebody had listened."

"Well, maybe next time. I'm sure you were just wonderful."

"I guess so. I'm waiting to hear from my parents. Mom listens a lot. She says she doesn't like it, but we talk a lot about things people have said on the shows."

"I think she likes talking to you a lot about the shows more than she actually likes listening to the shows, if you know what I mean. And she definitely wants to know what kind of language and topics you're being exposed to."

"That's for sure. I hope she was listening today."

"Well, as a wise man once said: Hope is all there is. Hope is what makes tomorrow worth waiting for."

Jimmy, whose head had been down, looked up quickly as Angela winked and walked out the door.

"You were listening!" he yelled. "I knew it all along!"

But he hadn't known. And now his smile returned, even bigger than it was when he had hung up the phone.

"This was a good day after all," he said aloud.

Angela walked down the hall with a spring in her step. This was not an easy job she'd had for the past fourteen years. She had touched a lot of lives, and a lot of lives had touched her. There were tremendous days of celebration, days she wouldn't give back for anything. But there were also so many children lost, children she had grown to love. The defense mechanism she tried to apply at the start of her days at the Dana Farber Cancer Institute had never worked. She had told herself not to grow too attached to these kids, because their deaths would undoubtedly pile up, each one with the potential to break her spirit. But it was the very spirit of the children that had provided her with a fulfilling life she might otherwise have never known. So, she surrendered herself to the inevitable, adopting a full risk, full reward approach to caring for children with cancer. She was determined to reach them, to connect with each and every one of them, to love them, and to mourn their deaths. The successes would provide her with the strength to carry on when the losses seemed too much to bear.

That was her approach, and it was shared by seemingly everyone at the clinic and at Six West. After all, how could anyone walking these halls intentionally keep their distance from beautiful children dying of cancer, dying of loneliness, and living in fear?

Angela certainly loved Jimmy. That's why she hoped for the day that she would never see him again. It would suit her just fine if he walked out of the hospital with a clean bill of health and never looked back. She'd understand if the pain and the memories kept him away, though she'd love for him to return with tales about his life, the life he was living without leukemia. That day was possible, though it was impossible to prophesize when. And until that day arrives, if that day arrives, Angela and the Macombers would have to find comfort in days like this.

"This was a good day after all," she said loud enough for others to hear, and those who did hear knew Angela had just come from Jimmy's room.

"Sports Overtime" Show Open, April 26, 2004

Announcer: It's Monday, April 26th, 2004. Do you know where your Red Sox are? They're in first place, buddy, that's where. The Red Sox just completed a three game sweep of the Yankees in New York, and now they lead those bummed Bombers by 4.5 games.

Sean from *Goodwill Hunting:* Do you like apples? Yeah? Well, I got her number. How do you like them apples?"

Announcer: By the time the Red Sox were finished dumping the pinstripers on their own turf, those boneheaded New York fans were booing Derek Jeter.

Harry Dunne from *Dumb and Dumber:* Just when I thought you couldn't get any dumber, you go and do something like this… and totally redeem yourself."

Announcer: And Pedro Martinez redeemed himself on the hill at Yankee Stadium. This was no Game 7 of the American League Championship Series. He shut down, shutout and shut-up those Yankees for seven innings. And Sox manager Terry Francona won over a few fans when he had the good sense to yank Pedro after seven innings. We bet Grady Little is still getting visitors at his home in North Carolina. Fun loving, well-intentioned, kind hearted Red Sox fans who just want to stop by and say:

Max Fischer from *Rushmore:* I'm sorry. I just came by to thank you for WRECK-ING MY LIFE!

Announcer: But life is good now. So, sit back and relax. Coming up right now on WTED, it's Bob Halloran and Fred "Freddie the Fredderman" Safreed. They'll be taking your phone calls, just as soon as they squeeze into the radio booth.

Homer from *The Simpsons:* Dear Lord, the gods have been good to me. As an offering, I present these milk and cookies. If you wish me to eat them instead, please give me no sign whatsoever....Thy will be done (munch, munch, munch).

Announcer: Join Bob and Fred in their happy place. The Red Sox are better than the Yankees. And with only 142 games left in the season, it sure doesn't look like the Yankees have enough time to catch up. If you think otherwise, tune in to "Sports Overtime" and get yourself an education.

Homer Simpson: And just how is "education" supposed to make me smarter?

Halloran: Well, I don't know about any of that. There's still time for the Yankees. I don't think they've been mathematically eliminated just yet. And that's still a pretty good team they've got.

Safreed: Over-rated.

Halloran: They're not over-rated! They put 8 All-Stars in that line-up, and the back of their bullpen can be lights out. Plus, they've got....

Safreed: They've got 8 FORMER All-Stars in their line-up. No way is Bernie Williams an All-Star anymore. And they just don't have the starting pitching. The Red Sox have won 6 of the 7 games with the Yankees this year.

Halloran: First time since 1913.

Safreed: Way to read the newspapers before you get in, Mr. History. But the point is that the Red Sox, when they go head-to-head with the Yankees, just match-up better. They've proven that. First, when they took three of four at Fenway, and just now when they swept'em in New York.

Halloran: Whoa there Fred. I mean, c'mon, it's a long season. You can't be ready to throw the Yankees under the bus already. They're just off to a slow start. They're three games under .500. If they were playing like they're capable of playing, like everyone expects them to play, they'd be right there with the Red Sox. And I guarantee you; the Red Sox won't win 6 of the next seven games they play against the Yankees. I'm not saying they'll lose six of the next seven. But these things have a way of evening out.

"Hi, honey!" Eileen announced as she and Glenn entered Jimmy's room. "Are you ready to go?"
"Just about. I don't want to leave anything behind, because I don't plan on coming back."

Safreed: I don't know, Bob. The Yankees don't have anybody as good as Curt Schilling. And they don't have anybody as good as Pedro. He was awesome yesterday. Seven shutout innings. 105 pitches. It was the best he's looked against the Yankees in a long time. And it's because he had something to prove. You don't think that with every pitch he threw yesterday, he wasn't thinking about what happened last October? He left disgraced.

"Thanks to Grady Little," Glenn said in disgust.

Safreed: And he went back there and he shut those terds down. And he'll probably always have that little edge against the Yankees. Don't you think he's going to be at his very best every time he faces them from now on?

"It was just as much Pedro's fault, Dad," Jimmy argued. "He's the guy throwing the ball, and he didn't come up big in the biggest moment of his career." Jimmy and Glenn had had this argument countless times before, so Glenn simply shrugged and emptied Jimmy's sock drawer into the suitcase on the bed.

Halloran: Fred, Freddy, Fredderman. A little reality check. Pedro's only 10-8 lifetime against the Yankees. They showed up here in a huge slump, and he just took advantage of that. I think the Yankees would have struggled yesterday if the Red Sox had thrown Bob Stanley out there. And I'm talking about Bob Stanley TODAY. The Yankees spent 183 million dollars for a team that can hit the ball. And right now, they're only batting .217 as a team. That's 29th in the big leagues. Do you honestly think that's going to continue? C'mon, Fred. Don't be fooled into thinking what you've just seen is what you're going to see the rest of the way – for the Red Sox or the Yankees.

Safreed: I agree with you there, because the Red Sox are only going to get better.

Did you see the line-up they threw out there yesterday? The last three guys were David McCarty, Cesar Crespo and Pokey Reese. The last five guys in the order didn't get a hit. Don't forget, the Red Sox are facing these guys without Nomar and Nixon. When the Red Sox get all their pieces back together, they'll be even scarier. I'm telling you, nothing I've seen so far this year makes me think any differently than I did when they signed Schilling and Foulke. This team is going all the way.

Halloran: Well, unfortunately for you Fred, you can't win the World Series in April. But I'll grant you, this is certainly a feel good day in Boston. The Red Sox pitching really did make the Yankees look hideous for three days in the Bronx.

"That's not the only reason it's a feel good day," Eileen glowed. *"Our boy is coming home!"*
"And we'll get you to Fenway just as soon as we can, Jimmy," his father promised.
"Let's sit in the monster seats. I haven't been up there yet! O.K.?"
"We'll try. I'll see what I can do."

Safreed: So, what's up with Jeter? He's like 0-for-his-last 25 now.

Halloran: Yeah, he's got that batting average down to .175. But can you believe the Yankee fans were booing him?

Safreed: Nothing surprises me about Yankee fans. Totally classless. That'd be like booing Larry Bird or Bobby Orr. Jeter's the captain and he helped them win four World Series championships. How can they just forget that and treat him like he's nothing. I mean, I understand the idea of 'what have you done for me lately', but they've got to give the guy a little slack. That was ridiculous.

Halloran: So, you don't think Red Sox fans would do the same thing?

Safreed: No I don't. They're too smart for that.

"Ha!" they laughed in unison, each of them knowing Red Sox fans would turn on their own grandmother if she ever struck out looking with a runner on third.

Halloran: So, if Manny Ramirez suddenly went into an 0-for-25 slump, you don't think he'd start hearing it from the Nation?

Safreed: No comparison. Manny isn't wearing four rings. You'd have to compare it to Bird or somebody like that. And no, if Bird missed 25 shots in a row, I don't think anyone would have booed him. He accomplished too much. He handled himself too well. He's too loved for any of that. And that's exactly how it should be for Jeter.

Halloran: Well, let's find out what some of the folks out there think about any of this. Let's start with M.L. in the car.

M.L: Guys, I feel like I won the lottery this time.

Halloran: Kind of a small lottery, I'm figuring. Maybe a scratch tickets for 20 bucks.

M.L: Whatever. It just feels so good to not only beat the Yankees, but to beat up on them! That's why I say it's okay to boo Jeter. He's the most overrated and overpaid player in baseball -- maybe in all of sports. I looked it up. An average season for him is a .315 average, 18 homers, and 82 runs batted in. And for that he gets 18 million dollars? You've got to be kidding me! Those are decent numbers if you're name is Dmitri Young. I say boo him. Move him to second base, and change his name to Knoblauch.

Safreed: Ouch!

"I love Jeter," Jimmy said. "I love Nomar more, but that Jeter always seems to come up with some way to win a game."

Halloran: Hey, what's the M.L. stand for? Miserable Loser? You're only jumping on Jeter because you're jealous. Jeter's always been a lot more than numbers. He's the heart and soul of a team that's won four championships. You can't just conveniently forget that.

M.L: Believe me. That's not something anyone around here lets you forget. People make it sound like the Yankees never would have won if they didn't have Jeter at shortstop. That's ridiculous. Last year when he separated his shoulder on Opening Day, the Yankees went something like 21-and-6 without him. Their team has been absolutely stacked since he got there. They could have won with just about anybody at shortstop.

"That's like saying the Patriots could win with anyone at quarterback," Glenn chimed in. Jimmy nodded and carefully pulled his Nomar Garciaparra poster off the wall. He rolled the poster into a tight, narrow tube. He taped it at both ends and placed it on the couch next to the similarly rolled up posters of Johnny Damon

and David Ortiz. These guys were coming home with him.

Safreed: Call us back when you get the rest of the parts for your brain, buddy. You're a fool. Don't talk to me about what a team or a guy does in April. Talk to me about what a guy does when it matters, when the game is on the line. Jeter comes through time after time. He's the new Mister October. And congratulations to Steinbrenner and the Yankees for recognizing that. They're paying him all that money to be a money player. And he is.

(From *Swingers*: Baby, you're so money, you don't even know it.)

Halloran: Yeah, but Fred, if you're going to tell me that April doesn't matter, then I have to remind you that what the Red Sox have just done – winning six of seven, and taking a 4.5 game lead in the East – doesn't matter. You can't have it both ways.

Safreed: Well, in Massachusetts you can. Not that there's anything wrong with that. But the Red Sox – Yankees rivalry is a unique situation. It does matter what the Red Sox are doing in April, because they're making a statement.

M.L: No way, man! Even Kevin Millar said after the game that there are no statements to be made at this time of year.

Safreed: Why do you throw me the ramblings of player like he's some kind of authority? So what if Millar says there's no statement to be made. He's wrong! Maybe he didn't think the whole thing through, or maybe he was just being diplomatic. I don't know. But I know the Red Sox have made a statement here, and stated very simply, it's that they're over last year.

"How does he figure that," Glenn wondered to no one in particular.
"Are you taking the magazines with you, Jimmy," his mother asked.
"Yeah, thanks. I'll sort them out at home."
"All right, I'll start putting them in your backpack."

Halloran: How do you figure that?

Safreed: Look, the rest of us can walk around with all this doom and gloom. We can talk about what happened last year, and throw ourselves a pity party, and believe it happens every year, and it's going to happen this year, too. But the Red Sox aren't doing that. They're not looking at the Yankees like this giant albatross they have to wear around their necks. They look at the Yankees, and they see a damn fine team, but that's it. They respect the hell out of 'em, and then they go out and beat 'em. And even if they're not making any kind of a statement to you, which is probably only because you don't want to hear it, they're still telling themselves that they're better than that evil team from New York. And when they face these guys again in September, or in October, they'll think back to THESE games in April, not that one game last October.

Halloran: Has anybody ever worn an albatross around their neck?

Safreed: What? Are you kidding me? I go on and on with some very profound and interesting stuff, and that's all you got out of what I just said? Some stupid thing about an albatross?

Halloran: Well, I hear that phrase all the time, and it just seems a little bizarre that's all. Can you imagine an albatross necklace? Some sailor's out there wearing a dead bird around his neck.

Safreed: Move on.

"Do you want to call the station again today before we go?"
"I was thinking about it, you know, if you guys were late, I was probably going to call. I don't feel tired right now at all. So, it might be fun."

Halloran: All right, fine. Irving from Berlin, Mass. You're next with Bob and Fred on "The Ted".

"Glenn, would you dial the number?"

Irving: Guys I've said it before, and I'll say it again: The toughest thing about success is that you've got to keep on being a success. And right now that goes for the Red Sox AND the Yankees. The Red Sox have had this early success, and that's wonderful. But they have to keep it up all season long and into the playoffs, or they'll just be considered another failure. Nobody's going to remember these games whether they win or lose later in the year. These games are just stepping stones toward real success. And the Yankees know that better than anyone. They have enormous pressure on them to succeed, because they've had so much of it, so much is expected of them.

Halloran: You know, I think you bring up an excellent point there. Because it's amazing to me just how much pressure the Yankees have on them day in and day out, and yet they always seem to be able to handle it. They don't have explosions that suggest they're some kind of pressure cooker or something. And they just go out there and win – consistently.

Safreed: Not right now. Maybe the pressure's finally getting to them.

Halloran: In April?

"Hi. Yes, this is Jimmy from Boston. Uh-huh. That was me who called a few weeks ago." Jimmy had been speaking into the telephone, but at this point he turned to his parents and said, *"I think they remember me from the last time I called."* Glenn and Eileen both welled up at the sight of their son so alive and excited. This was an uncommonly good day, and there was a good chance it was about to get better.

Safreed: You're the one who says they have pressure every day. Maybe it's too much for them. You know, they've got some new guys who might not be able to handle it as well as Yankee teams in the past. You've got Javier Vasquez – who was fine in Montreal. But what's he going to be like in New York. And A-Rod's a perfect example. He puts up great numbers in nowhere places like Seattle and Arlington, but now he's got to do it on the big stage. And maybe he'll fall flat on his pretty face.

Halloran: Pretty, huh? You like A-Rod there, do ya?

Safreed: It's time to move on again, Bob. Pretty is just a figure of speech, y'know?

Halloran: I'm not saying anything. I'm just saying, you know? Karl from Malden, if you've got a pretty face, Fred would like to talk to you off the air.

"What are they saying now?" Glenn asked soon after the radio had been turned down.
"They're talking to some guy from Malden."

Safreed: Don't listen to him Karl.

Karl: Well, I don't exactly have what you'd call a pretty face anyway. My nose is too big. But I called to tell you guys that my father, Barry, used to work on the waterfront with some guys who used to say the Red Sox biggest problem with the Yankees was that they were afraid of them. They could never beat them, because they were afraid of what would happen if they didn't, and they were afraid of what would happen if they did. And fear strikes out. And so do the Red Sox most of the time. But, Fred's right. These Red Sox are fearless. They're going right at those Yankees. And they're going to beat them this year. Can't you just feel it?

60

Safreed: I can. I really can feel it, right in my bones.

Halloran: I am loving this! I mean this is even more beautiful than most years. The Red Sox get off to a nice little start. They make everyone believe they can win it all. Folks start calling in to the radio station and telling us how good the team is, how great the chemistry is, and all this other optimistic, warm and fuzzy crap. And then these are the same people who call us back in August when the team has fallen out of the race and tell us that they knew all along that the team was a bunch of bums. It happens every year. You people are so predictable. You can't go looking at a 6 or 7 game stretch, or even a 15 or 20 game stretch. It's a long season, full of ups and downs, and with any luck at all, the Red Sox players will be able to keep a much more even keel than the fans who go from elation to depression like some crack whore. Bryan from Adams, am I right?

Bryan: I agree with everything you just said, Bob. I'm the crack whore!

Safreed: Congratulations. You're parents must be very proud.

Eileen, who sat down next to Jimmy on the couch and was trying to hear the radio conversation through the phone from several inches away asked, "Are they talking about whores?"
"No, mom. I mean, not really. They just said the word. Twice."
"Wonderful."

Bryan: Well, I mean I was driving home this evening, and I swear I had it all figured out. I knew how the Red Sox were going to get guys like Nomar and Nixon healthy again, and how Schilling and Pedro were going to be like one and two in the Cy Young race, and how Keith Foulke would be this great closer all season long. And I was just getting this great feeling of, like, nothing's going to stop this team.

Safreed: And then you remembered you're a crack whore?

Bryan: Yeah, something like that. I mean I was a big Mets fan during the summer of '69, and I had that same 'you gotta believe' feeling about these Red Sox. But then I came crashing down from my high when I heard that the Red Sox bullpen hasn't given up a run in 24 innings. And then I'm like, dude, there's no way they're gonna keep that up, you know? I mean, the Red Sox are clicking on all cylinders right now. They're going to have to fall back down to earth at some point. Right?

Halloran: Exactly. They won't play this well all year, and the Yankees won't play this badly. So why does everyone want to get caught up in all the emotion of 'Hey isn't this great', or 'This can't suck enough'? Everyone should just calm down. Keep it real. Keep it cool.

Safreed: Then you're not a fan. You're a robot. And that's no fun. I say, get excited. Get mad. And then take your ulcer medication or whatever you need to get you through. But don't try to tell me that beating the Yankees, even in April, isn't important, or fun, or great. Because it is. It just is. And if you don't get that, then it's your loss. Because I get it!

Jimmy rose from the couch and started pacing around the room a bit. He hadn't really considered yet what he was going to say, figuring he'd just respond to whoever preceded him. He threw his toothbrush, special soap, and a seldom used comb into his suitcase, and continued to wait for his turn. He desperately wanted to leave, but now he had a reason to stay for just a few minutes longer.

Bryan: I don't know, Fred. I think I'm going to try to take Bob's advice on this one. I mean, we all know how it hurts when the Red Sox stick it to us in the end, just like they did last year. I mean, those scars might not ever heal. I think it's better not to get our hopes up, because they're the Red Sox, ya know? They're gonna end up losing, somehow, some way, and it's gonna suck big time when it happens.

Safreed: You keep telling yourself that. And I hope you father a lot of children and you can bring them all up to look at life the same way. Look kids, try not to dream too much, because life just has a way of pooping on you. Nothing good has ever happened to me, and I'm going to pass that on to you, just like my father and his father. Now, run along and play, little kiddies. Have fun, but not too much, because remember, life sucks!

Halloran: End of lesson?

Safreed: Oh, I hate it when people call and tell me they're Red Sox fans, but they just want to wallow in their own misery. Stop following the team if you're just waiting for a chance to complain. What a bunch of babies!

Halloran: And we've got more of them right here on "Sports Overtime". Let's talk to John from Milton. John, what's on your mind today?

John: Well, I didn't really call to talk about sports.

Jimmy rested the receiver on his shoulder for a moment, and said: "Now it's some guy who doesn't want to talk about sports. They're gonna kill him."

Halloran: John, do you know what it is we do here? I mean, when you call a sports talk show, what do you think you're going to talk about? Gardening tips?

Safreed: This ain't a confessional, John. Don't go pouring your heart out to us about some nasty thing you did.

Halloran: Hey, that might not be too bad. John, go ahead. Tell us about your problems. Is you're boss cracking the whip? Or is it your wife?

John: Well, thank you gentlemen for reminding me yet again why I don't listen to this show or this station. I'm just calling because a friend of mine said you were talking about the origin of the phrase 'an albatross around the neck'. And it just so happens I can help you out with that.

Halloran: Oh, good. Let's get to the bottom of this. In fact, let's just put all the sports talk aside for the day. It's not like that's what we do around here.

Safreed: You started this.

John: I'll just tell you that it was Samuel Coleridge who first used the metaphor of an albatross in his poem, The Ancient Mariner, and then I'll hang up. Good-bye gentlemen.

Halloran: I'm going to miss him.

Safreed: Let's see if we can send him a nice fruit basket.

Halloran: We're going to have to talk to the producer about screening some of these calls better. But here's one up on the screen that we can take. We talked to this kid a few weeks ago. At least I think it's going to be him again. Jimmy is that you?

Jimmy: Yep, it's me. I'm surprised you remember.

Glenn and Eileen stared at each other, astonished, not sure if they should leave the room to hear both ends of the conversation, or to stay with Jimmy. They stayed.

Safreed: Oh, is this the kid who called a few weeks ago?

Halloran: That's what I just said. Nice to know you're listening over there.

Safreed: It's just that I find the days go by a lot faster if I occasionally tune you out. My therapist said it would help if I just mentally go away for a while. But go ahead. I'm listening now.

Halloran: Well, let's listen to what Jimmy has to say. Jimmy?

Jimmy: Yeah, um, my point today is just that I think it's time for everyone to just start treating the Red Sox better, you know, like you love them. I mean, when you ask people, they SAY they love the Red Sox, but then they rip'em the first chance they get.

Halloran: I don't think that's what's happening here today.

Jimmy: Well, yes it is, Mister H. Even the people who say the Red Sox are playing well are expecting them to fail in the end. It's like, even if it's a beautiful sunny day, everyone's just sitting around waiting for the rain to start. And it is going to rain from time to time. Everybody knows that. But maybe the sun will be shining or the stars will be out at the end of this Red Sox season.

Safreed: I don't even care if it's raining. I just want the Red Sox to win.

Halloran: I think you might have missed the Boy Wonder's metaphor there, Fred.

Jimmy: Don't you guys believe in the power of positive thinking, or the power of faith? It definitely works. I've seen it work for a lot of kids I know. For a lot of us, I mean, for a lot of people, just believing that things will get better makes things better. Because instead of being depressed and expecting the worst, you can be happy and not worry about any of the bad stuff that might happen.

Halloran: You're a little young there Jimmy. It's easy to be positive if you've only experienced a little bit of disappointment. You're talking to people who've had to deal with 1975 and 1978. Bill Buckner and Aaron Boone. And 86 years of what you want the most never happening. After a while, that frustration builds and builds...

Safreed: And then it builds some more.

Halloran: ...until it just boils over into anger. It's getting to the point where if the Red Sox ever do win the whole enchilada, I think there will still be some lingering anger from people who think, 'geez, it's about time, you big bums'. You can't just get rid of 86 years of anger with the snap of a finger.

Safreed: You're crazy there, Mister Crazy Face. If the Red Sox win it all, people around here will be walking on clouds forever. They'll be the ones who saw it happen, and they'll never forget it. People would be falling in love, helping people cross the streets, giving blood, hugging strangers...

(Dr. Peter Venkman from *Ghost Busters*: Dogs and cats living together. Mass hysteria!)

Safreed: ...everyone would love everyone. And nobody would be stupid enough to hold on to any amount of anger or resentment.

Halloran: Oh, there'd be a few people. Trust me.

Jimmy: I think there would be a few people, too. Because there's so many people who are so angry all the time. It's like they root against the Red Sox just so they can prove they were right about them.

Safreed: It validates their misery.

Jimmy: Right. And you guys do it, too. And so do the newspaper people, and all those guys on TV. Right now we seem really close to being positive.

Halloran: But underneath it all, there's a layer of negativity just waiting to rise up and bite everyone on the ass.

Jimmy: Which is why, all I'm saying is that if more and more people stayed positive, if they really, really believed something good was going to happen this year, maybe it would. That's what everybody tells me, and that's what I'm telling you. And, oh by the way, don't forget the Red Sox play their next 25 games against teams that finished under .500 last year, and those teams pretty much stink again this year. So, hopefully, the Red Sox will win a bunch of games, people will start believing in miracles, and then the team will feed off that, and then....

Halloran: And then the Red Sox will win the World Series, altering the course of human events, and life as we know it will never be the same.

Jimmy: Which wouldn't be such a bad thing.

Safreed: It's a beautiful thing.

Halloran: Well, Jimmy, maybe it's time for you to go back to training with the "Up With People" people, or whatever it is you've got planned for your Monday afternoon.

Jimmy: Nothing special.

Halloran: Don't you have any homework or tests to study for.

Jimmy: I take a lot of tests, but I don't have to study for most of them.

Safreed: Boy Wonder is also Boy Genius, I guess.

Halloran: You never studied for tests either, and look where it got you.

Safreed: Right next to you, Little Big Man. Seated at the right hand of Bob Almighty.

"You sounded wonderful, Jimmy," his mother praised. "You really did. I'm so proud of you. I love all that about the power of positive thinking. It..."
"And then you hit them with substantive stuff about the Red Sox schedule," Glenn interrupted. "Very impressive. No wonder they remember you. You're one of their best callers."
"I don't know," Jimmy said shyly. "I get a little nervous."
"You didn't sound nervous at all, honey. You were marvelous. And I think you showed them you have a little better understanding of the misery of Red Sox fans than most people."
"That's to be expected," Glenn said. "We've had our very own fellowship of the miserable off and on for two years. But not any more. Right?"
"I hope so, Dad. But nobody's promising anything yet."

Halloran: Who do we have next here? Ed's in Norton. Hey, Ed.

Ed: Hey guys. Um, well, I was just sort of wondering, you know, thinking, and well, I thought I'd call, and I don't know, maybe ask you guys, because you seem to know, and well, I'm not so sure if, I mean, it's kind of hard for me to put into words exactly, but...

Halloran: WILL YOU GET ON WITH IT ALREADY?

Ed: O.K. Sheesh, what a grouch.

Halloran: This is how you follow a 14-year-old kid? I mean, the kid made sense, and you just babble on.

(Al Czervik, Rodney Dangerfield, from *Caddyshack:* C'mon. While we're young!)

Safreed: Can we get Jimmy back on the line?

Halloran: Let's go to Paul in Revere instead. Paul, you've got it easy, all you have to do is sound smarter than Ed. Can you do that for us?

Paul: Sure, but I don't know if you guys are going to like what I have to say.

Safreed: As long as you can actually say it, I'll be happy.

Paul: Well, I'm enjoying the ride so far as much as the next person. But you just know the Yankees are coming. The Yankees are coming, people. You guys better wake up and get ready for it.

Safreed: So, what are you saying? You've seen the light? You know something the rest of us don't?

Paul: Seen the light? Yeah, I've seen the light. I've seen two lights. One says you're an idiot. And the other one says, so's that Jimmy kid.

The radio in Jimmy's room was never turned back up. Instead, Jimmy made one last search around the room, pulling out the drawers, looking under the desk and the bed, and checking the bathroom for a third time. Once he was satisfied he had everything, he picked up his suitcase and marched quickly out of the room, never looking back. He kept a brisk pace as he moved past the nurses' station. He had already spoken privately with everyone earlier in the morning, and while he knew he would miss these people who had grown to mean so much to him, he didn't want to go through another round of emotional good-byes. He gave a few desultory waves, acknowledged the cheers that erupted as he walked to the automatic double doors, and then stopped. He turned around, looked at the faces of the people who worked so hard every day to save his life, and tried to say "thank you". No sound came from his mouth, but it was clear to everyone what he had tried to say. Jimmy left to wait by the elevators. He was sure it would be a while before his parents had thanked everyone again and again.

Safreed: You're the idiot. Jimmy's fourteen. And he knows more about baseball than you do.

Halloran: And life.

Paul: Hey, I like that Jimmy kid as much as the next guy, but what a crock. I spent the last five minutes of my life listening to you guys talk about being all upbeat and positive – like it matters! I'm not gonna get that time back, you know. You still have to hit the ball. I don't care if you like the guy sitting next to you in the dugout, or if radio shows are flooded with angry fans, or if some player read something in the paper that morning. If there's a man on third with less than two out, you still need to bring him home. And you can have the positive energy flow of 35-thousand fans all sitting there and praying for you, and cheering like crazy, and it don't mean diddly. Because there's still a pretty good chance the hitter will still pop up to third. It happens. It's still baseball. And all this being positive crap is just that – crap!

Halloran: I'm going middle of the road on this one.

Safreed: Way to commit. Is it comfortable up there on that fence?

Halloran: Hey, it doesn't always have to be black and white. In this case, I can see both sides. Do I think it helps to be positive? Yes, I do. I think it's good for team chemistry. And I think it takes some of the pressure off, if guys are having fun. But do I think negativity from the fans and media is the reason the Red Sox haven't won in forever? No, I don't. Do I think being positive helps as much as you think it does? Probably not.

Safreed: Why am I even here, if you're going to ask and answer your own questions all day?

Halloran: Do I know why you're here? No, I do not.

Paul: Hey, I'll give that Jimmy kid a little credit, though. Because I went to my first game on the 18th of April in '75. And I thought that was going to be the year. The Red Sox were stacked with great players. And they had a great chance to win it all. And everybody remembers Carlton Fisk's home run in Game 6, but people seem to forget, the Red Sox gave up a run in the ninth inning of Game 7 to lose that thing, 4-3. Just another colossal collapse! Nobody's perfected losing like the Red Sox.

Safreed: You know, the Red Sox also gave up two runs in the ninth inning of Game

Two to lose that game, 3-2. I don't forget. Another bonehead move by a Red Sox manager. Bill Lee had elbow problems all year, and Darrell Johnson left him out there to start the ninth inning with a 2-1 lead.

Paul: And he gave up the double to Johnny Bench!

Safreed: Exactly. And that was the beginning of the end. Bench scored on an infield single. And then Ken Griffey won it with a double off Dick Drago.

Paul: I know. I know. Griffey called it the biggest hit of his life.

Safreed: Definitely not good times. What is it with Red Sox managers? You've got Johnson and Grady Little leaving pitchers in too long, and John McNamara taking Roger Clemens out too soon in 1986.

Paul: Yeah, but Clemens asked out of that game.

Safreed: Believe what you want. All I know is that...

Halloran: Guys, don't you see what's happening? Here it is -- in a nutshell. What bonds us, and what brings us all together every year is that we all share the memories of Red Sox collapses. Americans remember where they were when Kennedy got shot, or when the Challenger exploded. Red Sox Nation remembers where they were each and every time the Red Sox found some implausible way to break our hearts. And that, my friends, is the circle of life.

Safreed: Hakuna Matata!

Halloran: We'll be back right after this.

CHAPTER FOUR
Nomar Sits

Jimmy's ride home wasn't nearly as joyous as he expected it would be. He was going home.

"Isn't it supposed to feel better than this?"

He would sleep in his own bed tonight.

"Isn't that what I've been waiting for?"

But the rush he anticipated when the automatic doors opened and he stepped outside Children's Hospital for the first time in three months wasn't there. He felt the cool New England breeze slap him in the face, but it didn't give him the presupposed jolt. He felt the warmth of the sun embrace his skin, but it didn't bring the wonted smile to his face. The city's energy was evident in the quick-footed pedestrians and the hasty aggressiveness of the passing cars -- everyone with a place to go. There was noise, a buzz, a smell, a pace, a hustle, and a purpose to these surroundings. The excitement could be as contagious as a virus and linger just as long. It was just as Jimmy had remembered it. But this time, he wasn't a part of it. He wasn't caught up in it. He wasn't feeling empowered. Instead, he was feeling overpowered. It had been that way since he entered the hospital, and nothing had changed now that he was leaving.

Jimmy entered the hospital on day minus 7. He was leaving on day plus 78. The six to eight week stay he planned for himself turned into twelve weeks of the most debilitating and frightening time in his life. Nothing he'd been through in the previous two years had prepared him for this. Nothing he would ever go through could compare to the pain and the suffering, both mental and physical, that he had to endure. He was 14-years-old carrying the weight of a lethal disease, and the burden of trying not to let his parents know how terrified he was.

To arrive at the hospital on day minus 7 meant that the countdown had begun. There would be seven days of intense conditioning, a chemotherapy and irradiation process that far exceeded anything Jimmy had dealt with in the past. On day zero he would receive the bone marrow transplant, and every day after that was a plus day.

"Being alive is the plus, I guess," Jimmy had said when his brother had come to donate his bone marrow.

The minus days scared Jimmy in a way he hadn't foreseen. He had felt the punishment of chemo drugs in the past. But never, not once since he discovered he had leukemia, did he wish he were dead. That changed, albeit momentarily during those first few days of conditioning.

It all had happened so fast. The first few days involved high doses of cytoxan, 50 mg/kg. It's a Wonder Drug that suppresses the production of blood cells from the bone marrow. It goes after the cancer cells and it stuns the normal cells as well. As a result, Jimmy's entire immune system shut down. While he vomited enough to strain a neck muscle, and dealt with the embarrassment of incessant diarrhea, he also developed severe mucositis, an inflammation of the lining in his mouth and throat.

The cytoxan and its side effects were followed by four days of total body irradiation. During those four days, Jimmy received eleven total body irradiation treatments (TBI). It was a radiation level equivalent to over 500 standard X-rays. Jimmy stood up for the treatments, wearing a harness to keep him still, and custom made metal plates known as "lung blocks". Jimmy's bad marrow was being destroyed, and it was nearly destroying him. It was during a short visit with his brother that Jimmy mumbled, "I wish I were dead."

"Don't say that," Mark admonished.

"I can't help it," Jimmy moaned. "I feel so bad. You have no idea. The pain-killers aren't working. Everything they give me makes me feel worse. I feel like I'm dying anyway. And sometimes I just wish this would all be over."

"It will be over," Mark said. "Soon you'll get some new bone marrow, and you'll be feeling good again. You have to believe that."

Jimmy felt the surge of another profound stomach pain. He moaned wildly, and it frightened Mark. He was still just a kid himself. He had to be a kid. Why else would he be thinking about himself while his brother lay there before him in agony?

"Hey, you want to know what I've decided about college?" he asked. Jimmy wailed through another excruciatingly sharp pain. His cries were so loud, Mark was sure that a nurse would be in soon and catch him talking about himself. Mark felt guilty, but he didn't know what to do. So, he continued.

"I'm going to MIT. I haven't told Mom and Dad yet. I mailed my application a few months ago, right after the Super Bowl, and I just found out I've been accepted. Isn't that great!"

Jimmy wasn't focusing very well on the conversation. The pain was raging against his insides. He howled again, and the nurse, Jennifer, hastened into the room. Mark felt it was time for him to go.

"I'll see you Jimmy," Mark said as he was leaving. "I hope you feel better. I'll be back in a few days for the transplant. It's all going to work out. You'll see."

On the other side of the door, Mark fought back tears. He hadn't cried about Jimmy in a long time. He spent a disproportionate amount of time being angry with Jimmy for no good reason. He knew that, but he stayed angry anyway. Now, seeing Jimmy at his all-time worst was disturbing. He felt helpless, and he felt insensitive for talking about himself.

"I'm sorry," he whispered. Then, feeling a hundred eyes upon him and fifty hearts judging him, he skulked shamefully away.

Jimmy didn't hear his brother's last few thoughts. He had already bolted to the bathroom where he prayed he would find some relief.

Mark did return for the day of the transplant.

"Such an amazing event, yet so boring," Mark said. His parents didn't agree that it was boring, but they acknowledged that in this case the word "transplant" carried with it some misplaced expectations.

The bone marrow transplant was nothing like transplanting a kidney or a heart. Those were major surgeries. This was fast and easy. In fact, if someone walked into the room during a bone marrow transplant, they would probably assume it was a blood transfusion. Only the bagged marked "marrow" would divulge the actual purpose of the proceedings.

So, Mark arrived on day zero. During his procedure, six incisions about the size of his baby toenail were cut into two sides of his hipbone. A special tool known as a Jamshidi was used to work as a combination drill and syringe. The Jamshidi screwed into the bone until it hit the spongy marrow. The drill part of the Jamshidi was pulled out, and the syringe part was threaded on to that same end. The marrow was sucked out into the syringe, just as if the doctors were collecting a regular blood sample. But in this case, the fluid appeared more like jellied strawberries. In total, about two quarts of marrow were collected and squirted into a jar and strained over a filter to make sure there were no bone chips in it. Mark was told all of this later. He was out for the two-hour procedure. His work was done. He spent his first night in the hospital and returned home the next day. Jimmy's work was just beginning

He received his brother's bone marrow a few hours after the harvest was collected. The catheter served as a direct line into his bloodstream, allowing the marrow to migrate to the cavities in the bones where it is normally stored. The process was easy, and the procedures only took a matter of minutes, but no one would know for sure if the transplant was successful for several months. A lot of things could go wrong, and some of them did.

The greatest fear was graft versus host disease, so they waged war on that immediately. Cyclosporine, an immunosuppressive agent, was actually begun on day minus two. It was administered as part of the continuing effort to knock out Jimmy's immune system. This was important because after the transplant, Jimmy's white blood cells could try to reject the new marrow. Cyclosporine works to prevent that.

Despite receiving a series of antibiotics, and antiviral and antifungus medications, three days after the transplant, Jimmy developed a fever.

"And this rash around your catheter is called staphlyococcus epidermis," Dr. Fitzpatrick explained. "It's very common after a BMT. We know there's a pretty good chance it's coming. So, we get ready with a whole bunch of antibiotics." And since he knew Jimmy liked to hear the names of everything he took, Dr. Fizpatrick added, "They're called pipercillin, gentamicin, tobramycin, and amphotericin. And I'm ordering some rifampin as well."

"That all sounds good to me," Jimmy said.

But it wasn't good at all. Jimmy's fever persisted for nearly a week. The regimen of antibiotics continued along with around the clock blood and platelet transfusions. He was given additional medicines to reduce his nausea and vomiting. And still, his mouth sores bled incessantly. He couldn't even think about food. The fever and the drugs combined to make him feel lethargic and downright loopy. So, he barely remembered who came to visit.

Jimmy listened to his favorite sports talk radio station. He prayed for some kind of ending to his misery. He made constant use of the suction device at his bedside designed to vacuum his saliva because the mucositis had made it nearly impossible for him to swallow. And he spent hours psyching himself up to get out of bed, just for a few minutes, to avoid bed sores. That was his day – day after day. It was extremely difficult for him physically, but the psychological and emotional traumas were equally dreadful.

Finally, the fever broke, the lesions on his liver and gallbladder healed, and on day plus 20, he engrafted. Jimmy was producing white blood cells, and his blood type was gradually shifting from B-positive to A, which was Mark's blood type. A normal person's white blood cell count ranges somewhere between 5 and 11. Jimmy's was 0.3, and that was marvelous. It meant the new marrow was finding its way into his bones, and there was no sign of the dreaded graft versus host disease. But Jimmy knew that could occur at anytime, even much further down the road.

There were enough complications to keep Jimmy hospitalized for exactly 12 weeks. The neutropenia contributed to him getting various infections in his lungs, mouth, throat, sinuses and unsightly rashes on his skin. He also noticed blood in his urine, which was defined as hemorrhagic cystitis. It became increasingly uncomfortable to urinate, but it was treated simply with increased IV fluids.

And then there was the diffuse alveolar hemorrhage. Jimmy really didn't see that one coming. Just as he was allowing himself a minor celebration over the engraftment, he came down with a slight cough and shortness of breath. Minor inconveniences for most people, but the symptoms turned into a noninfectious pneumonia. Doctors ramped up the prednisone and administered additional corticosteroids in order to treat the DAH. There was grave concern the DAH could lead to overt respiratory failure, but Jimmy battled through.

Each complication added to the time Jimmy was spending in the hospital. Dr. Fitzpatrick had been adamant that Jimmy couldn't go home until his Absolute Neutrophil Count (ANC) was above 500 for three consecutive days. Jimmy learned the formula for figuring the ANC, simply multiply the number of white blood cells by the percentage of neuts. Somewhere near a thousand is preferred, but if the product is above 500, then a person can be effective in fighting infections, and Jimmy could go home to continue his fight there.

On three separate occasions, Jimmy's ANC was above 500 for two days in a row, but in each instance, the ANC dipped on the third day. More treatments were given. More blood tests were taken. More time passed and Jimmy's mood worsened. He had taught himself not to let his expectations rise too much, but he was living on hope – prednisone, cyclosporine and hope. Every piece of good news was tempered and eventually matched with bad news. Until today. Today, Jimmy went home.

"Sports Overtime" Show Open, July 2, 2004

Announcer: It's another Big Monday of "Sports Overtime" on "The Ted". After a spring time of feeling like the Alpha dogs of baseball, the Red Sox now have their tail between their legs after getting swept by the Yankees this weekend. So, today the Big Boys, Bob Halloran and Fred Safreed, will be discussing a little something folks in the sports world like to call payback. That BITCH!

Bob Barker in *Happy Gilmore*: The price is wrong, bitch!

Announcer: Yes, it sure looks like the Red Sox paid the price for feeling a little too good about themselves back in April. Note to Red Sox: Nobody's ever won the World Series in April.

Gary Sheffield, Yankees outfielder: The message is clear. We're not laying down for no one. We're trying to take it all. We're trying to send a message to everyone we play. Everyone was jacked up for this series. We wanted to sweep, and we did.

Announcer: Oh, but the sweep wasn't nearly humiliating enough. We also had to watch Yankee shortstop Derek Jeter dive face first into the stands with reckless abandon, no regard for his own personal safety, thinking only about the team, and coming out of those stands with a bloody cheek, a black eye, and the third out of the 12th inning. Oh, baby! That one hurt the Red Sox more than it did Jeter.

Jorge Posada, Yankees catcher: He says he's playing tomorrow. That's just the way Derek is. He has that intensity.

Announcer: And Nomar Garciaparra – not so much. In a 13-inning game destined for status as an instant classic, Nomar sat. And he sat. And then he got up… and sat back down.

Nomar Garciaparra, Sox shortstop: I just didn't get in. There was a time I might get a chance, but it just didn't happen.

Announcer: No, it didn't. So here's what's GONNA happen. Nomar's gonna get ripped today on these airwaves. They're going to throw him under the bus, and then back the bus up. Nomar's meat on a bone for a pack of hungry wolves. And we'll be waiting to hear from every fan who believed this was the year the Red Sox would pass the Yankees.

Happy Gilmore from Happy Gilmore: I'm stupid. You're smart. I was wrong.

You were right. You're the best. I'm the worst. You're very good looking. I'm not very attractive.

Halloran: That was ugly! UGLY!! Oh, my goodness. That was hard to stomach. What an absolutely abysmal weekend for the Red Sox. And that is so true. Not only did the Red Sox get swept and fall 8.5 games behind the Yankees, but we had to watch Jeter lay himself out like that while Nomar just sat there for 13 innings.

Safreed: He's dead to me! That was absolutely unforgivable! I mean, are you kidding me!

"They're going to crucify Nomar today," Mark said as he walked into Jimmy's room. "Are you sure you want to listen to this?"

Halloran: Well, they're saying he's still hurt.

"He is hurt," Jimmy said more to the radio than to Mark.

Safreed: Aww, hurt shmurt! Get in the game! Your teammates need you. I mean this is ridiculous. And you wanna know the number one reason why?

Halloran: Love to.

Safreed: Because Nomar's going to play tonight. Tonight! Do you understand what I'm saying? Tonight!

Halloran: Yes, Fred. I understand the concept of time.

Safreed: You mean to tell me that whatever was wrong with his Achilles is going to miraculously get better in like 12 hours! He couldn't play yesterday, but he'll be fine today?! Don't insult my intelligence with that hogwash!

"You have to admit that's a pretty good point. I know how much you love Nomar, but you can't love what happened yesterday."

Halloran: Well, rest does do a body good. Look, I agree with you, Fred. But we were told that he wouldn't be able to play everyday when he came back. We knew he'd have to take a few days off here and there. They're just following the plan.

"That's a good point, too, Mark. It's not entirely up to Nomar. Manager's make decisions, y'know."

Safreed: So take tonight's game off! You tell me what's the more important game, trying to avoid a sweep against the Yankees, or the Braves tonight! For crying out loud, Nomar ought to be ashamed of himself, and Terry Francona needs to grow some coconuts!

Halloran: You can't go blaming Francona for this one. If he's got a player who says he can't play, what's he supposed to do? He can't just send him out there, because what if Nomar really is too hurt to play, and then he goes and blows out the Achilles altogether, and they lose him for the rest of the season? This has to be all on Nomar. If he wanted to play badly enough, all he would have had to do was say so. But he didn't. So, either he was too hurt, or too chicken.

Safreed: I like the sound of chicken.

Halloran: I'm sure you do, big fella.

Safreed: Look, it's as simple as this: Nomar sits and sulks. Jeter plays and leads. 'Nuff said.

Jimmy tried to sit up in his bed, but it was still painful. On day plus 116 he had fallen while stepping out of the tub. It wasn't a hard fall, but the combination of radiation and steroids had weakened his bones. In that brittle state, Jimmy had suffered a compression fracture of his fourth lumbar vertebrae. He only required five days in the hospital, but was told the injury would take three months to heal. He was mobile again, but simple movements required time and a strategy.

Halloran: Well, I think there will be plenty more said in the coming days. And we'll get it started with MacLaine out in Shirley.

MacLaine: I can't help but think I've seen all this before. Isn't this exactly what Manny Ramirez did last year when he refused to pinch-hit during some big game?

Safreed: Yeah, I'd say yeah. You're right. It's basically the same thing. Manny had that pharyngitis thing that was going around. And Grady Little asked him to pinch-hit, I think it was against the Phillies, and Manny wouldn't even pick up a bat. That was pretty awful, too.

Halloran: And then they benched Manny for a game.

Safreed: Exactly. And I remember everybody was pretty upset at the time, including the Red Sox. Nobody went to bat for him, so to speak.

MacLaine: But all has since been forgiven, wouldn't you say? I mean, people say it's just 'Manny being Manny' like that's a term of endearment. But don't you think you'll ultimately forgive Nomar for this? Maybe that was just 'Nomar being Nomar'.

Safreed: If it was, I don't like it. Not one bit. I mean, I don't know. You make a good point. But I gotta be honest. I'm a little too upset to pay any attention to reason right now.

Halloran: So, you're admitting to being unreasonable.

Safreed: Yeah, right now I am. I'll tell you, I don't know how my TV survived last night. I just wanted to throw something at it every inning that went by and that guy just kept sitting there. And he wouldn't even join his teammates on the top step of the dugout when they were trying to get a rally going. It was like he just didn't care.

Halloran: But that's where you lose me, Fred. We know he cares. We've watched him for seven years, and he always plays hard. As upsetting as this was, I'm thinking it was really out of character for him. It was just so strange. Think about ANYBODY sitting in the dugout during a 13-inning game between the Red Sox and Yankees, and can you imagine anyone not wanting to play. I don't even have an explanation for it. Maybe Tim in Wakefield can help us out.

Mark helped Jimmy lift himself up. He had brought Jimmy's lunch on a tray and placed it on his brother's lap. Lunch today, and nearly every day consisted of a baked potato, carrots and an apple. In the early part of his recovery, Jimmy barely ate at all. More recently, his diet was limited to things that could be boiled or peeled. Eileen paid careful attention to cleaning the vegetables, and Mark delivered the meals whenever he was home.

Tim: Well, first of all, you guys are making yesterday's game out to be more important than it really was.

Halloran: You don't think trying to prevent a sweep against the Yankees, and being 6.5 games out of first place instead of 8.5 games is important?

Tim: Sure, it's important. But it's all about winning a certain number of games by the end of the year. So, let's suppose Nomar plays, but then he has to sit out the next three or four games, and the Red Sox lose those games. What good would a win against the Yankees mean then?

Safreed: Every win against the Yankees means more than any win against anybody else, and don't even try to tell me otherwise. That's the team you're trying to beat. They're the ones who put the monkey on the Red Sox back. The Red Sox need to knock that monkey off and prove to themselves and to the Yankees that they're the better team. Instead, yesterday the Yankees walked away feeling superior yet again. They've got a guy who'll throw his face into a metal railing to catch a ball, and the Red Sox have a guy who sits. And that sums it up perfectly. That's why the Yankees always beat the Red Sox.

Halloran: That, and they've always had a better team.

"Are you on hold with these guys again?"

Halloran: Hey, Arnold from Palmer, you're next on "The Ted" with Bob and Fred. How you doing today?

Arnold: Par for the course, I guess. Listen, I'm calling to defend Nomar.

"Yeah. I've been waiting about 45 minutes. Maybe they're not going to get to me this time."

Safreed: Oh, this ought to be good. Let's hear it. How can you possibly defend a guy who won't go to war with his team?

Arnold: Well, the guy's playing with a handicap, and it's obviously been affecting his play. He's been like a hacker out there. He came off the disabled list almost a month ago and he's only hitting .235 with one home run. He's not driving the ball well at all. And he made three pretty costly errors in the first two games of the Yankee series.

Halloran: That's right. And those errors led to four unearned runs.

Arnold: So, with all due respect to Nomar, he's been stinking it up. And since we know he doesn't stink, we have to figure that he's still hurt. And if he's hurt, and his play is hurting the team, and he knows his play is hurting the team, isn't it kind of a valiant thing to say, "I really want to be playing in this big game, but I honestly don't think I can help us win"?

Safreed: Valiant? You think it takes courage to sit around for 13-innings?

Arnold: Fred, let me ask you. Do you think Nomar would have helped the team if he played?

Safreed: As a matter of fact I do. I think he's a great hitter who's being paid a lot of money, and even if he's in a slump, he still poses a greater threat than anybody else the Red Sox might call off the bench. Even if his mere presence at the plate is intimidating enough that the pitcher walks him; that would be fine. But he's got to at least try. He's got to give us that much.

Halloran: Yeah, Arnie, I agree with Fred. It's one thing to not start the game, and that was bad enough. But once both teams start emptying out their rosters, basically using everybody, then it's all hands on deck. If he's healthy enough to suit up, then he should be healthy enough to grab a bat somewhere along the lines. Whaddaya say we take another call from our friend Jimmy in Boston?

"Quick! Turn down the radio," Jimmy said with his hand over the receiver.

Safreed: Shouldn't you be outside playing baseball or getting into trouble or something?

Jimmy: Yeah, usually this is my time to go out knocking over garbage cans and putting shaving cream in mailboxes, but I'm not feeling too well today.

Halloran: That's called Red Sox-itis. Symptoms include an upset stomach, occasional cold sweats, and throwing up just a little bit in your mouth.

Safreed: And it's brought on by watching the Red Sox lose 8 of their last 11, and 15 out of 26 games.

Jimmy: No, it's not the Red Sox who are making me sick. But you guys aren't helping when you're picking on Nomar like this. He's my favorite player.

Halloran: Well, then you must have been especially disappointed in him yesterday. Mister Role Model showed you how to be a selfish player, didn't he?

Jimmy: Not really. I think the problem is that you don't see his injury with your own eyes, so you don't believe it's that bad. But Nomar's been here for seven years, and in all that time, he's never given us any reason to think he's a quitter. Don't you think he deserves the benefit of the doubt?

Safreed: I gave him the benefit of the doubt for two months. This guy supposedly hurt himself in spring training, and we kept hearing it might be a day or a week, or he'd probably be ready for Opening Day, then the speculation was six weeks. Well, some TEN weeks later, he finally comes back. But he's not even really back yet! Oh, poor baby's got a little tightness in his Achilles. Suck it up, and get in the game!

Jimmy: When has Nomar not sucked it up? When has he not given 100 percent? When was the last time he didn't run out a ground ball? Has he ever done that? I think you have to remember who we're talking about, and what he's done, and how he's played over the years, and then try to keep everything in perspective.

Halloran: I think he's got you, Fred.

Safreed: Well, if he's got me then he's got you, but he doesn't have either one of us, because Nomar's different now. He's not the same guy who stood on top of the dugout to thank all the fans after the 1999 playoffs. He's not the quiet leader in the clubhouse we thought he was going to be. He's a loner. He doesn't talk to anybody. He never smiles. You can tell he's not happy here. He's been pouting ever since the Red Sox tried to trade him. The guy wants out. And I'm sure he's thinking, why should I put my body on the line, or my career in jeopardy for these guys. Ownership doesn't want me, so I'm not making any sacrifices for them. That's why he sat out yesterday's game. He thinks ownership quit on him, and he's been quitting on them ever since.

Halloran: Good point by Fred there, Jimmy. That would explain why it took him so long to come back from his Achilles injury. He certainly didn't seem to be in any great hurry to get back, kind of took his sweet old time, which he might not have done during happier times.

Jimmy: You say he took his time, but you don't know that. The problem is you guys don't see a surgical scar or a cast on his foot, so you don't believe his injury is serious. And I'm saying, first of all, his bad defense and crummy hitting prove he's not healthy, and second of all, you should believe him anyway – because it's Nomar. Besides, sometimes people are really hurting, but you might not know it by looking at them. Sometimes the pain is on the inside, and there's nothing anybody can really do about it.

Safreed: That's what they have doctors for.

Jimmy: Doctors can't fix every problem. Sometimes they just cross their fingers like evebody else, and then it's just a matter of time.

Safreed: All right, little Jimmy. You just keep living in your dream world where everybody tells the truth, and if Nomar says he's too hurt to play, then that's all there is to it. Me? I think I'll live in the real world where sometimes guys get a bug up their bum, and they turn into angry, bitter people who do spiteful things without any regard for their teammates.

Halloran: Like Fred.

Safreed: I'm not bitter. I'm just calling 'em as I see 'em.

Halloran: Are you sure? Because you sound a little bitter to me.

Jimmy: Me too.

Safreed: I'm fine. Don't you guys worry about me.

Halloran: Thanks for the call, Jimmy. Call back any time you want to wind Fred up again.

"I'll tell you, little brother, sometimes I don't know if you're talking about baseball or about yourself," Mark said. Jimmy just smiled.

Halloran: Bob from Tewksbury, you're next on "Sports Overtime".

Bob: Well, um, I kind of forgot what I was going to say. I guess I don't have much to offer.

Halloran: Thanks for the contribution, Bob. Let's try Rick in Providence.

Rick: I just called to say that I think all this negativity stinks, and it sucks, and it stinks. I'm living in Louisville, Kentucky now, and I can't tell you what a breath of fresh air it is. I was around when Jim Rice was booed, and when they booed Carl Yastrzemski. And it stinks. All the negativity that's in this town makes the greatest city in the world lousy.

Halloran: Well, it's nice to have you back.

Safreed: Yeah, can't tell you how much we missed you.

Rick: Your sarcasm only proves my point. Look, winning is a choice. And the only way the Red Sox are going to turn this thing around is by staying upbeat and positive. Cy Young's not going to walk into that clubhouse. Babe Ruth is not going to walk into that clubhouse. And if they do walk into that clubhouse, they're going to be dead. So, the Red Sox have to go with the guys they've got. And their fans need to be a lot more supportive.

Mark turned up the radio and sat on the end of Jimmy's bed waiting for him to finish his lunch.

Halloran: You're well within your rights to stay positive if you want to. But that's not our job. Our job is to talk honestly about what we see, and to be honest with you; I think our job is also to hold the local teams accountable. If the Boston teams do something the fans don't like, they'll hear about it on this radio station. Right now, you're voice is being heard, and you're telling the Red Sox that losing 15 of their last 26 games is all right by you. This team was 7 games over .500 on May 2nd. It's now two months later and they're still 7 games over .500. Is that what you expected from a team with a 120-million dollar payroll?

Safreed: Yeah. Do you see something positive in that?

Rick: I see a team that tries hard every day, and I see....

(EXPLOSION NOISE)

Safreed: That's right. Blow him up! A team that tries hard! C'mon. This isn't little league. These guys get paid to produce. And right now they're producing squat. And you're right, Mister State the Obvious. It's been two months, and all they've been doing is treading water. That's not a slump. That's a trend. This team is woefully underachieving.

Halloran: Meanwhile, the Yankees are running away with the division again. Since they were in here and got swept by the Red Sox back in April. The Yankees have gone 42-15. That's a winning percentage of .737. So, I guess all that talk about their pitching being questionable was a bit overstated.

Safreed: I don't think there's ever been any doubt that the Yankees are good. My point all along has been that the Red Sox are just as good, or even better.

Halloran: And how's that working out for you?

Safreed: Not well. I have to admit. Not well at all.

"How'd that bone density scan turn out?" Mark inquired.
"The counts were good, and I didn't need any transfusions. In fact, the last one I had was a whole blood transfusion when my hemoglobin dropped below eight a few weeks ago."
"So, you're feeling pretty good, except for the back, I mean?"
"Yeah, I guess so. It's just like always. I feel fine until I don't."

Halloran: Noah's in Webster. What have you got for us today, Noah?

Noah: Gentlemen, I can certainly approbate the palpable manifested truth of Nomar's extant circumstances. But I have to caution you concerning your attempt at physiognomy.

Halloran: What?

Safreed: Yeah, what?

"I love this guy. He's called a few times before. Cracks me up!"

Halloran: I swear the guy nibbles on a thesaurus before he calls.

Safreed: Just bring it down a notch, professor. When you were talking, all I heard was a dull tone of a TV test pattern.

Halloran: You heard that too? I thought it was just me.

Noah: What I mean by physiognomy is that you're trying to characterize Nomar's mood and temperament by analyzing his facial expressions. You don't see him smile, so you assume he's unhappy. You assume he's unhappy, so you leap to the conclusion that he's some sort of malingerer.

Halloran: Well, why didn't you just say that?

Safreed: I can't believe all these knuckleheads calling in here today to try to explain away Nomar's reprehensible decision to stay on the bench yesterday. It's as clear as the nose on his face. The Red Sox lost a game they should have won, except that one of their best players couldn't be bothered. And if he couldn't be bothered to play in a game like that, then I can't be bothered with him. Case closed.

Halloran: Sure, until he starts knocking the cover off the ball again.

Safreed: Then we may re-open the case. But for now, tell all these yahoos enough already with the defending of Nomar. It was just repugnant.

Halloran: Contemptible.

Noah: Odious, repellent, vile, wretched, lurid, abhorrent, ignominious.

Safreed: All right, all ready. Thank you, Mr. Vocabulary. I hate that -- people who use big words just to sound smart.

Halloran: Actually Fred, I think they use the big words because they ARE smart.

Safreed: Yeah, well, if you throw around too many ten-dollar words nobody's going to want you to throw your two-cents in.

Halloran: Wow! That was pretty good, Fred. You want to take a breather. I'm wondering if something that clever might have taken too much out of you. Do you think you can continue the show?

Safreed: I'm fine. It's not like I planned to say something clever. It was purely by accident.

Halloran: Well, stick around everybody. There could be more accidents in Fred's future. And you don't want to miss it. We'll be right back with more of your phone calls, and the Mixed Messages, next on "Sports Overtime".

Jimmy used the commercial break to gingerly rise out of bed and walk to the bathroom. By his calculations, he'd have between 15 and 20 minutes before the break was over. He hoped that would give him enough time. On his worst days, nothing could make him smile. But on his bad days, the Mixed Messages could get him feeling a little bit better. This was a good day, and he expected good things from his favorite radio show.

Halloran: We're back with some Mixed Messages, and let me tell you, the phone lines were jammed today with folks wanting to leave a message for Nomar Garciaparra and the Red Sox. Here's what we can share with you.

Recorded Voice: You have ten unheard messages. First message:

Message One: Hey, Nomar, this is Joe DiMaggio calling. Remember when Ted Williams said you reminded him of me. Well, I would have played. In fact, I saw what you did yesterday, and I rolled over in my grave.

Halloran: And, no doubt, rolled right into Marilynn Monroe .

Safreed: That's a nice afterlife.

Message Two: It's too bad Nomar doesn't play like a girl. You know -- LIKE HIS WIFE. She'd never bail on her team in a big moment. Next time you're rubbing up against her, Nomar, see if you can get some of her to rub off on you.

Message Three: Nomar, I used to hate the Fredderman more than anybody – THAT TALL BASTARD! But, now I'm not so sure. You SVELTE BASTARD!

Halloran: Nomar is svelte, isn't he?

Safreed: Sinewy, I think.

Halloran: Oh, Noah from Webster's got nothing on you.

Safreed: I could have gone with sylphlike, but I try never to look too smart.

Halloran: You do a nice job with that.

Message Four: The Red Sox are a horror show, like *I Know What You Did Last Summer* and *I Still Know What You Did Last Summer*. Except with the Red Sox, it's more like, "I Know What You Do Every Summer". You ruin it! YOU'RE RUINING MY SUMM-AHHHHHHH!

Halloran: First one of those in a while. And it won't be the last.

Message Five: Don't everyone get down on the Red Sox. Instead of following in the rich tradition of Red Sox teams of the past who like to wait until the last possible moment to pull the rug out from under us, this Red Sox team was much kinder and gentler – because they screwed it all up now!

Halloran: I didn't really look at it that way. This is easier to take than another one of those playoff debacles.

Safreed: It's not over yet. I'm mad, and I'm discouraged, but I haven't given up.

Message Six: Hey, Red Sox, is that all you got? You think you can hurt me with a shortstop who quits on his team? Heck, I lived through Bucky, Buckner and Boone, oh my! And those were only flesh wounds. Nomar's nothing but a pin prick, minus the pin, of course.

Safreed: Nice. Very nice.

Halloran: Did you see what he did there?

Safreed: Yes, I did. Very well done.

Message Seven: So, I'm sitting here alone in my mother's basement where I live. And I'm wondering what I'd like for my 37th birthday next week. I ask for a girl-friend every year, but Mom never gets me one. So, this year I'm going to ask for a blow-up Nomar doll. Then I'll put a tear in the Achilles heel, and I'll just sit it on the bench in my work room next to my soldier of fortune magazines, and I'll talk to it.

Halloran: This guy's got problems.

Message Seven (continues): I'll say: 'Nomar, you really disappointed me. That's why I have to punish you. I don't want to stick this C-4 plastic explosive in your mouth. But you've given me no choice.'

(voice from another room): Honey, are you in there?

Message Seven (continues): Oops, gotta go.

Halloran: Whoa, that was pretty bizarre. The guy sounds like Kathy Bates' character in *Misery*.

Safreed: More like Norman Bates. Are we sure he was kidding around?

Halloran: Let's hope so.

Producer's voice: Yeah, that guy calls every once in a while, usually with some kind of a gag bit.

Halloran: Even as a gag, you have to wonder about the guy.

Message Eight: Yeah, I'd like to leave a message at the beep. Nomar, you're a BEEP! Why don't you just BEEP my BEEP and BEEP BEEP BEEP, you

86

BEEEEEEP! Oh yeah, this is Mia. Give me a call when you get a chance.

Message Nine: Hey, Fred. First you pick the Red Sox to go all the way. Then you talk about how pathetic they are. Then you say you still think they can turn things around in time. You have more positions than the Karma Sutra!

Safreed: I do not. There are fifty-five positions in the Karma Sutra. Not even I flip-flop that much.

Halloran: Maybe if you did a little more flip-flopping, there'd be fifty-six positions. And how do you know something like that anyway?

Safreed: Oh, I know some things, Mr. Doesn't Know As Many Things.

Halloran: I worry about you, Fred.

Message Ten: You know what? Watching the Red Sox is like watching repeats of old *Seinfeld* episodes. I know what's going to happen, but I watch anyway. And I just can't help myself from laughing.

Halloran: Yankee fan. We get a few of'em.

(George Costanza from *Seinfeld*): I'm disturbed. I'm depressed. I'm inadequate. I've got it all!

Halloran: And that about sums it up, wouldn't you say? Red Sox fans have their low self-esteem and feelings of inadequacy back again. And all it took was getting swept by the Yankees.

Safreed: And the tale of two shortstops. On a one to ten scale for being a gamer or a leader, Jeter gets an 11, and Nomar gets a zero.

Halloran: Well, love him or hate him. He's the Red Sox shortstop, and that's not going to change until the end of the year. So, you better hope he turns things around for himself, and that the team kicks it into gear in a hurry. Pretty soon they'll be running out of time. And we're out of time for today. We'll be back tomorrow with more on the Red Sox soap opera. The Sox are in Atlanta for a game with the Braves, a game you can hear right here on WTED. And guess what Red Sox Nation? Nomar's in the line-up!

(MUSIC BURST AND COMMERCIAL)

CHAPTER FIVE
The Brawl

Jimmy read enough to know this could be an issue. But, he thought, maybe it's nothing. He woke up this morning with a pain in the side of his chest. It made his breathing difficult, and when he coughed, it was as if someone was stabbing him in the side. Combined with the dry cough that began yesterday, Jimmy was well aware that these were quite possibly early signs of pneumonia.

He lay in bed for several minutes trying to determine how much of this new information he would share with his mother and father. They would be in soon to check his neutrophil count. It had been in the 700 range for several days which meant Jimmy's body could be moderately successful fighting infection, but he couldn't have any visitors, and his parents liked him to stay in his room.

"The chest pain could easily be a pulled muscle or something," he thought to himself. "I threw up enough the other day to cause that kind of pain."

He also reasoned that his putrid breath could simply be caused by the cyclosporine he was taking. Those were the gray, football-shaped capsules that smelled like a skunk. They had never caused bad breath before, but it sure seemed to Jimmy like they had the potential.

Certainly, Jimmy felt ill. He had some aches and pains, and he hadn't felt like eating the past two days. But that was par for the course. Why would he assume that these symptoms were indicative of pneumonia?

"It's the rust-colored phlegm," he said out loud. "If I tell my parents about that, I know we're going to the hospital today."

It was almost too much to take. Everything the doctors had told him might happen – happened! He lost his hair, even his eye lashes and eyebrows. He lost his fingernails and his toenails. He had conjunctivitis. He hurt his back in what should have been an innocuous fall. He had cramps, and diarrhea. He found out the hard way that he'd become lactose intolerant. He had a bad case of mucositis that spread from his mouth to his digestive system. He was taking handfuls of pills. He was living like a prisoner in his room, washing his hands a dozen times a day, taking every possible precaution to prevent infection. And every set back made him feel like he was losing the battle.

He decided to tell his parents about his latest symptoms. His mom responded by taking his temperature, which was 101. And it didn't take his father long to pack Jimmy's bag. They all seemed to know what the diagnosis would be when they got to the hospital, and it wasn't likely that Jimmy would be coming home tonight.

In fact, Jimmy was still in the hospital when the Red Sox brawled with the Yankees in late July.

"Sports Overtime" Show Open, July 26, 2004

Announcer: Today on "The Ted" we'll be putting the wraps on a wild weekend between the Red Sox and their arch rivals from the Big Apple. The Red Sox did a little brawling with the Yanks on Saturday and came out on top – in the fight and in the game. Looks like our boys have got some fight in them after all.

Mickey from *Rocky*: You're gonna eat lightnin' and you're gonna crap thunder!

Announcer: Sure, the Red Sox are still 7.5 games behind the Yankees, but they went head-to-head, and toe-to-toe, and face-to-face, and a whole lot of other body parts to body parts. So, maybe this race will end up being neck-and-neck after all.

Adrian from *Rocky*: Einstein flunked out of school, twice.
Paulie: Is that so?
Adrian: Yeah. Beethoven was deaf. Helen Keller was blind. I think Rocky's got a good chance.

Announcer: If it sounds like crazy talk to think the Red Sox can still catch those Yankees, well then, welcome to "Sports Overtime", hosted by Bob Halloran and Fred "Freddie the Fredderman" Safreed. They're the ones who run the asylum.

McMurphy from *One Flew Over The Cuckoo's Nest*: I must be crazy to be in a loony bin like this.

Announcer: Ah, but we wouldn't have it any other way. Red Sox Nation was feeling the love when Jason Varitek shoved the glove, and told the Yankees: "We've had enough".

White Goodman from *Dodgeball*: You're going down like a sweet muffin!

Announcer: Oooh, and didn't that just make pretty boy A-Rod as mad as a wet hen, or some other kind of chicken.

Mr. Furious from *Mystery Men*: Don't mess with the volcano my man, 'cause I will go Pompeii on your butt.

Announcer: The brawl and ninth inning home run that beat the world's greatest closer should be the spark that ignites the fire back into the belly of the beasts from Boston. Hey, that sounded pretty good! Wish I wrote that instead of just getting to say it in this made up announcer voice that would be irritating anywhere but the radio. Why do I talk like this? I should get some help. Now, where was I?

Apollo from *Rocky III*: See that look in their eyes, Rock? You gotta get that look ɔack, Rock. Eye of the tiger, man.

Announcer: That's right. It's the eye of the tiger, and the Red Sox have it back. Who was right, and who was wrong in Saturday's fight? This one's gonna go to the judges, Big Bob, and Little Freddy.

Halloran: Little, huh?

Safreed: Had a salad today for lunch.

Halloran: Which lunch was that? The first one, or the second one?

Safreed: Just one lunch. Just one salad. Three days in a row now. I'm feeling real good, Mr. Can't Get Under My Skin. Real good!

Halloran: And real regular, I bet.

Safreed: It's all good. What a weekend! Jason Varitek, you're my new hero. That was just so perfect. You know, it had to be A-Rod. It just had to be, because he's the poster boy for all that Yankee smugness. He just shows up with his pretty face, and his pretty uniform, and his 25-million dollar salary, and thinks: 'Hello, world. What would you like to hand me today?' Well, Varitek showed him what loud-mouthed cry babies get in the real world.

Halloran: A two-hand shove to the face.

Safreed: You betcha! As soon as they started jawing at one another, I was yelling, 'Hit him! Smack him in the mouth!' And you could see what A-Rod was saying to him. I mean, they showed it a million times on TV, and they slowed it down, so there's no doubt he was dropping a bunch of F-bombs.

Halloran: Of course, we don't know exactly what Varitek was saying. But I heard a few rumblings after the game that what Varitek actually said was, 'we don't throw at .260 hitters.' God, I hope that's true. To get off a great line like that AND win the fight – that's just beautiful.

Safreed: Whether it's fact now, or will become fact down the road, it just doesn't matter. Who cares what he was saying! It was two guys getting up in each other's grills, and I don't know if Varitek was thinking everything through, or if he was just going on instinct, but once that thing got started, there had to be a fight. There's no way Varitek could back down. And I think he knew it. I think he knew that as uplifting as the fight might be for the Red Sox, backing down, NOT fighting would have been just as deflating. It could have ended the season right there. Instead, let's bring it on New York!

(Voice of presidential candidate John Kerry: Bring It On!)

"Bring it on," Angela said. She had come in to sit with Jimmy during her lunch break.
"It really was awesome, Angela. Best game of the year. First, they fought. And then Bill Mueller won the game with a two-run homer off Mariano Rivera in the ninth inning. It was awesome!"

Halloran: Yeah, and I guess we'll see how that works out for everybody. I do have to say that the Red Sox definitely brought the fight to the Yankees.

Safreed: What do you mean? Don't tell me you think the Red Sox started this?

Halloran: Well, walk it through. Bronson Arroyo hits A-Rod, who just happens to be the guy who had the game winning hit the night before. Did he do it on purpose? I don't know. But maybe A-Rod has a right to be suspicious.

Safreed: Yeah, well take your suspicions to first base and shut-up.

Halloran: Well, he barked, no doubt about that. But it was Varitek who stepped in front of him.

"Who cares who started it?" Jimmy asked. "The Red Sox won. And then they won again yesterday."

Safreed: Only because he was defending his pitcher. Who knows what A-Rod was up to? It's not like he was simply taking his base, or taking any of it lightly.

Halloran: Well, I'm going to work on the assumption that you think A-Rod is a big baby. So, with that in mind, do you really think there was any chance that A-Rod was going to charge the mound?

Safreed: I don't know. I guess, probably not. He's too big of a wussy.

Halloran: And I'm also working on the assumption that Varitek believes the same thing, that A-Rod's a big wuss. So, what I'm getting at here is that Varitek picked the fight. It was premeditated, maybe even hatched in the dugout the inning before, or maybe he just leaped at an opportunity. But I think Varitek, team leader that he is, forced that situation to develop in order to light a fire under the Red Sox.

Safreed: I'm not so sure I'd let your conspiracy theory go all the way back to Arroyo hitting him on purpose, but yeah, I think there's a chance Varitek seized the moment for the good of his team.

Halloran: Of course, he might also have simply been enraged. Maybe he hates losing to the Yankees enough that as soon as Mr. Wonderful started mouthing off, he just had had enough, and wanted to make him shut that cake hole. Who knows? Maybe Fred from Lynn knows something we don't. Good afternoon, Fred.

Fred: Good afternoon, gentleman. I hope what I'm hearing today is true, that this fight helps wake the Red Sox up. But I can remember the biggest Yankees-Red Sox brawl ever.

Halloran: May 20th, 1976.

Fred: Right. And that started with a pretty tough catcher as well. Carlton Fisk came up swinging when Lou Piniella crashed into him at the plate. And that scene turned ugly.

Safreed: So, what's your point?

Fred: The point is that the fight didn't turn out to be a turning point. The Red Sox finished 15.5 games behind the Yankees that year. And the reputation the Red Sox had of being '25 cabs for 25 players' never changed. So, the fight's only a good thing if the talent's there.

Safreed: I'll agree with that, and I'll tell you, the talent's there.

Halloran: Well, the talent was there in '76, too, Fred.

Fred: Not after the fight. After Bill Lee got hurt, the Red Sox didn't have the pitching. That fight was kind of a turning point in the wrong direction.

Safreed: Not this time. No injuries. Talent in place. New fire. Bring it on!

(John Kerry again: Bring It On!)

"Sounds like they're going to be playing that all day," Angela said. "By the way, has your doctor or one of the nurses noticed this rash on your upper arm?"
Jimmy looked away.

Halloran: And just in terms of a turning point, so far so good. You've got Friday night when Kevin Millar hits three home runs, but it's not enough, because the Yankees score in the top of the ninth. Then the Red Sox were hitless in the game on Saturday before the fight. Then they went on to win that game and the next one. Could it be a turning point? We will see what we will see. Now, let's hear from Curt in the car.

Curt: Hey guys, don't be stupid enough to think you can make something out of nothing. That's how dumb, idiotic rumors get started by those who don't know the game.

Halloran: Well, we're glad you called.

Safreed: What do you think we're making up?

Curt: That Arroyo hit A-Rod on purpose, or that Varitek planned the fight in advance. Don't say something stupid and something ignorant like that. It's a stupid idiotic comment to make. It's irresponsible. And you know what? It's ignorant, because you don't know. Obviously, you just made it up.

Safreed: I'd say we speculated, but…

Curt: Speculation turns to rumor turns to fact. It happens all the time. It's true the Red Sox and Yankees have a great rivalry going, but just because they're not out there playing grab-ass on the field doesn't mean guys are looking to start brawls. You had some valid points, but don't make up stupid stuff. I gotta go guys.

Halloran: And like a comet in the night, Curt in the car blazes through, and then he's gone just like that.

"Does it feel like alligator skin?" Angela asked.
"Yeah, I guess so. And I know what you're thinking, but this is day 168. I think I finally missed one of the side effects."

Safreed: I can't believe he called you stupid.

Halloran: Oh, and you think he was talking to me?

Safreed: I think the chances are better than even money.

Halloran: Let's see if Mike from Milbury is any kinder or gentler. Mike?

Mike: I don't know what was up with Curt. Time to switch to decaf, I think. But I loved what Varitek did. He was like a hockey player who gets a fight going to remind everyone on his team that this game isn't for girly-men.

"I'm not trying to worry you, Jimmy, but we have to take everything seriously. How long have you been on hold?"
"About a half hour. It's amazing how many people have nothing better to do than to sit on the phone all day."

Halloran: Can't you say the same thing about A-Rod? If he gets the game winning hit one night, and then gets hit the very next game, doesn't he have to stand up for himself and his team? And didn't he do that?

Mike: Ah, that guy's a gutless puke! In fact, it's too bad he lives in the city. He's depriving some small village of a pretty good idiot. I think Varitek should have taken off his spikes and hit him over the head with it.

Halloran: We've got some live ones today, Fred.

Safreed: I think the Red Sox have put the fight back into everyone, including the fans.

Halloran: Let's see what George from Clinton has for us today. George, you're next with Bob and Fred on "The Ted".

George: Hi, guys. Thanks for taking my call. Has anyone been talking about how Varitek left his mask on?

Safreed: Yeah, I heard some of that crap earlier today. Somehow Varitek is supposed to have been some sort of coward because he didn't take his mask off before he tried to forearm shiver A-Rod.

Halloran: So, what was he supposed to do, say 'Excuse me for a moment', take his mask off, and then start fighting?

Safreed: That's what some yahoos have been saying.

George: Well, don't you think it's a little gutless to get into a fight while you're wearing all this protective armor, and the other guy isn't? Sure takes a big man to throw the first punch at a guy while you're wearing a facemask, chest protector and shin guards. Typical Red Sox.

Halloran: And the colors have come out!

Safreed: Oh, I love this guy. So, now Varitek's supposed to not only take his mask off, but his chest protector and shin guards as well. How about his cup? Maybe you'd like him to strip down to his jock strap just to make it fair!

George: No, that might take too long. But the facemask can come off in no time. They do it all the time chasing after foul pops.

Halloran: George, don't you think that as soon as Varitek took off the mask, it would have provoked the fight. It would have been viewed as an act of aggression. I mean, that would be like a bird fanning his tail to say, 'You and me, bird. We're about to throw down.'

George: Sure I do. And the only reason Varitek didn't do that is because he knows A-Rod would have hit him first.

Halloran: So, what you're saying is that Varitek should have taken the mask off, so that he could take the first punch.

Safreed: You're calling him a coward just because he wasn't stupid.

"I'm going to go outside and listen at the desk for a few minutes. And I'll send someone in here to take a look at you. All right?"
"All right. But make sure they wait until after I get on."
A smile momentarily erased the concern Angela couldn't hide from Jimmy. She turned down the radio and left.

George: I'm just saying the pitcher threw a hard object at a nearly defenseless batter, and a well-armored catcher threw the first punch. I guess we shouldn't be surprised after your boy Pedro threw down Don Zimmer last October. I guess Varitek couldn't find any 70-year-old men to attack. You know what? If that's the Red Sox way, you can have'em.

Safreed: You know what? You can spin this any way you want. But things happen in sports, and sometimes things get out of hand. You don't have time to think. You just react. A-Rod reacted. Varitek reacted. And there you have it.

Halloran: Thanks for the summation. John from Dennis, you're up.

John: I printed out the picture off the Internet of Varitek putting the leather right up into A-Rod's face. And I guarantee you there are guys in New England this morning taking pictures of their wives out of their wallets so they can make room for that picture.

Halloran: So, you like what Varitek did.

John: Like it? I love it. Fred's right. Our season has now started. We're back to the days of 'Cowboy Up'. And as far as rivalries go, this one has kind of been of the hammer and nail variety, with the Yankees holding the hammer forever. And I gotta tell you, it feels good to nail them every once in a while. A-Rod's a little girl. And that's all there is to it.

Halloran: A little girl with the foul mouth of a longshoreman. Time to hear from our good buddy, Jimmy in Boston. Jimmy, I hope you know that fighting is wrong. We would never condone that, and we certainly don't want to improperly influence the youth of America.

Safreed: And you should never hit a man in anger, unless you're absolutely certain you can get away with it.

Jimmy: Well, I know violence is wrong, but sometimes there's just no backing down from a fight. And at the very least, the Red Sox reminded the Yankees that there is a fight, and that they're ready for whatever it takes.

Halloran: After the game, Sox General Manager, Theo Epstein said he was very, very proud of what his players did. And he added: 'We've been waiting all year for a feeling like this.' He's a boy wonder, and you're a boy wonder. Do you two boy wonders concur? Are you proud of the Red Sox?

Jimmy: I don't know if pride is the right word. I mean, it's not like they did something noble. They fought because they're ticked off. They know they're as good as the Yankees, but they haven't been able to prove it. And that gets frustrating, when you know you can do something, like maybe you just did it yesterday, and now you can't do it anymore, you start to doubt yourself, and you wonder about how strong you really are, and that's when you have to dig deeper and find whatever fight you have left. And that's what Varitek did.

Safreed: Is your father Knute Rockne? I mean, where do you come up with this stuff? When I was your age, I was still eating paste?

Halloran: And look where that got you. But it does make you think. Here we are, two relatively successful guys, and we're boneheads. So, what's the future hold for a bright kid like Jimmy? What's he gonna be when he grows up?

Jimmy: Maybe I won't grow up at all. I'll just stay a kid.

Halloran: Like Peter Pan. Makes sense since being a Red Sox fan is like living in our own little Never Neverland. Because they never ever win it all.

Jimmy: We'll see about that this year. At least hope is back that they're going to keep fighting to the end. And that's all we can ask of anyone.

Halloran: Enlightening and strangely philosophical once again, Jimmy. Until next time. We've got time for one more call. Here's Terry from Franconia Notch, New Hampshire.

Terry: I don't know how you guys have managed to leave out the most significant aspect of the entire weekend.

Halloran: I sense more enlightenment coming. Tell me, Terry. If it wasn't the fight, what was the most significant thing that happened this weekend?

Safreed: Other than you guys finally getting electricity in Franconia Notch.

Terry: Hey, it's beautiful up here in the White Mountains. But you guys haven't said word one about Bill Mueller's two-run homer off Mariano Rivera. That's what might turn this season around. Keep in mind; it's Rivera who shut down the Red Sox for three innings in Game 7 last year. He's been superman on the mound and every team has to be afraid when he comes into the game. But Nomar led off the ninth with a double. Nixon drove him home. And then Mueller got that celebration going at home plate. That fight doesn't mean anything if the Red Sox don't win the game. And to win it the way they won it, c'mon, three runs off Mariano Rivera in the ninth inning, and a walk off homer! That's what the Red Sox will build on. That's sticking it in the Yankees face. Think about it. The Red Sox proved to themselves that they can beat the Yankees no matter how dire the circumstances. And if these teams meet in the playoffs again this year, that knowledge, and that self-confidence is what's going to serve them the best, not the memory of some pushing and shoving.

Halloran: You done?

Terry: Yeah, I guess so.

Halloran: And so are we. You're listening to "Sports Overtime" on WTED.

98

CHAPTER SIX
Graft Versus Host

The rash that Angela noticed quickly spread all over Jimmy's back and stomach. It was a deep red rash that began to blister in several spots. Dr. Fitzpatrick also detected an appearance of white spots on Jimmy's tongue and bumps on the inside of his mouth. A new battery of tests was conducted, and the preliminary thinking was that Jimmy had developed graft versus host disease. This is what the Macombers had feared the most, and with good reason.

On day 170, nearly six full months after the bone marrow transplant, Jimmy had the worst night of his life. It began just after midnight when Jimmy began taking very rapid, shallow breaths. He wasn't getting enough oxygen. As his oxygen saturation plunged, his breathing rate accelerated. When Jimmy became quite pale and his eyes rolled back in his head, Glenn and Eileen, who hadn't left the hospital in two days, thought it might be time to call a priest.

Jimmy was close to blacking out when the night nurse gave him a high dose of Iloprost, which dilated Jimmy's blood vessels, allowing for increased blood flow. Jimmy's oxygen saturation levels came back quickly, and it appeared the worst was over. Jimmy had a few milder incidents the next day, and that's when his lab results showed elevated liver enzymes, and a confirmed diagnosis of GVHD.

Jimmy's GVHD was considered chronic because it occurred more than 100 days after the bone marrow transplant. Before 100 days, GVHD is considered acute. Both varieties are a common complication of bone marrow transplants in which the T-cells in the donor's bone marrow begin to attack the host's tissues and organs. That's part of the danger. The other, more serious part is that GVHD increases the risk of infection. It is the infections that are most often the cause of death for post bone marrow transplant patients. In one respect, Jimmy was fortunate. Because he developed GVHD nearly six months into his treatment, his blood counts were up, and he was stronger than most patients who had to wage war with GVHD.

Jimmy's new list of problems and conditions included dry, stinging eyes, because his tear ducts were compromised. He was unable to secrete enough saliva to lubricate his esophagus, so swallowing and eating were more difficult. He had a burning sensation in his mouth when he ate or brushed his teeth. He was jaundice. He had heartburn. He had it all!

And so the drugs started flowing through his veins at a hastened pace.

"My good friends prednisone and cyclosporine will help me through this," Jimmy told his parents. "And they've brought along a new guy called ozothioprine."

Glenn and Eileen tried to smile.

"Those drugs are supposed to suppress your immune system," Dr. Fitzpatrick added. "Meanwhile, we've got you on Bactrim and penicillin to help ward off infections. And just so you're prepared, Jimmy, you're probably going to continue these immunosuppressive drugs for about two more years. We can beat this thing but we are definitely in it for the long haul."

"And remember what Dr. Fitzpatrick told you, honey," Eileen demanded. "The most important thing is that you realize your immune system is not working correctly. So anything you're feeling, fever, dry mouth, cramps, anything, you let somebody know right away."

"She's right, Jimmy. Everything going on inside your body right now is very serious stuff. That's why we're not sending you home for a while. Get comfortable and crank up the radio."

"Get comfortable?" Jimmy said incredulously. "Doc, I haven't been comfortable in over two years."

They all nodded in agreement. They knew it was true.

The next day things got even worse for Jimmy. The Red Sox traded Nomar Garciaparra to the Chicago Cubs.

"Sports Overtime" Show Open, August 2, 2004

Announcer: Welcome to "Sports Overtime" where we'll be saying "adios" to Nomar Garcia-later."

The Terminator from *The Terminator:* Hasta la vista, baby!

Announcer: That's right. Theo Epstein has cured cancer, at least in the Red Sox clubhouse by dumping Nomar Gone-see-aparra on to the unsuspecting Cubbies, the Sox getting rid of some dead weight at the trading deadline.

Ace Ventura from *Ace Ventura:* I have exorcised the demons! This house is clear!

Announcer: In case you haven't heard, thanks for crawling out from under your rock and joining civilization once again. The Red Sox traded Nomar Garciaparra this weekend. Nomar was the face of the organization, you know, the face with the nose he borrowed from Witchy-Poo on H.R. Puffenstuff. Nomar, we hardly knew ye! But don't let the door hit you on the way out!

Freddy Benson from *Dirty Rotten Scoundrels:* Wow! Wow Wow Wow! All I can say is Wow!

Announcer: But that's only the beginning of this little soap opera. Soon after the trade, Red Sox CEO Larry Lucchino and Nomar got into a war of words. And we're wondering who's shooting it straight, and whose pants are on fire.

Fletcher from *Liar, Liar:* AND THE TRUTH SHALL SET YOU FREE!

Announcer: You're all free to decide for yourselves who you're going to believe, and whether trading Nomar was a good move or just plain CRAZY!

Rodney Dangerfield: My psychiatrist told me I was crazy and I said I want a second opinion. He said okay, you're ugly, too.

Announcer: So what do the big fellas on "Sports Overtime" think about all this? Well, stick around to find out. Bob Halloran and Fred "Freddie the Fredderman" Safreed are coming right up with your sports info-tainment on a silver platter.

Judge Stevens from *Liar, Liar*: It is only out of sheer morbid curiosity that I am allowing this freak show to continue.

Halloran: You know what? All I can say is 'Wow', too.

Safreed: I see your 'wow', and raise you a 'Holy Schnikies'.

Halloran: That really took some stones. I gotta hand it to Theo Epstein. Until now, most of his moves have been relatively safe. I mean, it doesn't take a whole lot of brains or guts to go out and sign guys like Keith Foulke and Curt Schilling. But trading Nomar? That's a ballsy thing to do.

Safreed: The man's got plums, and I say good riddance to Nomar.

"How many words do you men have for testicles?" Eileen thought while Jimmy pretended he was sleeping.

Safreed: Nomar was dead to me a month ago when he didn't bother to play in that Yankee game. This is a pure case of addition by subtraction. You get rid of the guy who's killing you in the clubhouse, and you pick up a couple of guys who can hopefully fit in.

Halloran: I think Theo said it best in his press conference over the weekend. Basically, he was left with the choice of having a combination of Nomar and Ricky Gutierrez at shortstop, because you never know when Nomar can play...

Safreed: And he threatened to go on the disabled list. Don't forget that weasely thing he did.

Halloran: We'll get into that in a minute. But Theo's got the Nomar slash Ricky shortstop combo, or he can pencil Orlando Cabrera's name in at shortstop for the next 60 some odd games. And I think, given that choice. It's probably better to try to upgrade your defense. Even if both Cabrera and the first baseman they got, Doug Mientkiewicz, are both hitting under .250 this year.

Jimmy stirred when Eileen wiped his forehead. He was still running a low grade fever, but at least his rash wasn't getting any worse. She appreciated moments like this, when Jimmy was just waking up, because it meant he wouldn't have to deal with the awful side effects of his new meds. And she wouldn't have to bear witness to it. It had been a rough couple of days as the doctors searched for the right combination of drugs, and Jimmy's mind and body reacted to each test run.

Safreed: They can do without the offense from Nomar, because they've still got plenty of guys who can hit. Plus, you saw what Cabrera did in his first at-bat with the Red Sox. POW! A home run! He'll be fine. If he can hit .275 and play a gold glove shortstop, I say Nomar won't even be missed.

"I miss him."

Halloran: But would you say the Red Sox are better today than they were before the trade?

Safreed: I think they're better without Nomar. I don't care if they traded him for a bag of balls. And besides, they can't be any worse than they were. How long could they keep playing .500 ball without the front office doing something to try to shake things up?

Halloran: Oh, they shook things up all right. And let's get to the phone calls to find out how the Nomar trade is playing in Red Sox Nation. Bryan from Adams, good to hear from you again.

"Mom, can you dial the number for me?"
"Are you sure you're up to it?"
"Yeah. Let's hope I get on before they come in here with that Thalidomide. That one knocks me out."

Bryan: Thanks guys. Wow! You guys said it. This is just unbelievable. The guy's here for seven years, putting up some Hall of Fame type numbers, and then POOF, he's just gone!

Halloran: Good trade or bad trade, Bryan. What do you say?

Bryan: I don't know. I always liked Nomar, so it cuts like a knife. But it feels so right at the same time. Maybe it's a good trade, since Nomar really didn't want to be here anyway. I'm just not convinced they got as much talent in return as they should have.

Safreed: Everybody knows Nomar's damaged goods and that he's in the final year of his contract. I'm sure the Red Sox got the maximum they could. Nomar's stock just isn't very high right now.

Halloran: Earl from Warren, did Theo screw this one up, or what?

Earl: Well, far be it from me to judge, but it doesn't look like good business to me. And it certainly doesn't strike me as a particularly gutsy trade.

Halloran: How can you say that? They traded the face of the franchise in the middle of a pennant race. This would be like trading Ted Williams or Carl Yastrzemski! This was as bold a move as you're ever going to see.

Earl: Not if you look at all the evidence put before you.

Halloran: Like what?

Earl: First, Nomar is injured. Second, Nomar is leaving the Red Sox at the end of the season. Third, Nomar's defense has been below average, and that's being kind. And fourth, Nomar's had a bad attitude ever since spring training. So, how much guts does it take to get rid of a problem that by most accounts was only going to get worse? Theo only did what he had to do. That's why he tried so hard to do it. And that's why he made the trade despite getting so little in return.

Safreed: Yeah, but when you say he got so little in return, it's like you're finding Theo guilty of making a bad trade. And I'd say the jury's still out on that.

Earl: Certainly. We might not know if it's a good trade or a bad trade until the Red Sox are home watching the Cubs play in the post-season.

Halloran: Which could happen. And that brings me back to Theo's stones. He knows there's a chance this trade will backfire. He's taking a huge risk. First, it could be a public relations nightmare based on how the fans react initially. And it could get a lot worse if the Red Sox go in the tank, and the Cubs go on to win the World Series. But Theo made the deal anyway, and that's…

Earl: But Bob, don't you see? The fact that he made the deal ANYWAY means that he knew he HAD to make it. That doesn't take terrific courage. In fact, it's just bad business. He traded his commodity when it was at its lowest. Consider; Theo almost traded Nomar during the spring for Magglio Ordonez, a 40-home run hitter. Now, all he can get is a light-hitting shortstop and a guy who won't even crack the line-up? You call it ballsy. I call it trading from weakness.

Jimmy was able to get out of bed and make his way over to the computer by the window. He remained overly sensitive to sunlight, so the shade was almost always drawn, as it was now. He began surfing for information about the trade while the phone stayed tucked between his left shoulder and ear.
"Fred's starting to get mad," he said.

Safreed: Earl, you're an idiot! Hang up the phone and go back to burying your head in the sand. You obviously haven't been watching what's been going on all season. Nomar's been a cancer in that clubhouse, and an average player at best. So, don't talk to me, either of you guys, about whether this move was ballsy or not! It had to be done. It got done. And Nomar can kiss my lily-white derriere on his way out of town.

Halloran: As if he didn't already want to leave badly enough. Now he's got that offer to motivate him. But I don't think anybody's really gotten to the main point of this story yet. And that's that Nomar apparently told the Red Sox that he might have to go on the disabled list in August.

Safreed: Not 'might have to'. He said he'd PROBABLY have to, which I think adds a little more certainty.

Halloran: Yes, absolutely. Probably is much more certain than 'might'.

Safreed: And that whole Larry Lucchino phone conversation just ticks me off to no end. I mean, how could...

Halloran: Well, hold on a minute, Fred. Let's explain that before we get into it. In case, people hadn't heard. Larry Lucchino, the Red Sox President, has come out and said that he called Nomar right after the trade, basically to wish him well. And in the course of that conversation, Lucchino asked Nomar how his foot was, and according to Lucchino, Nomar said, 'It's fine now.'

Safreed: Yeah, it's fine NOW, meaning if I were still with the Red Sox, it wouldn't be fine. But since I'm going to the Cubs, I've just had a miraculous recovery.

"That's not what it means at all. I can't believe they're giving Nomar the Bledsoe Treatment," Jimmy said, *referring to talk radio's incessant insults of the Patriots former quarterback.*

Halloran: That's certainly the insinuation. And keep in mind, this was apparently just a few days after Nomar had told the Red Sox that he'd PROBABLY, O.K. Fred? -- that he'd probably have to go on the disabled list and miss a few more weeks of the season. And now he says he's fine. Hard to think of anything sleazier than that – if it's true.

Safreed: Of course, it's true. Nomar as much as said it was, but he tried to say he was being sarcastic. Yeah, right!

Halloran: Now, that was sarcastic. Rafer's in Johnson, Rhode Island, and he's next on "Sports Overtime".

Rafer: You guys are making a miscalculation of Olympic proportions. I can't believe you're taking Lucchino's side in this.

Halloran: They both gave the same account of the story. Nobody's denying that Nomar said his foot is fine now. It's just a matter of interpretation. And you're free to interpret it any way you want, just like we are.

Rafer: Sure, and isn't it convenient that you would interpret it in favor of the man who you have to deal with on a regular basis?

Safreed: That's got nothing to do with it. It has everything to do with watching the way Nomar acted for the past few months and being able to deduce that the guy has been trying to stick it to the Red Sox ever since they tried to trade him.

Rafer: Well, that's a bit off track as far as how I wanted to approach this. You see, Lucchino's the one who revealed the particulars of a private phone conversation first, right?

Safreed: So?

"So – everything! This is the point I was gonna make. Go get'em, Rafer!"
Eileen loved to watch Jimmy's enthusiasm. It had become more and more infre-quent, because of the various complications he'd had to endure. She fought back a tear, but it was a happy one.

Rafer: Well, first, don't you think that's a crappy thing for Lucchino to do, especially when his only intention would be to make Nomar look bad. And secondly, why would he want to make Nomar look bad? Because he knows the trade is a bad one. Therefore, he has to make it look like Nomar's a bad guy, that he can't be trusted, that he was lying about how hurt he was, and that he didn't really want to try to help the team win.

Halloran: Well, if those were Lucchino's intentions, he succeeded. Because regardless of how the story got out; it's out. And Nomar said what he said.

Rafer: Of course he did. And I love the fact that Nomar didn't deny it. He told the identical story, almost word for word. The only difference was the tone. Nomar says that a guy he doesn't much like, and who just traded him, called him up. Nomar was being very short with him, because he didn't really want this guy calling him. And then when Lucchino asks him about his foot, he says 'It's fine' as a way to brush him off and end the conversation.

Safreed: But he didn't just say 'It's fine'. He said 'It's fine, NOW!' That's a huge difference. It's fine NOW that I don't have to play for you anymore. That's the proof you need to know that Nomar was a malingerer.

Rafer: Nomar denies saying 'It's fine now'. He says he told Lucchino it bothers him, but it's fine. Take a moment to read the quotes. Anyway, nice talking to you guys. I gotta run.

Halloran: Good stuff so far. You told the last guy to hang up, and this guy hangs up on you. Nice to see you haven't lost your charm.

Safreed: Charm schmarm. Who's next?

Halloran: Well, let's take a look at a couple of e-mails. This one's from Larry in Johnson, Rhode Island. 'I can't believe how stupid Red Sox management is. They traded away one of the best shortstops in the American League for an obvious scrub who's also a free agent at the end of the year. Their big problems are in the bullpen. This was a very dumb move by Theo and he'll wind up paying for it. The 2004 season is down the tubes. The Red Sox are not going to the World Series with this team of losers.'

"They can still win it," Eileen said hopefully. Jimmy nodded while his eyes tried to focus on the computer screen. It was becoming increasingly difficult, because he could feel his headache returning.

Safreed: Put down a 'no' for that one. Here's a 'yes' vote from some lady in Avon, Connecticut. 'I think the Red Sox made a great trade. Nomar wasn't going to sign with the Red Sox anyway. And now we have a younger and healthier gold glove shortstop and someone who can actually play first base. How can this be a bad trade?' Then she points out that the Red Sox also got Dave Roberts in a separate deal to give them some speed off the bench.

Halloran: And here are the quotes Rafer was talking about. This is Nomar's side of the story. He says: "I was being sarcastic. I'd just gotten traded. He said, 'What do you mean, it's great?' I said, 'It bothers me, but it's fine. Yeah, it bothers me, but I'm fine.' I never said, 'I'm fine now.'" Then he goes on: "I was talking to my parents. Do you think I really wanted to talk to him right now? He was the last person I wanted to talk to, to be honest with you." I gotta tell you, Fred, that all sounds plausible.

Safreed: Too much time is being spent on this 'he said, he said' garbage. The guy's gone, and I'm glad he's gone.

Halloran: But listen to this, and this is where maybe a couple of these phone callers might be right about Lucchino. Lucchino was asked if he thought Nomar was being sarcastic, and he said: 'I'm not going to go there. That calls for too much speculation on my part.'

Safreed: Which basically hangs Nomar out to dry, I know. So, there you have it. Lucchino threw Nomar under the bus. Big whoop! What's any of this have to do with whether the Red Sox are better today than they were two days ago?

Halloran: I just find it interesting, that's all. Maybe Jimmy does as well. Jimmy, how goes it?

Jimmy: Oh, I'm fine NOW.

Halloran: Ha-ha. Yeah, I guess we're all fine now. I guess we have to be fine anyway. The deal is done, and we'll just have to live with it.

Jimmy: Or suffer through it, as the case may be.

Halloran: Fan of the trade, Jimmy? Or not so much?

Jimmy: Well, it's all about winning the World Series. Mr. Epstein said it again this weekend. The Red Sox are going for it all this year, and I for one sure hope it happens this year. I can't wait much longer.

Halloran: None of us can. And that's probably the first time Theo's ever been called MISTER Epstein.

Jimmy: Well, Theo said he didn't think the team was good enough to win the World Series, especially the way they were playing defense. So, they picked up two real good defensive players.

Safreed: And they got rid of Nomar. So, they've got that going for them.

Jimmy: But this wasn't really about getting rid of Nomar the way you like to think it is, Fred.

Halloran: Uh-oh. He's coming after you, Fred.

Safreed: I can handle it.

Jimmy: It's just that you think this is about Nomar being a bad guy in the club-house. But it's really about not wanting to go into September and October never knowing if you're going to have Nomar in the line-up or Ricky Gutierrez.

Halloran: Right. It's about not knowing if you have a great player at shortstop, or 75 percent of a great player, or if you have Gutierrez who's probably a below aver-age player.

Jimmy: That's what I think. For instance, I don't think Mr. Epstein makes this deal if Pokey Reese is 100 percent healthy. Pokey could give them the great defense that Cabrera is supposed to on the days that Nomar can't play. So, I think they could have gone with Nomar and Pokey, but not Nomar and Ricky.

Halloran: Might be some truth to that.

Safreed: Well, then Jimmy, O smart one! Explain to me why the Cubs would make this deal. You see, I think the Cubs are expecting Nomar to play just about every day and that he'll have a great attitude just because he's out of Boston. He's got no reason to stick it to them, and plenty of motivation now as he enters free agency. He'll be auditioning, and the Cubs will benefit. But if it's more about his health and availability, as you say it is, why would the Cubs take on a guy who might be on his way to the disabled list?

Jimmy: Because before the deal they had Alex Gonzalez as their shortstop for the next 60 games of a pennant race. Now, they've got Nomar for probably 40 of those games. They're better off. And maybe the Red Sox are better, too.

Halloran: The kid's been boning up on the box scores and reading the papers, Fred.

Safreed: Ah, the kid's still living in his little kid dream world. Theo made this move to cure cancer, plain and simple.

Jimmy: Now, who's living in a dream world?

Halloran: Jimmy, it's always a pleasure. Have you got anything else for us today?

Jimmy: Nope. Just that I hope the Red Sox start playing better. It's a shame for them to be wasting so much potential. They've got a great team, but they haven't been playing great. And not everyone gets opportunities like they have this year. They should take advantage of the time they have.

Halloran: And that's all the time we have. Back after this.

CHAPTER SEVEN
The Sox Get Hot

It was the side effects that were the hardest to take these days. Jimmy had learned to ignore the rash. If he closed his eyes and dreamed about being at Fenway Park, he could go for hours without feeling his head pounding. If he watched what he ate, his stomach pain was manageable. But he was taking new drugs, and more drugs, while the doctors performed a balancing act of nurturing his new marrow while suppressing its effects on the rest of his body. And he didn't like what was happening to him.

He didn't like the biopsies of his stomach, colon, and intestines. He didn't like the colonoscopy, the cystoscopy, the bronchoscopy, or any of the other endoscopies that he'd had or would have in the near future. He didn't like having his picture taken from the outside, what with his emaciated frame, his minimal amount of hair, and what hair he did have was going prematurely gray. And he definitely didn't like having his picture taken from the inside.

But it was the mind-altering side effects that were most disturbing to Jimmy and his family. They were all used to the nausea, fatigue, hair loss, and overall body aches. But they had never seen Jimmy freak out like this.

It started harmlessly enough. Jimmy was watching television when it suddenly appeared as though the TV were 50 feet away.

"What's going on!" Jimmy yelled.

Mark was with him the first time it happened and Jimmy's volume startled him. As Jimmy held his head with both hands and continued to wail in horror, Mark called for the nurse. It took two nurses to settle Jimmy down. He was shrieking, "I don't understand what's happening! Help! Make it stop!"

In his mind, the nurses were very large and very far away. They were reaching for him in slow motion. The sounds of their voices were slow and droning. He felt like Alice in Wonderland falling down the rabbit hole. More than the first time he heard he had leukemia, more than the first time he underwent chemotherapy, and more than the night he almost died, Jimmy was frightened. His mind that had protected him with courage and reason and hope for nearly three years was now betraying him. For all he knew, the stress or the drugs or both had made him crazy. His body was constantly being beaten down, and now the leukemia had gone to his brain. It was terrifying!

But it was temporary. Jimmy's therapy for chronic GVHD included cyclosporine and prednisone. They were administered on alternating days, and the dosages had been increased. It was important to be as aggressive as possible when treating chronic GVHD, because as the Macombers knew, the disease was fatal in more than 25-percent of affected patients. That's why they stood by as Dr. Fitzpatrick prescribed thalidomide, azathioprine, cellcept and others. The treatment of GVHD is very stepwise. It begins with steroids, and if they don't work, another agent is introduced. No one knew for sure what would work, and in Jimmy's case,

110

they eventually tried all of them. As the guinea pig „Jimmy went through bouts of depression, confusion, and high anxiety. His family, as the helpless spectators, could only watch in powerless agony.

The most stressful side effect for the Macombers was when Jimmy went through cycles of exaggerated emotions. Not prone to anger, there were times when Jimmy announced that he hated everyone in the room and he wanted them all to leave. Helplessly, they left. There were times when Jimmy's depression sunk to near suicidal levels. Nobody left at those times. But the stress was wearing on the entire family. Glenn and Eileen aged in dog years. They had never envisioned their lives would turn out like this. They leaned on each other, and fortunately when one of them was having an especially bad day, the other one usually was having a good day. That's how they got through it. They weren't sure how Mark got through it. They were pretty sure they weren't doing a wonderful job parenting him. The turmoil was too disruptive and distracting to properly focus on their older child.

Still, Mark was growing up nicely. His rounds of jealousy were less and less frequent now that he was trained on beginning his college career at MIT. The proximity gave a measure of relief to his parents, and he was glad he'd be nearby in case anything happened.

'In case anything happened'. That was the phrase that permeated nearly every decision the family made. Should they go to the movies, or out to dinner? What if something happened? Can Mark go on a ski weekend with his friends? Can Glenn and Eileen go to her cousin's wedding? What if something happened? The stress was constant, and it was only bearable because it was. They had all been through more than any of them thought they could handle, but they handled it. Now, watching Jimmy's mood swings, especially his heightened fears, it was getting harder and harder to handle.

Eventually, Dr. Fitzpatrick was able to achieve the delicate balance of medications, thus lessening the negative side effects. Things were looking up for both Jimmy and his favorite baseball team.

"Sports Overtime" Show Open, September 4, 2004

Announcer: Welcome everyone! And thanks for tuning in to another edition of "Sports Overtime" with Big Bad Baby Boy Bob Halloran and the even bigger, badder, baby-er, and boy-er Fred "Freddie the Fredderman" Safreed. And they've got a little proposition for you today.

Fletch from *Fletch:* This little proposition doesn't entail me dressing as Little Bo-Peep, does it?

Announcer: That would be entirely up to each individual in our listening audience. However, Bob and Fred would like you to call in today and try to explain why the Red Sox are on such roll right now.

Mitch from *City Slickers* (singing): Rollin', rollin', rollin', keep them doggies rollin'. Man, my ass is swollen, Rawhide!

Announcer: We're pretty sure it was the Nomar trade that turned this season around. In fact, we know that's why the Red Sox have rolled out 21 wins in their last 23 games.

Mitch from *City Slickers* (singing): Round'em up, ride'em in, get'em up, get'em dressed, comb their hair, brush their teeth, Rawhide! Tie me down, tell me lies, pull my hair, slap my thighs - with a big wet strap of, Rawhide!

Announcer: And isn't it just too bad that Little Nomie's not around to enjoy this. The Red Sox are right on the Yankees tail, while the pouting shortstop has his tail between his legs in Chicago. And those Cubbies ain't going nowhere!

Terry Malloy from *On The Waterfront:* I coulda had class. I coulda been a contender. I coulda been somebody, instead of a bum, which is what I am. Let's face it.

Announcer: Now the Red Sox are left with just a bunch of self-proclaimed idiots. And they might just be the best group of idiots ever assembled on this rock we call Earth.

George from *Seinfeld:* Is that right? I just threw away a lifetime of guilt-free sex and floor seats for every sporting event in Madison Square Garden. So, please, a little respect. For I am Costanza, Lord of the Idiots!

Announcer: Now, if you've got another explanation of why the Red Sox are suddenly red hot other than the Nomar trade, we'll be happy to listen. We'll be surprised. We'll think you're insane. But we'll listen, at least for a minute or so before we cut you off for not making any sense whatsoever!

Clark from *National Lampoon's Christmas Vacation:* If I woke up tomorrow with my head sewn to the carpet, I couldn't be more surprised.

Announcer: It doesn't get any better than this, folks. The Red Sox are absolutely SMOKIN' HOT. And we've got Bob and Fred sitting up like good little boys with their headphones resting on their over-sized heads, and they're ready to listen to whatever you've got to say. So, say it! Don't be afraid.

Therapist from *Old School*: This is a safe place. A place where we can feel free sharing our feelings. Think of my office as a nest in a tree of trust and understanding. We can say anything here.

Announcer: Anything except BLEEP, BLEEP, and BLEEP, or BLEEEEEEEP! Remember, we've got the FCC constantly crawling up our BLEEEEEP!

Halloran: Well, we've been here before. Red Sox Nation is feeling pretty good about itself right about now. No self-esteem issues. Not a care in the world.

Safreed: Why do you say we've been here before? I can't remember a time when Red Sox fans felt this good about the team. I mean, usually fans have their fingers crossed that maybe something good will happen. Now, they just expect it to happen. And it usually does.

Halloran: I know, I know. It's almost like being a Yankee fan. There's so much confidence right now, it's bordering on cocky. But we have to remember, they still haven't won anything. In fact, they're still chasing the Yankees by a couple of games. But what I mean about us being here before, is that today's optimism is pretty similar to when the Red Sox took six of those first seven games against the Yankees in April.

Safreed: It's not the same. It's...

Halloran: Oh, it's the same, Fred. Of course, it's the same. Back then folks were expecting a hundred wins, easy. They thought the Red Sox were destined for greatness. Then, there was that malaise that took over for nearly three months.

Safreed: Until the Nomar trade. Since then, the team's been playing loose. They're having fun. And they're winning games. Don't even try to tell me that's a coincidence. That was the best possible thing that could have happened to the Red Sox. You could just feel the pressure being lifted right away.

"Will they ever let that go?" Mark asked. He had been at the hospital a lot lately, recognizing that once school started for him tomorrow, he might not be able to make it around quite as much.
"Nope. They'll be killing Nomar forever. It's a wave that can't be stopped.

Halloran: I'm agreeing with you, Fred. I do think this team, almost to a man, started playing better immediately after the trade. But let me ask you this. Doesn't that kind of suck? I mean, you can throw Nomar under the bus if you want, but aren't you upset with the players who weren't able to play up to their potential simply because Nomar was in a snit?

Safreed: What are you talking about?

Halloran: I mean, it's not just the defense at shortstop that's better. It's the defense everywhere. Suddenly guys are moving runners over, stealing bases, doing all the things that it takes to win. And if they're doing all this just because Nomar's gone, I think that's pretty awful. How dare they not play as well as they can, just because of one guy's foul mood!

Safreed: No. They're winning games, because Orlando Cabrera is a better short-stop than Nomar, and because they don't have his bad karma dragging everybody down all the time.

Halloran: I'm just saying that maybe professional athletes should be able to play their game no matter what. I mean, do you really think that before the trade if David Ortiz failed to get a runner home from third it was because of Nomar sitting in the dugout. And that if Ortiz drives home that run today, it's because Nomar's gone?

Safreed: Yes, I do.

"What an idiot," Mark said. "I'll never understand why you love these guys so much."
"They make being a Red Sox fan better," Jimmy explained. "Even when they say stupid things."

Safreed: It's called chemistry, Bob. And you never know how it's going to affect a team, or when.

Halloran: I don't know. Baseball seems like it's more of an individual game. You're at the plate all by yourself. And even if you hate the guy in the on-deck circle, you've still got to hit the ball.

Safreed: Look, the defense is better, because Nomar's gone. And that's made the pitching better. And the offense is clicking, because everybody's picking each other up, and that's because Nomar's gone. That pretty much sums it up, Mr. Completely Missing The Point.

Halloran: Well, then, let's find out what Abe from Lincoln is thinking.

Abe: I'm thinking the Red Sox are extremely good theater, and I used to love going to the theater.

Halloran: Yeah, but we're only in the second act. We'll have to wait and see how it ends.

Abe: The reason I called was just to say that it's clear that all men are not created equal. This Cabrera has brought a whole new energy to the team. He's been sensational on defense, and I think he's been a real pleasant surprise with the bat as well. When he first got here, I said, I don't like that man. I must get to know him better. And now I love him. Great move, Theo!

Halloran: Let's find out if Ben from Franklin agrees. Ben?

Ben: No, I can't say that I do agree. I'd like to take you up on your opening proposition, and tell you the Red Sox recent success is NOT due to the Nomar trade.

Safreed: We got our first crazy of the day. Ben, did you go off your meds, today?

"I hope they give him a chance to speak before they shout him down," Jimmy said. He'd been feeling much better lately. His rash was almost gone, and his blood tests were improving. He wondered if he'd be able to go home in time for the baseball playoffs.

Ben: A great man once said, 'To succeed we should jump as quickly at opportunities as we do to conclusions', but I see you guys being certain about something that just isn't supported by the evidence.

Halloran: Enlighten us.

Safreed: If he does, I'll be as shocked as if I were struck by lightning.

Ben: Well, I took the time to look up some numbers.

Safreed: Great, a numbers guy. Let's have it, Ben.

Ben: See if you can follow along. In the last 23 games, the Red Sox have committed 11 errors, two of them, by the way, were committed by Cabrera. Now, in the previous 23 games when the Red Sox only went 13-and-10, they committed 13 errors, and only one of them was committed by Nomar.

Safreed: But Cabrera gets to a lot more balls.

Ben: Actually, he gets to exactly one more ball every four games. That's according to his average number of chances. But nevertheless, the point is that the Red Sox overall defense has been about the same directly before and after the trade.

Safreed: You can look at the numbers all you want. I know what I see, and this team is much better than it was.

Ben: Think what you want, but there's more here. During the last 23 games, the Red Sox starting pitchers have gone an average of just under 7 innings per start and their ERA is 3.37. In those 23 games before the trade, the starters' ERA was 4.89. That's a remarkable difference.

Halloran: How do you explain that, Fred?

Safreed: Easy, the defense IS better, regardless of what Ben says. And the pitchers are throwing with more confidence that the guys behind them will actually catch the ball.

Ben: Necessity is the mother of invention, and I think you invented that rationale because you need it to explain what you want to be true. But it's not true. Unless you think the starters hated Nomar so much, they just refused to pitch well while he was on the field, you have to agree that the reason the team is winning now is because their entire pitching staff is throwing exceptionally well.

Halloran: Then how do you explain this comment from Kevin Millar who said, 'We hadn't played so great before the trade happened. Now we're playing better. I don't know what the reason is. It would be unfair to say that trading Nomar is the reason, but is it part of it? I think so, yeah.' Then he goes on to say, 'There isn't anybody doing their own thing now and that's different. Nomar had a lot of things going on and he's introverted. He had the Achilles'. He had the contract. And it was its own story. Every day with the trade, that changed the atmosphere immediately in here.'

Safreed: And what about Johnny Damon's quote? Read him that one, Bob. Listen to this, Benny. Go ahead. Read it.

Halloran: All right, Fred. Calm down. Damon said: 'We see the revolving door all the time, but I do think we're better than before, in every way. Defensively, we can count on those guys all the time. I think we're better.'

Safreed: Even the players are saying it. What more do you need?

Ben: Those are cop out quotes. Of course the players are going to say they're better now, or that it was Nomar's fault. If it's not his fault they were mediocre for so long, it would have to be their own. They need to find a reason they weren't winning just like you guys. So, they find the simplest one, just like you guys.

Jimmy felt like going for a walk. So, he rose with moderate ease and comfort out of the bed, threw on a pair of slippers and ventured out into the hallway. He continued listening to the radio on his new cell phone. He had wanted one for a long time, and he was looking for every opportunity to use it. Mark went along with him. He didn't like being cooped up in that room any longer than he had to. Truthfully, he had no idea how Jimmy did it for so long. Day after day. Week after week. And now, month after month. His brother's courage often made him doubt his own.

Halloran: All right. Good call. The guy came in with some information. He had a viewpoint and he backed it up. Now he can go back to his rubber room and spend his days staring out the window. Because he can come up with any bunch of numbers he wants. The trade was made, and the team is playing much better. That's not just a coincidence. Those are two inter-related facts.

Safreed: Are you going to talk to Jimmy in Boston again today? I kind of remember him defending Nomar, and I'd love to get on his case a little bit.

Halloran: You feel the need to pick on a 14-year-old kid? What's wrong with you? Did you miss a meal or something?

Safreed: No, it's just that the kid calls a lot, and we haven't heard from him in a while. I'm guessing it's because he's one of those Nomie rump swabs, and ever since the Red Sox started winning, which proves they were all wrong, those guys haven't been calling. Where's Jimmy today, y'know? Where's he been while the Red Sox have won 10 in a row and 16 of their last 17?

Halloran: I don't know, Fred. Why don't you ask him yourself? Jimmy's on the line right now.

Jimmy: Hey guys.

Safreed: So, what's the story, Jimmy? Didn't have the guts to call before now?

Jimmy: Honestly, been a little sick. Without getting into a lot of detail, I yakked so much I hurt my voice.

Halloran: Yeah, you don't sound so good right now either.

Safreed: Well, I gotta hand it to you. A lot of the people who bum-kissed Nomar on his way out of town have gone into hiding. Takes a 14-year-old kid to be man enough to admit he was wrong. Go ahead, Jimmy. The airwaves are yours.

Jimmy: I'll admit I miss Nomar. I always liked him, and I wish he could be a part of what's been happening. But Fred, I never said it was a terrible trade or that it would ruin the Red Sox. I only said Mr. Epstein made the trade mostly because Nomar was hurt, not because he was really hurting the team, or that he was bad for team chemistry.

Safreed: And you were wrong. Why can't people just say it! Is it so hard to say I was wrong?

Jimmy: O.K., Fred. You were wrong.

Halloran: That wasn't so hard.

Jimmy: It was kind of easy, actually.

Safreed: Are you guys finished?

Jimmy: Fred, not to be disrespectful or anything, but you want everything wrapped up in a nice little package, or one easy sentence. But life's not like that. People sum up what happened last year by saying, Grady Little messed up. I've asked people what happened in the 1986 World Series, and all they tell me is that a ball went through Bill Buckner's legs. But I know there has to be more to it than that.

Safreed: There isn't.

Jimmy: There has to be. But anyway, now you need a simple answer for why the Red Sox are winning. So, you say it was the trade. You're happy with that answer, but it's really, really incomplete.

Halloran: People want solutions that can fit on a bumper sticker. Forget the totality of the issue. Solve it in six or seven words.

Safreed: There's just no other explanation. I mean, how else would you explain it?

Halloran: Well, don't forget, Fred, the last two years the Oakland A's got real hot in August, and it wasn't because of some trade. They just got on a roll, and both times it was in August. Nobody tried so hard to figure that one out.

Safreed: Well, there wasn't a humongous trade right before they got on a roll. If there were, then I'm sure people would have pointed to that as the reason.

Halloran: And maybe they would have been wrong.

Jimmy: It's just hard for people to accept sometimes, I mean I know it was for me, but sometimes things happen for no reason at all. Sometimes those things that happen are incredibly good, and sometimes they're incredibly sad. But they happen, and nobody really knows why.

Safreed: And sometimes things DO happen for a reason, and that reason is as clear as day.

Jimmy: And sometimes the reasons aren't so clear. That's all I'm saying. But even if I don't agree with your reason, I'm still super glad the Red Sox are playing so well. I just hope it lasts right through the regular season and the post-season.

Halloran: Yeah, some folks are worried about the team peaking too soon. But they're well on their way to the post-season, and once you're in the tournament, anything can happen. Thanks again for the call, Jimmy.

Safreed: Thanks for calling to admit you were wrong, and then not really doing it.

Halloran: Are you done?

Safreed: Until next time.

Halloran: All righty then! Until next time. Jimmy, get well soon, all right?

Jimmy: I'm trying.

Halloran: And we'll be trying to talk some sense into our callers, right after this.

CHAPTER EIGHT
The Rematch

Eileen and Glenn sat together on the back porch of their home. Their hooded sweatshirts were an apt response to the sudden temperature drop. There were no words for several minutes, each content to stare out beyond the maple trees and into the early October sky. A look of concern furrowed Glenn's brow. A smile parted Eileen's lips. Their hands touched, but their minds were worlds apart.

Eileen was remembering Jimmy's expression when the Red Sox had clinched a playoff spot. It was an otherwise uneventful victory against an overwhelmed Tampa Bay team at the end of September. She had been with Jimmy in his hospital room, and the two of them watched as the Red Sox players doused each other with beer and champagne.

"It seems like an odd way to celebrate something," Eileen recalled saying.

"Well, that's exactly how I'm going to do it when they tell me I don't have cancer anymore," Jimmy responded. "I can't drink the stuff anyway. I might as well pour it all over myself."

Eileen smiled then, and she smiled now. Jimmy had never let her see him in his moments of hopelessness, and her smile was an acknowledgement of his courage. She knew he must have moments of despair. She had them. Glenn had them. And they both felt guilty afterwards.

Glenn was feeling a little guilty now. He was thinking about the words he had said over Jimmy's bed just a few days earlier. Jimmy was enduring his fifth straight day on a ventilator after having contracted pneumonia for the second time since his bone marrow transplant. Dr. Fitzpatrick described it as pneumocystis carinii pneumonia (PCP), which is a kind of fungal infection that most often attacks people with compromised immune systems. It was a potentially deadly opportunist.

It began like so many of Jimmy's other ailments, so how was anyone supposed to know that this time Jimmy's dry cough and occasional shortness of breath were indications of something so perilous? But Jimmy developed a slight fever and chills, and over a period of a several days, he grew more and more tired. Finally, a bluish discoloration was detected around his mouth and his feet, and doctors had a much clearer indication of what was wrong. Chest X-rays, an induced sputum test and another bronchoscopy were done to confirm the diagnosis.

Jimmy was immediately started on Bactrim and more steroids, but after a week of unimpressive response to the medications, Jimmy was placed on the ventilator to improve his oxygen levels. Once again, Jimmy appeared to be dying and there was no telling when or if he'd be taken off the ventilator.

"Take him," Glenn whispered to God. "Show him some mercy, and just take him. Please, don't make him live like this."

Glenn sobbed more than at any time since Jimmy's original diagnosis. He had been strong, and he had been practical. He continued working and put his trust in the doctors to make his son better. He knew there were lots of children who suffered from leukemia, but were eventually cured. And he assumed with confidence that Jimmy would be one of the growing number of success stories. Jimmy would get through this, and so would each of the Macombers.

Like Eileen, Glenn had moments of weakness and doubt, but he had never felt as weak as he did that night in the hospital. He stood over his son listening to the rhythm of the ventilator. Jimmy was breathing on his own, but the machine was facilitating his efforts.

Glenn counted the breaths as Jimmy struggled to inhale. He counted the moments that passed before Jimmy finally exhaled. He watched the various medications drip through the IV tubes into Jimmy's chest. The site was all too familiar and painful. This is how Glenn's mother looked several years earlier when he watched her die in a hospital room just like this.

Glenn asked God to take his son, but by the time he stepped into the elevator, he was scolding himself. "If you're not hopeful, you're hopeless," he said, telling himself what he had told Jimmy so many times before.

As the elevator doors closed, a nurse walking by heard a teary-eyed man say in a loud voice to no one in particular, "Hope is all there is, you idiot."

"Sports Overtime" Show Open, October 11, 2004

Chris Berman, ESPN: "Back it goes…and the Red Sox are moving on!"

Announcer: Moving on all right, thanks to Big Popeye who patiently waited for his pitch and dropped a game winning home run into the Monster Seats Friday night.

Popeye from *Popeye*: I ain't no doctor, but I'm losing my pay-shkence, aah, ga-ga-ga-ga-ga-ga."

Announcer: And after Big Popeye's home run swept the Angels, it was time for… What? What do you mean it's not Popeye? Papi? What the heck's a Papi? Oh, all right. Big Papi was the Game 3 hero. Fine!

Popeye: I ought to busk you right in the mush. I is disgustipated!

Announcer: Anyway, once Big Papi propelled the Red Sox in to the American League Championship Series for a second straight year, the Red Sox waited to see if they'd have a return date with the Yankees. And we got'em!

Hans Gruber from *Die Hard*: Do you really think you have a chance against us, Mister Cowboy?
John McClane: Yippee-ki-yay.

Announcer: It's the Red Sox and Yankees, Part Deux! And they're going to keep "deux"-ing it until we get this thing right. These two sworn enemies have played each other 45 times in the past two years. The Red Sox have won 23 games, and the Yankees have won 22. Pretty even match, wouldn't you say?

Eddie Felson from *Color of Money:* It's even, but it ain't settled. Let's settle it.

Announcer: And certainly Pedro Martinez will have a score to settle. Yankee fans will be waiting for him to 'Come to Papa!'

Pedro Martinez: I just tip my hat and call the Yankees my daddy. I can't find a way to beat them at this point. You just have to give them credit and say, 'Hey, you guys beat me, not my team.' I wish they would disappear and never come back.

Announcer: That was Pedro's humble and perplexing response after he blew another lead in his last start against the Yankees. Now, it's a father and son reunion. So, get ready for the mother of all series as the Red Sox try once again to overcome their nemesis, the Yankees. Ahh, the Yankees. Why is it always the Yankees?

George from *My Best Friend's Wedding:* It's amazing the clarity that comes with psychotic jealousy.

Announcer: The Yankees are in our heads. The Red Sox are in our hearts. And I've got this queasy, uneasy feeling in the pit of my stomach. So, let's belly up to the microphone with two of our favorite heavy hitters, Bob Halloran, and his sidekick, Fred "Freddie the Fredderman" Safreed. It's time for "Sports Overtime" on WTED!

Fat Bastard from *The Spy Who Shagged Me:* I can't stop eating. I eat because I'm unhappy, and I'm unhappy because I eat. It's a vicious cycle.

Halloran: And now the cycle is complete. We've gone full circle. Amazing, really. Predetermined, probably.

Safreed: Couldn't have it any other way.

Halloran: Oh, there were plenty of people who would have preferred to bypass the Yankees and get the Twins.

Safreed: Yeah, and those people are affectionately called losers, and chicken bleep little babies. They whine about not wanting to lose to the Yankees again. Defeatist jerks. I've got no use for them whatsoever, and I'm glad they didn't get their way.

Halloran: I'm with you on this one. Just say it out loud, 'Red Sox-Yankees' or Red Sox-Twins'. If they were reality shows, which one would you watch?

Safreed: Depends on which one has the hot chick. But assuming the 'hot chick factor' is equal, I'd go with Sox-Yankees.

Halloran: You've got issues, Fred. And so, apparently, do the Red Sox. They're going up against the Yankees, just like you wanted, but their two aces aren't exactly at the top of their games. For Schilling, it's his health. And for Pedro, it's his head.

Safreed: I think I'd worry more about Pedro than Schilling. Schilling's a proven big game pitcher. He's 6-and-1 now in the post-season. He shared World Series MVP honors with Randy Johnson just two years ago. I'm not worried about him gutting it out.

Jimmy was sitting up at his computer reading as many stories as he could about the Red Sox and Yankees getting ready to play each other. He had been off the ventilator for ten days. He was still weakened by his infection, but in many respects he felt better than he had in months. Now, it was as if he was recovering from pneumonia instead of battling cancer. Pneumonia wasn't even in cancer's league. Sure, it almost killed him, but the treatments were easier to handle and bouncing back seemed much more immediate and probable. He was still restricted to one or two visitors at a time, but his spirits were lifted by his improving health and the current state of the Red Sox.

Halloran: Oh, there's no doubt Schilling will go out there. But that ankle was clearly bothering him in Game One against the Angels. He only gave up the one run, but he allowed a base runner in every inning, and didn't make it out of the seventh. If the ankle isn't any better tomorrow, I wouldn't expect that Yankee line-up to let him off the hook so easily.

Safreed: I'll grant you, it's a concern. But the Red Sox aren't making too big a deal out of it. And he'll be pitching on 6 days rest. I think he'll come up huge in Game One. Pedro's the guy you're not sure of what you're going to get right now.

Halloran: It's the first time he'll be facing the Yankees since he called them his daddy, and of course, the game would have to be in New York. So, the crowd will be riding him from the moment he goes out to the bullpen to warm-up.

"It's gonna be awesome," Jimmy said. His father agreed.

Safreed: That's just one more thing that makes this such a dream scenario. Pedro returning to Yankee Stadium in the ALCS after what happened last year, and what happened last month, I mean, it's just perfect. And it's all just going to motivate Pedro. If he's got anything left in that arm, and if he's as proud a competitor as everybody thinks, then he should pretty much pitch the game of his life.

Halloran: Saying 'They're my daddy' and 'I can't find a way to beat them, I wish they'd disappear' isn't exactly sounding like a proud competitor. You just may have to face it that the Yankees have gotten into Pedro's head, and he might actually be a liability in this series. Think about it. The advantage the Red Sox have going into this series is the one-two punch of having two aces. If the Yankees beat either one of those guys, the advantage swings their way. I mean, the Sox are left with Bronson Arroyo, still a question mark, or Derek Lowe, who was so bad he got dumped from the starting rotation for the playoffs.

Safreed: That's a lot of words that basically just say, 'Play the games'.

"Yeah, play the games," Glenn echoed. "They're going to sap the fun right out of this with all their pre-game analysis. Are you sure you want to keep this on all day every day?"
"Dad, can I tell you something?"
"Sure, son. What is it?"
"Well, I don't want you to start worrying about me, but when I was on the ventilator, there were a few times when I prayed that God would let me give up."

Safreed: We don't know what's going to happen. There are no guarantees. Let's get it on! You know what I mean?

"You did?" Glenn asked without revealing he had done the same.
"Yeah, sometimes I just get so tired of being in the hospital and feeling bad so much of the time."

Halloran: Burt from Lancaster, do you know what he means?

Burt: Yes I do. Hey guys. Tell me this isn't our own little Field of Dreams. You know? As soon as the Red Sox lost Game Seven last year, I started praying for a rematch. I just wanted these guys so bad, I could taste it. I didn't know if there was enough magic out there to make this dream come true, but it happened. I'm ecstatic!

"But it was like I could feel you and Mom, and Mark standing over me, and I knew you guys were praying for me to keep going. The next thing I knew, I was coming out of it and breathing better."

Halloran: And you're not worried, Burt?

*"Now, I'm glad I kept fighting, because I'm going to get to see the Red Sox and Yankees in the ALCS for the second straight year. Thanks, Dad.
Glenn blushed and looked away."*

Burt: Of course, I'm worried. That's why I love this team. They're never dull. You gotta give'm that. And I believe in these guys, because they wanted this match-up. You guys are right that a lot of fans would have just as soon skipped the Yankees and hoped for an easier match-up with the Twins. But I don't think the Red Sox wanted that. They want this fight, and they're going to take it to them. Woo-hoo! Go Sox! Yeeeee-haaaaah!

Safreed: Well, right before Burt morphed into Howard Dean, he made a good point. The Sox aren't going to back down at all. I don't think they're going to feel the pressure, or carry the burden of Red Sox failures – including their own last year. It's good that they're a bunch of idiots. They'll be loose, and play their best.

Halloran: Rick from Middleton, you're next with Bob and Fred on "The Ted".

Rick: Hi, I think it's important that the Red Sox were able to skate right through the Angels as easily as they did. The Yankees had to struggle a little bit against Minnesota. They had to win two of their games in extra innings. And that might tell you something about where the Yankees are right now.

Safreed: You're exactly right. Bob, you talk about the Red Sox pitchers, but what about New York? Who can they count on? No one, that's who. Even if Schilling and Pedro aren't at their best, the Red Sox are going to score plenty of runs. Look at them, they just scored 25 runs in three games against Anaheim, and their pitching is probably better than the Yankees!

Jimmy returned to his computer screen. He was reading a story in the New York Post. The earpiece from his cell phone was lodged securely in his right ear, and with his left ear, he heard his father say, "Do they know it's you when you call? I mean, are you considered one of their regulars."

Rick: The Yankees are gonna end up coming up short of their goal this year. No doubt about it. Go Red Sox!

"I think so. The guy who answers usually says, 'Hi, Jimmy', or something like that."

Halloran: Thanks, Rick. Now, let's hear from Ed in Norton.

Ed: The honeymoon's over for this Terry Francona guy. Wouldn't you say?

Halloran: Now, what are you going to get on his case for today of all days? He just led them to a sweep in the ALDS, and you're going to go after him anyway?

Ed: Well, who's the guy who pitched to Vladimir Guerrero with the bases loaded? The only guy in their line-up who can hurt you, and he lets Timlin throw him a meatball with a 4-run lead. And what the heck did they take Arroyo out for anyway? He was pitching beautifully, and then he didn't even come out for the seventh inning.

"I can't listen to that guy," Glenn said. "Give me a break! I think I'll turn down your radio, and I'll just sit here until you get on."

Safreed: We're not really going to start dissecting Game Three against the Angels, are we?

Ed: We could go back to that 'Who's your daddy' a few weeks ago. That's when Francona did the same stupid thing that bum Little did a year ago. Pedro's got a 4-3 lead after seven innings. He's thrown 101 pitches. I mean, the situation is almost identical, and he sends him out there for the 8th inning.

Safreed: And history repeats itself, I know.

Ed: That's two years of being managed by Dumb and Dumber.

Jimmy laughed and Glenn, wondering why, turned the radio back up.

Ed: If Francona can't figure that out by now, how can you expect him to out-manage Joe Torre? Even if you look at the teams and figure it's an even match, Torre versus Francona is a huge mismatch, and that's probably how the Red Sox will end up losing this series. They're gonna do it to us again, boys. That thud you're about to hear will sound a lot like the thuds you've heard every year for the last 85 years. Like we say in the sewer, 'Time and tide wait for no man'. The Red Sox are going down the drain.

Halloran: Somebody stepped on his rose-colored glasses.

Safreed: Yeah, and then rubbed the chards of glass in his eyes. Now, he's blinded by anger.

Halloran: I love it when you extend a metaphor.

Safreed: You inspire me, Mr. Willing To Share Your Feelings.

Jimmy stared at his computer screen, but couldn't recognize any words. He was thinking about death, and dying before the Red Sox won a World Series. He knew that if he relapsed again, he would almost certainly die before next October. The bone marrow transplant was his last, best chance. So far, the cancer was staying away, and he was winning his battles with infection. Still, the Red Sox just have to win this year, he thought. He began to think 'God owes me that much', but he thought better of it.

Halloran: Let's look for more inspiration from David in Wells, Vermont.

David: I'll come right out and tell you I'm a Yankee fan, but I'll give up the props to the Red Sox. They scare the 'H-E double hockey sticks' out of me, especially Ortiz. That one guy called and said Francona was an idiot for pitching to Guerrero. What about Mike Scioscia pitching to Ortiz in the 10th inning Friday night?

Halloran: Yeah, but he brought in a lefty to face him. At least he played the percentages there.

David: Anybody remember what Ortiz did against a lefty in Game Seven at Yankee Stadium last year? I sure do. He homered in that game against a hefty lefty to make it 5-2 in the top of the eighth.

Safreed: Anybody remember what happened after that?

Halloran: I sure do.

David: Seriously guys, perfect, I'm not. But I really didn't call to rub your nose in last year. I just think that Ortiz is a monster. He's the only guy on either team that can really carry a ball club, especially in a short series. I hope Torre pitches around him every chance he gets.

Halloran: That's an interesting point you bring up. And as a Yankee fan, it tells me you don't have an awful lot of faith in any of the Yankees to carry the team, even though A-Rod just came up big for you guys. He had the game tying double in the twelfth inning of Game Two. And then in the clinching game, he's the one who doubled in the 11th inning, stole third and then scored the winning run on a wild pitch.

Safreed: Typical Yankees, by the way.

Glenn was staring at the radio and wondering why. After all, it was a radio. But it helped him to keep his eyes focused on something other than Jimmy, because if he stared at his son, his mind would race, and the race never ended in a good place.

David: What do you mean typical?

Safreed: The other team threw it away. They handed it to you. Don't think for a minute the Red Sox are going to do that.

David: And that's typical Red Sox whining. Woe is you, I know. But hey, I'm the friendly Yankee fan. I didn't call to fight with you guys. I'm just admitting that Ortiz scares me, and I'll add that, yes, the Yankee pitching staff is a real concern. Thanks for taking the call.

Halloran: That was not your typical fan. An almost likable Yankee fan. Objective even.

Safreed: Vermont must have mellowed him. If you get away from New York long enough, I guess you can actually become a human being after a while.

Halloran: Let's keep going with the phone calls. Next up we've got Joe in Sandwich. Do people call you Sloppy Joe?

Joe: No. Why?

Halloran: No reason. What's up, Joe?

"How are you, Jimmy?" There was no response.

Joe: Well, I'm probably more like the typical Yankee fan. Arrogant. Cocky. Self-assured. And I frequently just blurt out '1918' for no apparent reason.

"Jimmy?"

Safreed: I bet that gets big laughs from all your other I.Q. challenged Yankee fan friends. Very original stuff. Don't you guys realize that after a while those taunts lose their meaning? We're numb to it. I couldn't care less about history. We're in the here and now, buddy. And right here and right now, the Red Sox are gonna smack those condescending smirks right off all of your faces.

"Jimmy?" Glenn tapped his son on the shoulder, startling him. In a flash, Glenn could see his son's despondent look replaced with a big, toothy smile. Jimmy's teeth weren't as white as he'd like, because he hadn't been able to brush with any kind of authority in several months. But in that moment of changing expressions, Glenn knew that Jimmy was prepared to pretend he was happy and carefree. In that moment, Glenn knew his son was lying to him.

Joe: Say it loud often enough, Fred, and you might actually start to believe it. The Red Sox have never been able to beat the Yankees when it matters. It almost takes the fun out of it. I mean, where's the suspense? I guess the only suspense is not knowing how the Red Sox are going to lose. Watching the Red Sox struggle is like watching a turtle rolled over on its back. Just helpless. And hopeless.

"Sorry, Dad. I wasn't listening. What did you say?"

Halloran: Now that's a Yankee fan. They just love to talk trash about the future by bringing up the past. Get in the moment, pal. And be sure to call us back when you're big mouth is full of humble pie.

Glenn paused before dismissing the question, "It wasn't important. They'll probably only take a few more calls. Better get ready."

Safreed: Good one, Mr. Biting Wit. I'm glad you're on my side.

Halloran: Always and forever, Fred.

Safreed: Do you have any pie? I'm a little hungry.

Halloran: Try to focus. Just a few more minutes before we get to the break.

Jimmy was growing tired. Depression has a way of doing that to a person, and so does all the medication Jimmy was taking. He had started to drift away, nearly falling asleep, when his father jolted him to attention with a gentle tap. He hoped his Dad hadn't seen his worried, sullen look. He hoped his reflexive smile had returned in time. But as he looked at his father now, he knew his father was worried about more than his physical health. Jimmy sighed and considered hanging up the phone.

Joe: And one more thing before I go. You guys are in big trouble now that the Yankees are up in Pedro's head.

Halloran: You don't think there's a chance he was simply using reverse psychology? Maybe lulling the Yanks into a false sense of security?

Joe: Beaten man. That's what he is. He doesn't have the 95-mile an hour fastball to fall back on anymore. And remember, he didn't go on the DL at all this year. That little frame sure has thrown a lot of innings. And you know what? I think he pitched through the season in order to keep his value high as a free agent. He'll make his money, but it's going to cost the Red Sox dearly. Not to worry though. He'll have plenty of time to rest when his 'Daddy' sends him to his room.

Halloran: Oops, I think we just lost the connection with Joe. How'd that happen do you suppose? Not to worry though. We've got Alan from Jackson, New Hampshire on the phone.

"It doesn't look like I'm going to get on today," Jimmy said. "Once they get to the commercial break, I'm gonna take a nap."

Alan: Hey guys. Y'know where I come from there aren't a whole lot of Yankee fans, and most of the Red Sox fans I know are feeling pretty good about our chances this year. But I gotta say, I'm not sure all the optimistic folks are living here in the real world.

Safreed: And why not?

"All right, kid. That's when I'll get going. You're mother and Mark will probably be here by the time you wake up."

Alan: For me, it all comes back to Pedro. How many home run pitches has he floated right down the middle this year? 26? That's more than he gave up the three previous years combined. Then after he slumps into the post-season, he throws seven average innings, giving up three runs, and he declares himself the ace again. Aces who have three Cy Young Awards and make 17.5 million dollars are supposed to be better than that.

Halloran: For those of you who might have missed it, Alan's bringing up a good point here. After Game Two against the Angels, Pedro said, and I'm quoting here:

'I was the number one today and that's all that matters. I don't care what the experts have to say. They were talking trash. Every time they give me the ball, I'm special.'

Safreed: Sounded like he was over the 'Daddy' stuff, and got his confidence back.

Halloran: And his confidence was shaken, not stirred. Remember, Pedro finished out the regular season by giving up 21 runs in his last 23-and-a-third innings. He needed a strong outing, and he delivered.

Alan: Delivered what? He delivered the kind of performance you'd love to get out of Arroyo. But I couldn't believe after he pitched such a mediocre game that everyone was saying, 'Look at Pedro. He's back!' Give me seven or eight shutout innings, and I'll say he's back. He may be confident again, but I'm not.

Halloran: It's pretty clear you've got something against Pedro. Can't you just be happy with the win?

Alan: You're darn right I've got something against Pedro. His 'me first', and 'I play by my own rules' act got old a long time ago. This guy didn't even join his teammates on the field during pre-game introductions. Get your butt out there, buddy!

Halloran: Yeah, what was up with that?

Alan: Look, all I know is this guy ain't a big game pitcher. If Schilling's ankle makes him less than 100 percent and God forbid he loses Game One, I could see us losing the first two games and having the season resting on Arroyo and Tim Wakefield. I don't mind telling you, that scares me a little.

Halloran: Alan, you are right on the money. Schilling's ankle and Pedro's head, especially against the Yankees, are genuine concerns. Thanks for the call. Let's talk to Jimmy who's in Boston. Jimmy, are you nervous?

In an effort to infuse a little energy into himself, Jimmy stood up from his chair.

Jimmy: A little bit. I feel like if we beat the Yankees, we'll definitely win the World Series. So, it's all kind of riding on the next seven games.

Halloran: What's your gut telling you?

Jimmy: To stay away from fried foods. And that we're gonna need a little help from up above.

Halloran: You're not going to get religious on us now, are you Jimmy?

Jimmy: Not really. I mean, people have been praying for years, and it's never done any good. I don't know if praying has ever done me any good either. I think it's probably true that God answers every prayer, but sometimes he says no.

Safreed: Well, I'm not buying the idea that the winning team somehow had God on their side. I can't believe even really religious people think that God has some sort of vested interest in the outcome of sporting events.

Jimmy: I didn't mean to get us going in that direction, guys. Really. When I said 'help from above', I was talking more about magic and fate. The Red Sox seemed to have a lot of it last year, and then it ran out on them. But this year, they either dominated games or they lost them. They've gotten where they are with superior talent. But talent alone won't beat the Yankees.

Safreed: All right; that I'll buy. Now, you're making a little more sense. You're right. They're definitely going to need some hits that kick up some chalk, or a bloop hit off a check swing somewhere along the line. I don't think that's God getting involved, but a little bit of luck could go a long way.

Halloran: Jimmy, sounds like you've been staying up a little too late watching these games. You're voice is weak, and you're energy's a little lower than we're used to hearing from you. Take a nap today, and get yourself ready for two more weeks of history in the making. I think we all might just live to see the Red Sox win a World Series.

Jimmy: That's what I've been praying for. No offense, Fred.

Safreed: None taken.

Halloran: Talk to you later, Jimmy. Now, here's Jones from Quincy.

Jones: All this talk about the Red Sox and Yankees going at each other's throats again is music to my ears. I love all that jazz. This is the way it had to be, because the Red Sox could never make things easy.

Glenn took the cell phone from Jimmy and laid it on the desk. He helped his son

132

over to the bed, sat him down, lifted his legs and pulled the covers up over him. He looked upon his son for a moment, and then kissed his forehead, but Jimmy didn't feel it. He was already asleep.

Safreed: They just swept the Angels, what could be easier than that?

Jones: How about a sweep that didn't include blowing a 5-run lead, giving up a grand slam, and going into extra innings?

Halloran: That would be easier.

Safreed: C'mon! The other guys get paid too, you know. The Angels are a good team, and the Red Sox needed to prove that they're a great team in order to beat them.

Jones: I hope they're a great team, because that's what they're going to have to be.

Halloran: Well, they've been assembled to be a great team. And they're going to face the Yankees this year with a strong bullpen and a strong closer. Did you see what Foulke did in that first series? In the ninth inning, the Angels had runners on second and third with one out, and Foulke struck out both Garrett Anderson and Troy Glaus, two of the Angels most dangerous hitters. He really had that change up working, spotting it on both corners, changing speeds, and his arm speed and arm slot are identical no matter what pitch he's throwing.

Safreed: You kill me, Mr. Talks A Good Game.

Halloran: What are you talking about?

Safreed: Arm slots? Spotting the change? You talk like you've been a big league pitching coach for thirty years – like you even have a clue what you're talking about.

Halloran: I can see what's happening out there. And it looks wonderful on my Hi-definition television from Tweeter, by the way.

Safreed: This is exactly how you get when you talk about football. You sound like you're scheming defenses saying things like 'cover two' and 'eight in the box'. And you probably don't have any real understanding of what you're saying.

Halloran: I know what cover two and eight in the box mean. Why are you trying to pick a fight over this?

Safreed: Because I know the only thing you know about 'eight in the box' is that you ate the first four!

Halloran: Oh, I see what this was now. You set this whole thing up just to get in a little punch line. Have you been saving that one up for a while?

Safreed: Actually, yes. But since we haven't talked about the Patriots in a while, I didn't know when I'd get to use it. So, yes, I set it up. Thank you for playing along.

Halloran: What do you say we send out for pie and doughnuts?

Safreed: Sounds good to me.

Halloran: All right everybody. This is the day before the Red Sox and Yankees get together in what promises to be another epic battle. We'll talk more about the moment we've all been waiting for when "Sports Overtime" on WTED returns – right after these messages.

CHAPTER NINE
The ALCS and CMV

This was another disappointing car ride in a seemingly never-ending series of disappointing car rides. Glenn and Eileen were supposed to be picking up Jimmy from the hospital and bringing him home. They planned to have a quiet family celebration, because Jimmy still wasn't supposed to have any visitors. But Mark was going to be home from school. Glenn had received permission to leave work early. And Eileen had prepared a variety of desserts, not knowing which one Jimmy's stomach might be able to handle, and she was fully prepared for the possibility that Jimmy might pass on all of them. It wouldn't matter if Jimmy couldn't eat much, or if his enthusiasm didn't match the excitement of the others. Jimmy was finally coming home. And then he wasn't.

Dr. Fitzpatrick had told the Macombers that once Jimmy was over his latest bout with pneumonia, and his blood counts were high enough and consistent enough, he could leave the hospital. Eileen and Glenn were at the hospital yesterday when his Absolute Neutrophil Count (ANC) was above 500 for the third straight day. They rushed home and began preparing for Jimmy's arrival. Jimmy was certainly strong enough to continue his recovery at home. But the phone rang early the next morning.

"Cytomegalovirus. CMV," the doctor said blankly. "It's a virus that infects most people worldwide, but it doesn't usually present."

"Except in people with weakened immune systems," Eileen assumed correctly. "Jimmy's not coming home, is he?"

No, Jimmy wasn't coming home any time soon. CMV used to be one of the most life-threatening transplant infections there are, but it can now be treated with ganciclovir, an antiviral medication, and pooled antibodies. Patients typically stay in the hospital for fourteen days of therapy and then get discharged if they're doing well.

Soon after Jimmy came down with pneumonia for the second time, Dr. Fitzpatrick noticed Jimmy's breathing was more rapid and labored than his first go round with pneumonia, and his chest X-rays showed bilateral pulmonary infiltrates, which were all indications of respiratory distress. Further examination revealed Jimmy's spleen was slightly enlarged. That's when Dr. Fitzpatrick ordered the tissue biopsy to determine if Jimmy had CMV. The results came in the next day.

Glenn and Eileen had known about the tissue biopsy and what Dr. Fitzpatrick was looking for, but they noticed Jimmy's condition vastly improving. His breathing had become easier. His response to the antibiotics was relatively uneventful, and what they chose to focus on was that his ANC was within acceptable boundaries for three straight days. They knew CMV usually occurs within the first two months following a transplant. So, they let their own optimism deliver a diagnosis prematurely. Dr. Fitzpatrick had heard the Macombers were expecting to take Jimmy home, so he called to remind them that Jimmy might still have another battle on his hands.

So, instead of heading in to the hospital to bring Jimmy home, Glenn and Eileen were sitting in the middle of traffic on their way to console their son – again. Stopping and rolling along on the Southeast Expressway, the mother and father of a boy who had seemed to be dying for the past two years empathized with their son. They felt his pain, and they knew his heartache. They knew that today would be especially hard on him, because the Red Sox had just fallen three games down to the Yankees in the American League Championship Series. Glenn turned on the radio.

"Sports Overtime", Show Open, October 17, 2004

Roy Orbison singing *It's Over.* (The song continues throughout the show open): "It's over...over...ooooh-ooooh-ver!"

Announcer: Come one. Come all. Join us today for "Sports Overtime" on WTED. It's going to be one great big pity party.

Judge Rayford from *And Justice For All:* I found out what the meaning of life is.
Arthur Kirkland: What's that?
Judge Rayford: It sucks.

Announcer: It sure does. Red Sox fans, you can come as you are to this party. And when you respond to your very special invitation, make sure the RSVP stands for Red Sox, Very Pathetic!

Kurtz from *Apocalypse Now:* The horror. The horror.

Announcer: Oh, sure. We thought RSVP was going to stand for Red Sox Victory Parade. But that's not going to happen now. The Red Sox have fallen into a three-nothing hole, and they can't get up.

George from *Seinfeld:* My father was a quitter. My grandfather was a quitter. I was raised to give up. It's one of the few things I do well.

Announcer: We really don't like to give up before it's over. But let's face it. It's over. No team in the history of baseball has ever climbed out of a hole this deep. So, you can either start kicking yourself for letting the Red Sox suck you in again, or you can start waiting till next year – again!

Grinch from *The Grinch:* Seven o'clock, wrestle with my self-loathing; I'm booked! Of course, if I bump the loathing to nine, I could still be done in time to lay in bed, stare at the ceiling and slip slowly into madness. But what would I wear?

"Are you sure you want to listen to this? Aren't we depressed enough already?"

Announcer: Let's see. To sum up the Red Sox and Yankees series so far: Curt Schilling was knocked around like a billiard ball in Game One and might be done for the year. Pedro Martinez was out-pitched by Jon Lieber in Game Two. And then there was the incredible embarrassment of Game Three. The Yankees did more scoring than a sailor on leave in that one. The Sox lost 19-8 last night. And the misery's not over yet!

Nick from *The Big Chill*: Wise up, folks. We're all alone out there and tomorrow we're going out there again.

Announcer: The series that held so much promise, the re-match that seemed both improbable and pre-destined, the hope for Red Sox glory just once in our lifetimes, well, it's all kaput! Once again, the joke's on us!

Alvy Singer from *Annie Hall*: There's an old joke. Uh, two elderly women are at a Catskills mountain resort, and one of them says, 'Boy, the food at this place is really terrible.' The other one says, 'Yeah, I know, and such small portions.' Well, that's essentially how I feel about life. Full of loneliness and misery and suffering and unhappiness, and it's all over much too quickly.

Announcer: It can't be over soon enough for our lovable hosts of "Sports Overtime", Bob Halloran and Fred "Freddie the Fredderman" Safreed. These guys know a little something about sticking a fork in things, and they're here to tell you, the Red Sox are done! Oh, well. It's only a game. Right? It's not as if it were something important that people have been waiting their whole lives to see. So, that's a good thing.

Roy Orbison (up loud): "It's over. It's over. It's over. It's over."

"As depressing as it is, maybe it'll also serve as a distraction for Jimmy," Glenn said. "I hope he's listening."
"I hope he's calling in right now. If this city had even a fraction of Jimmy's heart, they'd never give up on the Red Sox, not until the final out."
Eileen stared out the window praying for a miracle for the ten-thousandth time. For a while, she didn't even hear the radio blaring inside the car."

Homer from *The Simpsons:* Son, when you participate in sporting events, it's not whether you win or lose, it's how drunk you get.

Halloran: Words to live by today. Not that we condone getting drunk.

Safreed: Not at all.

Halloran: But you've got to think more than a few Red Sox fans will be looking to drown their sorrows, maybe even as early as tonight. It could all be over just like that.

Safreed: I can't believe it. I feel like I've been zapped with a stun gun. I sat there watching the game last night thinking this just can't be happening. I think I threw up in my mouth a half dozen times.

Halloran: Wonderful imagery. But it's just amazing how fast it turned ugly. You're thinking, 'All right. So, Arroyo's a little nervous. He gives up the home run to Matsui and the Red Sox are down 3-nothing. But then the Sox scored four runs off Vasquez, and you're thinking this could be O.K. Then Arroyo can't get out of the third. Leskanic and Wakefield give up five more runs in the fourth. Matsui ends up with five hits, five runs scored, five RBI and two home runs. And it's like, my God, what just happened here!

Jimmy had just said good-bye to Angela who had been the bearer of the bad news.

"Chances are, it's not CMV," she said. "And you'll be getting out of here in a couple of weeks."

Jimmy accepted the news as he often did, quietly. He sat and thought for a moment, "What are the chances I DON'T have CMV. I get everything they think of around here."

But Jimmy took the news fairly well, Angela thought, probably because he was so tired from watching the game the night before that he wasn't ready to get up and do any packing anyway.

Safreed: Just a nightmare. It's one thing to be down three-nothing, which is bad enough. But it's another thing to go down three-nothing with a loss like that -- at home. How demoralizing is that?

Halloran: For everyone, the players and the fans, it's gonna be tough going back out there at Fenway Park tonight. And they're going out there with Derek Lowe as their starter, and he's a guy who pitched so poorly at the end of the year that he was knocked out of the rotation for the playoffs. He's only pitching, because Tim Wakefield had to go four innings last night to save the bullpen.

Safreed: It's not looking good.

"He's a genius," Glenn said aloud, though Eileen didn't hear him.

Halloran: Excellent point, Fred. And when you say it's not looking good, do you mean 'not good' in a way that 25 teams have been down 3-0 in a best of seven series, and all 25 have lost? Or do you mean 'not good' in a way that 20 of those 25 teams were swept in four games?

Safreed: I just mean it's not looking good. I don't even know if my mouth is working today, or if any words are actually coming out. All I hear is a dull ringing in my head and my mind keeps having flashbacks to Yankees crossing home plate, one after another after another. Shoot me now. Please put a tiny little bullet in my brain!

Halloran: And I'm not one for ranking the different levels of pain the Red Sox have put their fans through over the years, but in a way, maybe this one hurts the most. I know the signature moments of Buckner and Dent and Grady last year still exist, but I think when you consider the expectations for this team were so high this year, and the rivalry with the Yankees being as high as it's ever been, and now losing to them in back-to-back years, and just getting blown off the field like that, this has got to be the worst one yet.

Safreed: Maybe. I don't know. Last year was a crusher, because we were so close to victory. You know? We could taste it, kind of like in '86 with the Mets, except this was the Yankees, and it was gonna taste so sweet! This time, they didn't even get close. So, it's different. But I definitely feel just as empty today as I did when Aaron Boone hit that home run last year. And it's not even over yet. This could actually get worse. And it already hurts so much, it's gonna leave a mark.

Halloran: Just a mark, I hope, not a stain.

"I can't believe how often they mistake crude for funny on this show," Eileen said. "Oh, you're back!" Glenn smiled. "I didn't know you were still listening." "Glenn, what if…" Eileen paused as Glenn checked his mirrors in an effort to change lanes.

Safreed: Geez, it just sucks that we have to spend every year comparing which loss hurt the most! It's like asking someone if it hurt more when they got that needle stuck in their eye, or when they got kicked in the plums. How about winning for once? Is that possible? I mean, just once!

(**The Bishop from *Caddyshack:*** There is no God!)

"What if Jimmy has CMV? How do we talk to him? I mean, with the leukemia there was always talk of being cured, putting it behind him forever. But this CMV can be like AIDS. It can cause blindness. And it could kill him! What do we say to him about this? My God, this is as bad as the day we learned he was sick."

Halloran: And you have to wonder what hideous surprises they have in store for us tonight. Maybe they'll prolong the agony for a couple of days. Maybe…

Safreed: I just don't want to get swept! They've got to win at least one game. They just have to!

"He doesn't have CMV," Glenn said definitively. "He doesn't. That's all there is to it. And by the way, the Red Sox aren't out of this thing yet. I refuse to prepare for the worst, because I want to be ready when the best happens."

Halloran: So, it's up to Derek Lowe. That's gotta make you feel a little better, huh, Fred?

Safreed: That dull ringing is back in my head.

"You don't want to talk about the 'what if's'?"
"No, I really don't."

Halloran: Maybe that was the phone ringing. We've got Ben from Franklin on the line. Did you hide all the sharp knives in your home, Ben?

Ben: This is gonna be a rough one guys. I felt like it might be over when the Red Sox lost the first two games. If they couldn't win with their aces on hill, how were they going to win this series? I mean, the one-two punch of Schilling and Pedro was supposed to be our secret weapon this year.

Halloran: But you can't really blame either guy, can you? I mean Schilling's clearly pitching on a bad ankle. Something's terribly wrong there. And how's Pedro supposed to win if the Sox only score one run?

Safreed: By throwing a shutout. That would've been nice.

Halloran: You can't really get on him for not throwing a shutout. C'mon, Fred. He pitched well enough to win. It's just that Lieber had the night of his life.

Safreed: When's Pedro gonna have the game of his life? Answer me that. You just can't accept being out-pitched, out-manned by Jon Lieber! For crying out loud! It's not like he was out-pitched by Sandy Koufax. It's Jon 'freakin' Lieber! And can you believe what he had the nerve to say after the game? After the Red Sox lost both games in New York! He starts talking about mango trees and feeling good! Don't tell me you're feeling good after you just lost! That was terrible!

Halloran: I thought we might get to that today. For those of you who might have missed it, here's what Pedro said about hearing the 'Who's your Daddy' chant at the Stadium the other night.

Pedro (on tape): It actually made me feel really, really good. I actually realized that I was somebody important because I got the attention of 60,000 people. Fifteen years ago I was sitting under a mango tree without 50 cents to actually pay for a bus. And today, I was the center of attention of the whole city of New York. I thank God for that.

Safreed: You know what? He's got to understand the situation. Go ahead and thank God for your good fortune some other time. At the post-game news conference after you just let your team down, that's the time to talk about wishing you could have done more to pick up your teammates. Save the mango tree garbage for your memoirs, Pedro!

"I just don't know how much more of this I can take," Eileen said. "We keep trying to look strong for him. He keeps trying to look for strong for us. And every single one of us knows the others are crying inside. I'm certainly not going to fool Jimmy if I go in there with a big smile on my face."

Ben: I agree with you, Fred. It was like after Schilling only went three innings, and the Red Sox showed such great heart by rallying back with five runs in the seventh and two more in the eighth – that was incredible – they almost came back to win that first game, and when they didn't, they needed Pedro to be gi-normous! And he wasn't. Yes, he got through the "Who's your daddy" stuff. But three runs in six innings just isn't good enough.

Halloran: He could have given up two runs in nine innings and it wouldn't have been good enough. The fault in that game lies with the offense. Fred, you get so indignant about Pedro being out-pitched by Lieber. What about the hitters who were out-classed by him?

Safreed: They all suck. Right now, that's how I feel. Everyone's to blame. When's Johnny Damon gonna step up? He's 1-for-13, so far. And he came in smoking hot! Manny doesn't have an RBI, and he drove in SEVEN runs in three games against Anaheim. How does that happen? The Red Sox have scored sixteen runs and Manny doesn't have an RBI? What's that all about?

Glenn had been thinking for a long moment when he pulled up to a stop light on Melnea Cass Boulevard, turned to his wife and said, "You won't fool him, not a chance. He's never been fooled by our phony smiles. But we're going to go up to his room again today and smile, because even if he isn't fooled by it, he still needs it."

Halloran: Maybe John from Milton can tell us what it's all about.

John: Sure. I think I can. It's all about doing what it takes to win on that given day. Look, the Red Sox have had two games where they scored seven runs and eight runs, and they lost both games. And they had another game where they only gave up three runs, and they lost that one, too. So, it's like when they're hitting, they're not pitching. And when they're pitching, they're not hitting.

Safreed: That about sums it up.

John: But the Yankees have been able to find ways to win. And I hate to say it, but that's what they always do. This is the same sad old story that keeps getting re-told with new chapters added on. Beating the Yankees would be paradise, and now it's lost.

Safreed: Yup, that about sums it up.

Halloran: You're contributions to the show today, Fred, have been really exceptional. If you don't mind I'm going to occasionally put a mirror under your nose just to make sure you're still breathing.

Safreed: (silence)

Halloran: All right. While somebody gets me that mirror, let's talk to Fred from Marion.

Fred: I just have a quick question. What's the deal with Schilling's ankle? Is he going to be able to pitch again, or what?

Halloran: That could be kind of a moot point if the Red Sox don't win tonight.

Safreed: And tomorrow.

Halloran: That's right. At this point, the Red Sox are keeping their fingers crossed that Schilling could be ready to pitch again on Tuesday in Game 6.

Jimmy sat alone in his bed with the phone tucked under his left ear. He'd move it to his right ear when he heard his name, because he liked to gesticulate with his left hand when he made an especially cogent point. He really wanted a chance to be heard today.

Fred: So, who's going to pitch Game 5?

Halloran: Looks like that would be Pedro. He'd have four days rest. And by cutting in front of Schilling in the rotation, Schilling would have six days rest, which still might not be enough. But we might be getting ahead of ourselves a little bit. They still have to win tonight. Isaac in Newton, you're next on "The Ted" with Bob and Fred.

Isaac: I'm sure everyone understands the gravity of the situation, so I won't repeat how dire it appears. But what really ticked me off last night was when Dale Sveum sent Bill Mueller home and he was thrown out at the plate.

Halloran: Third inning.

Isaac: Right. The bases were loaded and Cabrera hit that double. It tied the score, and if Sveum doesn't wave Mueller home, we might have scored a few more runs that inning.

Safreed: It was 19-8! Are you seriously going to sit here and look at one play as the one that lost the game? Unless the Red Sox were going to score twelve more runs that inning, I don't think Sveum has to feel too badly this morning.

"What an idiot," Glenn said, and Eileen nodded.
"What an absolute idiot," Jimmy said.

Isaac: Well, it's not like we're doing calculus here. This is pretty basic stuff. If the

Red Sox added a couple of runs there in the third, it could have changed everything that happened after that, and maybe the Yankees don't end up with 19 runs.

Safreed: And maybe monkeys will fly out of my Aunt Fannie! It was 19-8! It's not even worth talking about. In a few hours, Game Four will be underway and if the Red Sox lose by eleven runs again, you can call back tomorrow and complain about when the Red Sox didn't sacrifice bunt in the second inning. All right, Isaac?

Isaac: You know, the more you say 19-8, the more it sounds like 1918.

Safreed: My head hurts.

Halloran: We'll be looking forward to your call tomorrow, Isaac. Now, let's talk to Joe in Sandwich.

Safreed: Oh, not this guy, Bob.

Joe: Oh, don't feel bad, Fred. I just called to say I really hope you guys win one someday.

Safreed: Thanks for your sincerity.

Joe: No, really, I am being sincere. You know, I would normally have loved to call and gloat and poke fun at you guys, but I just can't. It would be like teasing you when your dog dies or something. I can't even imagine what it's like to be a Red Sox fan today.

Safreed: Hey, you know what? You're probably being very genuine right now. And it sounds nice, and maybe I should apologize in advance for saying this, but what I don't need right now is the patronizing sympathy of a Yankee fan. I'm telling you, I'm not in the mood.

Joe: All right, all right. I promise I won't call when the series is over. But I'll be thinking about you. And one thing you should be thinking about – you should be thinking about the feeling you have right now. Hold on to that feeling, and remember it the next time I do call and you try to tell me all the reasons why the Red Sox are going to win it this time. 'Coz I think if you remember how this feels you'll always know that no matter what's going on, no matter who's hot or hurt or whatever, the Red Sox just can't beat the Yankees. It'll never happen, not in a million years.

Safreed: Yeah? How about this, Joe Joe? How about when you're dog dies, you hold on to that feeling. And remember it. Take that feeling around with you every day. Be my guest.

Halloran: And our next guest, not here to talk about dead dogs, is Jimmy in Boston. Those of you who listen regularly might know Jimmy as a very bright, and very hopeful Red Sox fan. Do you have any hope left, Jimmy?

Jimmy: Not a lot. But my dad says there's no such thing as hopeless. There's only hope. So, I guess there's a little bit.

Glenn and Eileen smiled. They had parked the car, but they wouldn't be getting out for at least a few more minutes.

Halloran: And what are you holding on to? What's your source of hope these days?

Jimmy: One day at a time. That's all there is. Today could be the end, or maybe tomorrow. But if it's not today or tomorrow, then who's to say when it will be? There's always a chance for a miracle.

Safreed: Leave it to a wide-eyed little boy to be the one person who hasn't faced reality here. Hey, Jimmy, I don't want to be the bearer of bad news, but it's all over. It's over for you. And me. And for every Red Sox fan who was foolish enough to believe this year would be different. Face it, kid. It's inevitable. No team comes back from being down 3-0. I was with you there for a while, but now I'm just dying a slow, painful death.

Jimmy: Sometimes I feel the same way. And I can see the people around me losing hope, too. But I hang on because it's a dream. It's really the only dream I have these days. I want to be able to cheer when the Red Sox win it all. And who knows how many chances I'll have to see it happen.

Halloran: You're right. These opportunities don't come around that often. And this is two years in a row that the Red Sox have blown it. It truly is an Evil Empire that can snatch the dreams away from great, young kids.

Safreed: I'm hurting over here, too, Mr. You Can't Make Me Cry.

Halloran: Yes, the Evil Empire also takes dreams away from overweight, loud mouth radio talk show hosts who tend to sweat while trying to unwrap a DVD.

Safreed: You've got to admit those DVD's are a bitch to open.

Halloran: Jimmy, thanks for calling and keep the faith. No harm in that. Here's Terry from Franconia Notch. Good to have you back with us, Terry.

Terry: Thanks you guys. And I know you're gonna laugh, but this thing is far from over.

Halloran: What's far from over? The series?

Terry: Yeah. This team has shown so much heart all season long. You had guys making good at-bats right to the very end last night. Tim Wakefield jumped into the game to help out and give up his start. I mean, everyone in that dugout still believes. I don't know why nobody else does.

Halloran: Do you need to hear the stats on the number of teams in any sport that have come back from being down three games to none?

Terry: Look, if the Red Sox are going to win the World Series…

Safreed: Can you believe this guy?

"I wish I had said that," Jimmy said. "I wanted to tell them it wasn't over, but I lost my train of thought and then they said good-bye. Shoot!"

Terry: Hear me out. If they're going to win the World Series, they'd be making history, right? First time since 1918 and all that. Well, who's to say they can't make a little history along the way and become the first team to come back from such a big hole? Just because it hasn't been done before, doesn't mean it can't be done.

Safreed: Actually, I think in this case, that's exactly what it means.

Terry: Again, hear me out. These two teams are pretty evenly matched, wouldn't you say?

Safreed: Not any more. No.

Terry: Well, at the start of the series you thought they were. So, when you've got two evenly matched teams, the outcome of any one game is like a coin flip. It could pretty much go either way. And if you've ever flipped a coin a bunch of times in a row, then you'd know that sometimes you might get three heads in a row, and then a bunch of tails. It's not just heads, tails, heads, tails.

Safreed: So, we've just had three heads come up, and now you think we're gonna see four tails?

Terry: Exactly. At least, it's possible. And look at how it's all stacking up. Derek Lowe tonight against Orlando Hernandez. That's a coin toss. Then you've got Pedro going in Game Five, maybe Schilling in Game 6, and now we've come to Game 7, and the Yankees are wondering what just happened. They're the team with all the pressure then. They'd be the ones faced with the greatest choke job in sports history.

Halloran: Sure, Terry, but you've got 'if they win Game Four, and if Schilling comes back'. That's a lot to ask for.

Terry: So? That's what I'm asking for. And I know you guys think I'm the crazy one. And I might be the only one to call here today saying there's still a chance, but that ballpark is going to be filled tonight with 35-thousand fans who are hoping for that miracle Jimmy talked about. There's more hope in Red Sox Nation than you guys would want to believe.

"He's talking about you," Glenn said as he entered the room. "We were listening in the car. You sounded great!"
"Hi, Jimmy," Eileen added with a great big smile, and Jimmy smiled back.

Halloran: Is there a chance? Of course, there is. It's a fat chance.

Safreed: I prefer to say a slim chance.

Eileen instinctively put her hand to Jimmy's forehead. He didn't feel warm. That was good. She pressed his stomach and Jimmy didn't groan. That was also good. She felt the glands on his neck, and looked closely at his eyes, noticing more redness than jaundice. Her examination was thorough and almost satisfying. Certainly, Jimmy didn't have CMV. He should be coming home today, she thought.

Halloran: So, there you have it. Fred and I agree. Yes, there's a chance. But don't count on it, folks. Instead, let's hear the Mixed Messages folks have been leaving on our WTED answering machine today.

Recorded Voice: You have nine unheard messages. First message:

Message One: This team makes me sick! For the first time all year, I've taken off my Red Sox hat. And I'm bald! But when people look at me and laugh, I'd rather it was because I'm bald than to let them know I root for that pack of losers.

Halloran: Now, that's someone whose faith has been shaken.

Message Two: I bought a bottle of champagne in 1986 and it's still unopened. I won't drink it until the Red Sox win it all. I'll drink everything else, of course, just not the champagne. In fact, after last night's embarrassment, I'm going to start drinking like it's my job.

Message Three: People say this is a baseball town. It's not a baseball town. It's a drinking town with a baseball problem.

Safreed: Sounds a little like, 'You lose, you booze'.

Halloran: And if you win, switch to gin. But really, we don't condone the excess spirits.

Message Four: I loved this team. I brought them into my home. I cared for them. I gave them the best years of my life. Now, they're gone, and my wife is still here. What's fair about that?

Glenn looked at the clock, noticed the time, and went to retrieve Jimmy a cup of water. It was time for his cyclosporine. Jimmy grimaced but swallowed the foul tasting pill dutifully. It never got any easier.

Message Five: I've been wearing my lucky shirt ever since the start of the Anaheim series. It worked for a while, but now that shirt is burning. It's burning in hell where the Yankees can find it when they die. And God, I hope that's soon!

Message Six: Yes, um, I just called to say that I still believe the Red Sox can beat the Yankees. You see, I had a long conversation with my dolls who said they heard it from the gnomes in my backyard that the Red Sox are going to win. So, there's nothing to worry about. Toodles.

"Such strange people," Eileen blurted. She wanted to turn off the radio, but she knew better than to do so during the 'mixed messages'. That was Glenn and Jimmy's favorite part of the show. The two of them were laughing, in part, because it struck them funny, and they were laughing, in part, because she wasn't.

Message Seven: It's a good thing I root with my heart, but I bet with my head. This team can crush you, but when I'm out fishing on my new boat next spring, I expect to feel a whole lot better. Thank you, Red Sox. Thanks for sucking so dependably.

Halloran: Smart man. He went with the sure thing.

Message Eight (song parody of Bruce Springsteen's Born in the U.S.A.): Born down in a Red Sox town. The first kick I took was when I hit the ground. You end up like a dog that's been beat too much. Till you spend half your life just covering up. Born in a Red Sox town. I was born in a Red Sox town. I was born in a Red Sox town.

Safreed: A little diddy from the OTHER boss, the one that doesn't own the Evil Empire.

Message Nine: I finally figured out what the problem is with the Red Sox. I've traveled the world asking questions. I've sought the advice of experts and scholars. I've made computations and employed the services of the Big Blue computer. And after dedicating my life to this quest of finding out what's wrong with the Red Sox, I believe I have finally found the answer. THEY SUCK!

Halloran: It's an angry Red Sox Nation out there today, Fred. Have you just about woken from your coma?

Safreed: I'm getting there. And you know what else? That guy who called and laid it all out, and said if the Sox win tonight, they could have Pedro and Schilling in Games Five and Six, he's starting to get to me. Jimmy, too. I mean, what if, Mr. Giving Up To Soon? You know, maybe it is possible for the Sox to come back. I mean more incredible things have happened than that.

Halloran: No they haven't. Never. If the Sox come back, it would be the most incredible thing that has ever happened on planet Earth.

Safreed: And we would be there to see it. Wouldn't that be great?

"Yes, that would be great," all three Macombers said in unison.

Halloran: Don't ever change, Fred.

CHAPTER TEN
Battling Back

Jimmy didn't make it into the family room of Six West very often. There was a television there, but Jimmy had one in his room. He also had PlayStation II and a computer. The family room did have an electric keyboard under a painting of a sunlit waterfall, but Jimmy didn't play. So, the only reason for Jimmy to visit the family room was to be bored somewhere else. Instead of feeling run down and queasy in his room, Jimmy meandered down the hall and felt run down and queasy in the family room. That's where he was surprised to find an old friend of his, Tom Bartley.

Jimmy, Tom and another boy named Mark Ericson were inseparable during a field trip to Camden Yards last summer. It was a Dana Farber sponsored "Teen Trip" to see the Red Sox play the Orioles. About 35 kids took the trip, feeling more like healthy and free teenagers instead of like cancer patients. Tom was every bit as big a baseball fan as Jimmy. The two boys challenged each other's baseball knowledge with pop quizzes all along the 12-hour bus trip. Mark was less informed on stats and baseball history, but he was easy to get along with and loved to laugh. The three boys sat with each other at the game, and Tom just missed catching a foul ball. He would have had it except he had a hot dog in one hand and a soda in the other. He reached for the ball with his hot dog hand, but the ball bounced away and someone else ended up with a mustard stained official Major League baseball.

Tom's arrival at the hospital was met with both joy and sadness for Jimmy. He was glad to see his old friend, but he knew if Tom was back in the hospital, it wasn't a good thing. Tom, like Jimmy, had acute lymphocytic leukemia. He had been in remission when the two boys met last summer. But, like Jimmy, his cancer had returned.

"I'm going to get a bone marrow transplant," Tom said. "My mom told me you just had one."

"Yeah, about 8 months ago. It wasn't so bad," Jimmy lied.

"Eight months ago? Wow! The last time I saw you was on that trip to see the Red Sox play the Orioles. You looked so good that day."

"Yeah, we all thought I had this thing beat. Same with you, I guess."

Tom explained that he had been in remission for nearly three years when his cancer returned. The initial blasts of chemotherapy weren't effective enough, so the BMT was advised. Without a sibling, it took Tom nearly four months to find a suitable donor. Now, they had one, and the conditioning phase would start tomorrow. Tom was predictably nervous and asked lots of questions about what it was like for Jimmy. Jimmy tried to be truthful, but couched his honesty with encouraging toughness.

"Look," he said. "It's going to be the worst thing you've ever been through. I can't lie to you about that. But what choice do you have? It's not like you can give up. Your will to survive is stronger than anything they can do to you. You almost always feel beaten, but as long as you're alive, you're not beaten. You're beating it. So, you just keep living."

The two boys sat and thought about that for a moment. In truth, Jimmy had never thought about that before. He just blurted it out in an effort to help his friend through a tough time. Then he remembered what his mother had told him once; sometimes the advice you give other people helps you the most.

"Did you hear about Mark?" Tom asked and Jimmy nodded indicating that he did. "He didn't beat it."

The two teenage boys with cancer put their heads down and remembered an old friend. They had only known Mark for a short time, but they knew him well because of the common and profound life experiences they all shared. They knew Mark was courageous and scared. They knew he smiled through his pain, that he was smart, that he had to grow up faster than most kids, and that he had given some guy at a baseball game twenty dollars for a mustard stained baseball before handing it over to Tom.

Jimmy and Tom silently recalled that same memory. Then, Tom broke the silence with another disquieting question: "What was the hardest part of the BMT for you?"

The question startled Jimmy who was still reflecting on that thrilling and very wet baseball game at Camden Yards. There were two one-hour rain delays that 35 deliriously happy teenagers sat and sloshed their way through, never bothering to run for cover. In between the heavy raindrops, the Red Sox hit six home runs, including two from David Ortiz, and they beat Baltimore 7-5. It was also Tim Wakefield's 100th win for the Red Sox. What a spectacular day, Jimmy thought. Then he shifted gears and considered the question Tom had posed.

"Well, beyond all the embarrassing stuff like losing my hair, and having to put creams all over my butt rashes – don't laugh, it'll happen to you, too – I think the hardest part is definitely the loneliness. My family visits a lot, but I don't see my friends. Heck, I don't even know if I have any friends anymore. Sometimes I get e-mails, but it happens less and less the longer I stay in here. So, there aren't a lot of chances to talk with a kid your own age."

Tom understood.

"I'm really sorry you're here, Tom," Jimmy added. "But in another way, it's really nice to see you again."

Tom understood that as well.

The two boys laughed together for the next two hours or so, before Tom was called back to his room. As Jimmy walked him back down the hallway, Tom felt a little less nervous about the impending BMT process. And Jimmy felt a little more hopeful about his own situation.

Yes, there was always hope, for Jimmy, and for the Red Sox.

"Sports Overtime" Show Open, October 19, 2004

Announcer: All right, Red Sox fans. Remember when we were talking about how you could stick a fork in the hometown team. Well, never mind. They're still cooking, and they're cooking with gas!

Tim Wakefield, Red Sox pitcher: The last two nights show the depth, the character, the heart and the guts of this ball club. It took every ounce of whatever we had left to win tonight's game and to win last night's game.

Announcer: That's right, back-to-back classics. The Red Sox battled the Yankees for 26 innings and nearly 11 hours of baseball over two unbelievable nights.

Willy Wonka from *Willy Wonka:* The suspense is terrible. I hope it lasts.

Announcer: Today on "Sports Overtime" with Bob Halloran and Fred "Freddie the Fredderman" Safreed, we're gonna find out who thinks the Red Sox really have a chance to pull off the greatest comeback in the history of sports, and who thinks they're just yanking our chain.

Song Parody of *Ebony and Ivory:* Agony and Ecstasy. Live together with the Sox and Yankees. Side by side in another play-off series. Oh, Lord woe is me. Agony, ecstasy, living in perfect harmony.

Announcer: So, what's it gonna be, agony or ecstasy? And how much longer are we going to have to sweat this thing out?

Jane Craig from *Broadcast News:* People called in complaining about your sweating?

Aaron Altman: No, NICE calls, worried that I was having a heart attack.

Announcer: Bob and Fred aren't sure how much more of this they can take. The joy is excruciating.

Donkey from *Shrek:* I just know before this is over I'm gonna need a whole lot of serious therapy. Look at my eye twitchin'.

Announcer: And now the series shifts back to the Bronx with Red Sox fans waiting on a miracle. And maybe the miracle of modern science will provide it. Curt Schilling will head to the mound after a surgical procedure on his ankle that was first attempted on a cadaver. You know, like a dead guy. You heard me.

McCroskey from *Airplane:* Looks like I picked the wrong week to stop sniffing glue.

Announcer: And it looks like the Red Sox have done it to us again. They've given us a reason to believe. Boy, I hate that!

Michael from *Godfather, Part Three:* Just when I thought I was out, they pull me back in.

Announcer: And we welcome all of you back in for another fine edition of "Sports Overtime" with Bob and Fred on "The Ted". This is the land of hope and dreams!

Andy Dufresne from *Shawshank Redemption:* Remember, Red, hope is a good thing, maybe the best of things. And no good thing ever dies.

Halloran: I hope hope is a good thing.

Safreed: That last one was from Shawshank Redemption, and I can tell you one other line from that movie, one that might make more sense today. It was, 'Hope is a DANGEROUS thing. Hope can drive a man insane.'

Halloran: Thank you, Roger Ebert. So, which is it? Is hope good or is it dangerous?

"It's good," Angela said. She had come to find out if Jimmy's CMV test results were back yet. They weren't.
"Definitely good," Jimmy agreed. "My Mom and I watched 'Shawshank' the other night. That was definitely good, too."

Safreed: It's both. It's good to be able to watch these games just completely wrought with emotion. It's not even good, it's just awesome! I'm exhausted when these things are over, and not just because it's like one in the morning. They're absolutely draining. Then when the Red Sox win, you barely have the energy to jump up and cheer.

Halloran: That's because the instant you're happy about another David Ortiz game winner, you also realize the position the Red Sox still find themselves in. One more loss and they're out.

Safreed: And that's the danger. We're all caught up in this again. I mean, I was as low as I can go after Game Three, and I was ready to accept what fate was going to deliver. So that when the Red Sox lost a fourth game, I don't think it was going to hurt that much. My mind was already there. Now, I'm back into this thing. I'm pumped and jacked! So now if the Red Sox lose this series, I'm gonna sink even lower than I was before. A baseball season is a roller coaster ride, but the highs and lows of this post-season are just killer!

Halloran: And you may never be the same again. That Shawshank line said, 'No good thing ever dies'. But if the Sox make fools of us again, I could see a lot of people letting go of hope in the future. The next time the Red Sox are close to doing something big, folks might just be indifferent to it as a kind of self-defense mechanism.

Safreed: Fool me once, shame on you. Fool me a hundred times, and I'm just gonna punch you in the face.

Jimmy and Angela both laughed. He was feeling especially good today. His concerns about his own health were diminishing as the days passed without incident, and his concerns about the Red Sox had turned into overwhelming confidence. He was a believer once again.

Halloran: Right now it's hard not to have hope. The tide has definitely turned in the Red Sox favor. Can you believe the number of times the Red Sox could have lost the past two games, but didn't? I mean, we're talking about three passed balls in one inning, Mariano Rivera blowing two saves in two nights, the Yankees stranding runners all over the place...

Safreed: Trot Nixon sliding to catch that sinking line drive from Matsui with the bases loaded against Pedro. Tony Clark's ground rule double last night...

Halloran: Yeah, that might be the biggest one. If that ball stays in the ballpark and rattles around in the right field corner, then Ruben Sierra would have come around to score in the ninth inning, and the Red Sox are out of this thing. But it didn't happen. It just feels like something very different is happening out there right now.

Safreed: It's the Yankees more than it is the Red Sox. Don't get me wrong, the Red Sox are playing good baseball, and they've shown incredible resiliency to come back from that pitiful Game Three. But it's the Yankees' bad play and missed opportunities that are giving this that different feel. It starts with Rivera. He's the unbeatable foe. Then Dave Roberts comes up with the greatest stolen base in the history of baseball.

Halloran: Everyone knew he was going. Three pick off throws, the tension was mounting. And then he pops up safely at second base.

"That was incredible," Jimmy exclaimed. "I stayed up for the whole game. No amount of chemo could have knocked me out. It was absolutely unreal. The best game ever!"

Safreed: Huge! Just immense! But Mueller still has to drive him home, and he does. So, Rivera has a chink in the armor. Then you look at the Yankee hitters. They stranded 14 runners in Game Four, and then they went 1-for-13 with runners in scoring position last night. I think they're feeling the pressure.

Halloran: As soon as Roberts stole that base and Mueller shot that line drive right back at Rivera, it put the Yankees back on their heels.

Safreed: And while you've got the heart of the Yankee order taking a nose dive, the Red Sox have David Ortiz with three game winning hits now in the post-season.

Halloran: If the Red Sox come all the way back to win this thing, they're going to have to put a statue of Ortiz right up there next to Ted Williams outside the ballpark. This guy is reaching folklore status.

"Ortiz is my favorite player, now that Nomar's gone," Jimmy said, and then added with a trace of sadness: "I wish Nomar was still here."

Safreed: That two-run jack in the 12th inning Sunday night is something I'll never forget. I was just so thankful the Sox didn't get swept. I just wanted one moment to hold on to from this series. Now, we've got the homer, the steal, the Ortiz game winning single last night and so much more in between. It's just been incredible!

Halloran: All right, are you ready to talk about Schilling and what could happen tonight?

Safreed: No, not yet. Let me live in this warm glow a little while longer. I'm sure the phone callers will be ready to get right into it anyway.

Halloran: Let's find out. Samuel from Jackson, New Hampshire, you're first on "Sports Overtime" today.

Samuel: Love the show guys. No doubt about it, this Red Sox team dies hard with a vengeance. They're spirit is unbreakable. But I actually did call to talk about Schilling. What's his story? Is he all right to pitch tonight?

Halloran: It's an amazing story already and the guy hasn't even stepped on the mound. You know, he tried to wear a special shoe for Game One, and it didn't do the trick. So, they've actually performed a surgical procedure on the ankle in which, I guess, they stitched the tendon, the one that kind of slips back and forth over the bone. They've stitched that into place, so it won't move and cause him any discomfort.

Safreed: Tell him the best part, Mr. Wanted To Be A Doctor.

Halloran: Well, this procedure has never been done before, so they practiced it on a cadaver.

Samuel: And was the dead guy able to pitch two days after he had the surgery?

Halloran: No, he was still dead. But we'll find out about Schilling tonight.

Safreed: And considering how much the bullpen has worked over the past two nights, they really need him to go deep into the game, if that's possible.

Halloran: Right now, we don't even know for sure that Schilling will pitch at all. He's going to try it out before the game to see how it feels, and then he'll make the decision.

Safreed: Good, because this series needed a little drama.

"Don't you think it's amazing what doctors can do to help people these days?"
Angela asked.
"Yes," was Jimmy's response, knowing that the question was designed to lift his spirits. So, in an effort to lift Angela's spirits, he added: "And nurses, too."

Halloran: Bill's in Clinton, Mass. What do you have today, Bill?

Bill: Nothing but good, good feelings. I think we're witnessing the law of averages coming back to bite the Yankees in the rear. You guys saw what A-Rod, Sheffield and Matsui did in those first three games. And now look what they're doing. They couldn't hit a bull moose with a bass fiddle right now.

Halloran: Analogy aside, he makes a good point. I've got the numbers right here. In the first three games, those three guys you mention went 24-for-42 with 19 runs scored and 18 RBI. That's just ridiculous.

Bill: And what were they in games four and five?

Halloran: They went 4-for-30.

Bill: That's the law of averages. They couldn't keep up a .500 pace. So, it was inevitable that they'd struggle. And while they failed to produce, the Red Sox had time to come back and win those games in extra innings.

Halloran: I don't know if it's as simple as the law of averages, but their ineptness has been a big part of what's happened the past two nights.

Safreed: Don't forget to give the Red Sox bullpen some credit. Those guys have gone something like 14-and-a-third straight shutout innings. And it's not just because the Yankees suck, even though they do. It's because the Sox pitchers have been making good pitches when they've had to.

Angela could tell that she was becoming little more than a distraction for Jimmy who had immersed himself in the conversations on the radio. She didn't mind being ignored. She was only there to help and encourage Jimmy. If he didn't need her, that was quite all right. She patted his head and unsuccessfully attempted to mat down a cowlick. Jimmy looked up, recognized Angela was leaving, and tilted his head in a half-hearted attempt to say good-bye.

Halloran: And I hope that law of averages catches up to Johnny Damon. He's only 2-for-24 so far in the series. This would be a good time for him to start picking things up. Here's Darren in Dalton.

Darren: It's obvious the Yankees are blowing it. You take a look at Game Four the other night. Bernie Williams comes up in the 11th inning with the bases loaded against Leskanic. For crying out loud, I could hit Leskanic, and Williams flies out to end the inning. Yankee teams in the past, heck, Bernie Williams in the past would have won the game right there. The Yankees just have more holes than the Red Sox and they're finally being exposed.

Halloran: Sure. You may be right. And then the Yankees might come out tonight and lay another 19-8 score on the Red Sox.

Darren: Not likely. The Yankees don't have that clutch guy anymore. A-Rod can pad his stats all season long, but when it really matters he's going to line out to second base like he did in the 11th inning two nights ago. He's nothing. Sheffield's hurt. And Matsui had his one big game. All they've really got is Jeter, and he came up with the three run double against Pedro in Game Four, but Torre's got him batting lead-off, so he doesn't get nearly enough RBI opportunities. Throw in the fact that they only have three reliable guys in the bullpen, and even they've been unreliable so far, and the Yankees are ripe for the picking.

Halloran: It's amazing the Yankees were able to win 101 games as bad as they are.

Darren: They're not bad. They're just the second best team in the American League.

Safreed: I agree with Darren. The Yankees are a flawed team. Now, it's just a matter of whether the Red Sox dug too deep a hole, and if Schilling's able to pitch tonight.

Halloran: It all comes back to Schilling. And the risk is that if Schilling starts, but is ineffective, how quickly will Francona pull him out of the game? Jon Lieber's going for the Yankees, and judging by how well he pitched in Game Two, I don't think you can wait too long with Schilling if he's not getting it done.

Safreed: The man's got the weight of a nation on his shoulders tonight.

Halloran: And that can't be good for his ankle. D.H. in Lawrence, what can you contribute to this conversation?

D.H: Just that I love to play right. And for the past two nights the Red Sox have played right. Once Millar drew the walk in the 9th inning of Game Four, and it ignited that whole chain of events, the Roberts steal, and Mueller's single that knocked Rivera on his butt. It was all beautiful. It was a perfect response to the night before when the Yankees embarrassed us. Now, we've done it to them, and after tonight it will all be even. Then, let the better team win. And that's the Red Sox.

Halloran: I can't even believe we're talking about this today. Do all of you know what you're suggesting? You're talking about the Red Sox actually winning this series! Can we get back to the fact that it's never been done before, and it's highly unlikely that a Yankee team is going to be the first victim of it, especially a Yankee team with a 180-million dollar payroll? Are we seriously talking about this?

D.H: I know I am. I wasn't after Game Three, and I still wasn't after Game Four. But you can't deny what you're eyes have just witnessed. The magic is back, baby! All they need is one more win, and that last one will be easy.

Safreed: You betcha! If the Yankees lose Game Six, they'll be toast. They'll go out there like the Red Sox in Game 7 of 1986. They won't stand a chance.

Halloran: So, it's all on the line tonight. Pretty much the way it's been the last two games. Jimmy's back with us before we head to break. Jimmy, let me ask you, is hope a good thing or a dangerous thing?

Jimmy: Sometimes it's the only thing. But right now, it's definitely a good thing. Because for a while there it was like hoping to be ten feet tall or to live forever, hoping for the impossible. But now, anything's possible. And that's a real good thing.

Safreed: I'm still in awe of what's been happening. The Red Sox were so close to being done so many times, and then they survived to play another day. It's like a death row inmate waiting for a reprieve from the Governor, and while they're strapping him in, he can hear the phone ringing. Nobody answers it. But they just keep letting it ring. Who's on the phone? Pick it up! Are we gonna win, or is the damn Governor calling to say 'Keep up the good work'? Finally, I think the guy just dies of suspense.

(Homer Simpson: I like stories!)

Halloran: The suspense isn't killing me. I'm loving every minute of it.

Jimmy: Me, too. And to go back to The Shawshank Redemption, my Mom watched that with me the other night, and we both liked the line when they said: 'Get busy living, or get busy dying.' I think you need to get busy living, like the Red Sox, Fred. Dying's no fun at all.

Safreed: I just wish the Sox and Yankees would get busy. Start the game. The only thing worse than the suspense during the game is the suspense of waiting for the game.

Halloran: Well, it won't be long now. The series is back in New York where the chants should be 'Who's Your Papi' instead of 'Who's Your Daddy' tonight. But we'll never hear that from the Yankee fans. Will Curt Schilling be able to pitch and pitch effectively, or will it all come to a crashing halt in Yankee Stadium for a sec-

ɔnd straight year? We'll find out tonight. And we'll take more of your phone calls
after this. You're listening to "Sports Overtime" on WTED.

CHAPTER ELEVEN
Taking Down the Empire

With so much time spent alone in a hospital room, Jimmy had become rather proficient surfing the Internet. He clicked and keyboarded his way around his favorite sports websites devouring as much as he could about the Red Sox, Yankees and the rest of Major League Baseball. He also had become a student of his disease.

Initially, Jimmy avoided any information about ALL figuring the less he knew the less he'd be afraid of. But his curiosity got the better of him, and now he believed knowledge was empowering. Yes, he read about such cases as the "16-year-old female patient, who had undergone bone marrow transplantation… and presented with dry cough, dyspnea, and fever for 4 days." He knew that her "chest radiography showed poorly-defined bilateral opacities", that a "high-resolution CT revealed bilateral ground glass opacities with superimposed septal thickening and intralobular linear opacities," and that "laboratory results were nonspecific and empiric treatment with multiple drugs was initiated."

He didn't completely understand all the vernacular, but he had no trouble comprehending the last sentence: "The patient had no response to therapy and died 12 days after the admission."

He had read about at least a hundred such cases, but he'd also learned about the inspirational stories of survival. Families supported each other on Internet blogs by sharing their feelings and experiences, and answering questions for each other. Jimmy spent hours pouring over the passages that detailed the lives and deaths of other cancer families. He was sometimes saddened, sometimes reassured, but always moved. Tonight, he would type out his own blog knowing that his good news would be shared by so many others who needed a little bit of good news, even vicariously.

Jimmy never got used to the idea of a negative being a positive, but he was certain of what Dr. Fitzpatrick meant when he said the CMV tests were negative. It meant he didn't have it.

"I knew it all along," Jimmy said unconvincingly. "I've been feeling too good lately. Does this mean I can go home?"

"Yes, it does. But not right away. You're temperature spiked a little bit yesterday, so as long as we've got you here, we might as well keep an eye on that. Plus, you're due for another round of platelets later this afternoon. So, I think you can look more realistically at leaving on Thursday, assuming we get you up over a thousand calories a day by then."

Jimmy knew what that meant, too. It meant he'd be watching Games 6 and 7 of the ALCS from the same hospital bed from which he saw the Red Sox improbable extra inning victories in Games 4 and 5. Strangely, he was starting to think of this as his lucky hospital bed.

"Sports Overtime", Show Open, October 21, 2004

Announcer: You grow up in this town and your parents are Red Sox fans, your grandparents are Red Sox fans. So, you become a Red Sox fan. And you get tortured for the rest of your life. Until today!

Neil Diamond singing *"Sweet Caroline":* Where it began I can't begin to knowin'. But then I know it's growing strong.

Announcer: Welcome to a Thursday edition of "Sports Overtime". The Red Sox dream the Impossible Dream, and this one was even "impossibler". Whatever. You get my meaning.

Neil Diamond, *Sweet Caroline:* Was in the spring. And spring became the summer. Who'd have believed you'd come along.

Announcer: World Series here we come.

Neil Diamond, *Sweet Caroline:* Hands, touchin' hands. Reachin' out. Touchin' me. Touchin' you.

Announcer: Being a Boston fan is totally wicked awesome!

Neil Diamond, *Sweet Caroline:* Sweet Caroline, ba-ba-ba! Good times never seemed so good. I've been inclined to believe they never would.

Announcer: The Red Sox are the first team in baseball history to rally from three games down and win a playoff series. Call it out around the world. There's gonna be dancing in the streets!

Venkman from *Ghost Busters:* This city is about to face a disaster of biblical proportions.
Mayor: What do you mean, 'biblical?'
Venkman: Riots in the streets, dogs and cats living together, mass hysteria!

Announcer: And the Sox did it against those Yankees. Man, that's the really cool part. After so many years of coming out on the losing end, this provides a little closure, wouldn't you say?

Primo from *Analyze This:* Get a dictionary. Find out what this closure thing is. If that's what he's going to hit us with, I want to be ready.

Announcer: Hey, A-Rod now that the series is over who's your Caddy? Yes, Yankee fans predicted another title for the Yankees, and they were right. They own the title of the biggest chokers in the history of sports.

Steff from *All The Right Moves:* We didn't quit! You quit!

Announcer: Well, I guess a lot of us quit, but that doesn't matter now. Hey, Nomar. Two words for you. Thanks, beautiful.

Al Michaels' famous Olympic hockey call: Do you believe in miracles? Yes!

Announcer: Three words for you Yankee fans, Mark "bleepin'" Bellhorn. This is "Sports Overtime" with the Bob Bobber the Bobberman and some guy named Fred. Ladies and gentlemen, boys and girls, welcome to the Yankees elimination party!

Halloran: Plain and simple, this instantly becomes the most amazing sports story ever. I've always said the U.S. Olympic hockey team winning the gold medal in Lake Placid was the best sports story, but this has now topped it.

Safreed: Because you've toppled the dictatorship. That's what you did.

Halloran: We're talking about coming from six feet under to beat and humiliate the Yankees, the most hated of all rivals. There is nothing on this planet that could possibly be sweeter for a Red Sox fan. There can be no finer moment. There never has been and there never will be a finer moment than this.

Safreed: Wrong. As great as it is, it's not enough. Yes, they beat the dreaded Yankees, and they accomplished something that no other team has done before. And that's great, but there's got to be that one more step.

Halloran: You're right. The fact that the Red Sox haven't won a World Series in 86 years, that's still in play. And you can tell the players aren't satisfied. I'd say last night's celebration was the most subdued of the three they've had so far. Clinching the wild card was bigger. Beating Anaheim was bigger. Last night, they celebrated, but they didn't go crazy.

Safreed: Not as crazy as a lot of Red Sox fans, I can guarantee you that.

Jimmy didn't hear the beginning of today's program. He had walked down the hall to see his friend, Tom. It wasn't a well thought out plan. Tom was already heavily involved in his pre- bone marrow transplant conditioning program. He wasn't re-

ally up for any visitors today.

Halloran: I thought it was very nice of all the Boston beat writers to go down and help the Yankee writers work on all their choke leads. And I would invite all of our listeners to get copies of the New York headlines. Hey, Joe from Sandwich, are you listening? You fruitcake! Daily News, front page: The Choke's On Us. And who do they have choking? A-Rod.

Safreed: A-Fraud. His legacy's going to be that girly hand-slap in Game 6 knocking the ball out of Bronson Arroyo's hand, and then acting like he didn't do anything wrong. That was such a Bush League move. He's a jerk!

Halloran: Here's the second page of the Daily News: This is even better. Pain Strikes, Fans Curse Historic Collapse Against Hated Sox. Page three, Babe Ruth with a Yankee cap on crying! It's a full page with a little tear falling out of his left eye.

Safreed: Wonderful detail.

Halloran: Hey, Babe, there's no crying in baseball! And here's the back page with Pedro Martinez pointing a finger up to the sky with the headline: Hell Freezes Over. That's beautiful.

Safreed: You're like Regis Philbin today, just reading the papers to folks at home.

Tom didn't see Jimmy, but Jimmy saw him, and it was horrifying. The first time he met him, Tom was relatively healthy, and bouncing around with excitement on that trip to Camden Yards. A few days ago, Tom appeared to be about the same. Certainly, he was more sullen, but he still looked good and laughed from time to time. Today, it was entirely different.

Halloran: This is just so perfect. You think the Boston media is tough. The New York media is crucifying them. A team with 26 championships, and they are ripping them a new one.

Safreed: There sure was a loud sucking sound last night.

Halloran: I want to get to the phone calls, because these people deserve to be heard. This will be their day. Let's start with William in Randolph. How are you feeling today, William?

William: Like a 19-year-old kid who just had sex for the first time. What do I do now?

Safreed: Apologize, as I recall.

Halloran: Or just cuddle.

William: I tell you, Charlie Brown just kicked the football, and he broke a couple of Lucy's fingers while doing it. This is unbelievable. Y'know, the greatest right in the world is the right to be wrong. And I don't care that we were all wrong about this team when they were down 3-0. I just think it's great. The other shoe never fell!

Safreed: I wouldn't be surprised if good old Charlie Brown is smoking a cigarette right now with the Little Red-Haired girl still breathing heavy in his arms. That's about what this is like. Charlie and Sox fans have always played the part of the lovable loser. Well, not anymore! We've been the losers. We've lived with anxiety, and pain, and frustration. This is better. It's about time Charlie got some!

Halloran: And the Red Sox got theirs by stomping all over the Yankees right there in Yankee Stadium.

Jimmy stood in the doorway motionless. In Tom, he could see himself. Jimmy had avoided mirrors when he was at his most ill, but now he could see how others must have seen him. Pale, withdrawn, patches of hair missing, sweating and freezing at the same time. He knew what Tom was going through, and he cried a little for his friend, and for himself.

Halloran: This was a series of redemption. It was for all the Red Sox teams that lost in the past, but more specifically last year's team. A lot of these guys went through so much and to lose in a Game Seven and then come right back the next year and win in a Game Seven, it's unprecedented poetic justice.

Safreed: Which is exactly why one of the greatest moments last night was when they gave John Henry the American League trophy.

Halloran: The Gene Autry trophy.

Safreed: Whatever. They gave it to Henry and he turned to give it to Johnny Damon. But Damon said he didn't want to be the first one to hold it. So, he walked around the corner and found Tim Wakefield, and said 'You should be the first one o hold this, old man'. And Wakefield was visibly moved. Remember he gave up the home run to Aaron Boone. More than anyone, he wanted to get to the World Series. That was a great moment.

Halloran: There were just so many great moments, whether it was during the celebration or during the series itself. Not only after Game 3, but Game 4 when you're down 4-3, and you're going up against the best closer in the history of the game. And you get out of that. And then he's got you by two runs in the next game, and you get out of that one. I mean, Schilling, after he goes down in Game One, you could feel the air go out of the balloon. And you're saying to yourself, 'No way'. And then they did something I've never heard of them doing. I mean, they take Schilling in and give him a little minor surgery.

Safreed: Don't forget the cadaver.

Halloran: Right. Abra cadaver! Like magic, he's ready to go. It's like they got some help from a dead Sox fan.

Safreed: I heard the team doctor, Bill Morgan describe it last night, and it sounded pretty gross to be honest with you. Taking a tendon and sewing it down so that it wouldn't snap across the bone. Schilling deserves so much respect. You talk about a guy who backs it up.

Halloran: He delivers the goods man. Ninety-nine pitches the other night, and every one of them had to hurt. Not only did he pitch, but he pitched fantastic! What a stud!

Angela was waiting for Jimmy as he returned to the room. Jimmy had left the radio on, and she was listening to it, thinking to herself, "They think these athletes are heroes, just because they play in a little pain. Here comes a real hero right now."

Safreed: I don't think a whole lot of players would have put themselves through what he did. They should put a statue of him right now on top of the Prudential building.

Halloran: Easy, boy.

Safreed: So, the whole city can see it. There would be this giant 24-carat gold statue of Schilling on top of the roof, so when airplanes come in they can see it.

Halloran: The guy gets it, that's for sure. But I don't know if he'll be getting a gold statue any time soon.

(Schilling on tape) That's a stupid, idiotic comment to make.

Safreed: No, it's not. I'm telling you, watching that guy out there with his red sock of courage, it gave me goose bumps. It was like when Roy Hobbs was bleeding into his shirt in The Natural. How could you not love that? The guy bleeds Red Sox red, literally.

Halloran: I agree with you there. That sock ought to be on its way to the Hall of Fame right now. Right next to every jock strap of every Red Sox player who just pulled off the greatest comeback ever.

Safreed: You don't see a lot of jock straps behind glass. That might be a nice touch.

Halloran: Dusty from Springfield, you are on the air.

"How are you feeling today, Jimmy?"
"I was feeling great, but I just went to see Tom. Is that how I looked?"
"Afraid so. But you got through it, and so will Tom. Just look at you now."
"I know. I can't believe I'm going to get to see the Red Sox win the World Series."

Dusty: I'm walking on air. These guys are the first team to genuinely be able to stand up and say nobody believed we could do it. Because nobody believed they could do it. Unless they believed in themselves, they couldn't accomplish this. It's never been done before.

Safreed: Did you guys here what Posada said after the game? You've got to play that tape. Go ahead, the one where he talks about nobody believing in them.

(Posada on tape): As a group, we were tough at times. Nobody believed we could be here. It says a lot about this team, a lot about these guys.

Halloran: Oh, shut-up, you Jorge Posada you! Nobody believed you would be here? Are you kidding me? What an absolute fraud. Who didn't think they'd be here?

Jimmy, more animated than Angela had ever seen him, paced about the room. He was already dialed in and on hold with the radio program. The last two years of his life were filled with grave concerns and disappointments. Now, everything seemed

o be going his way. It was beautiful. Angela treasured these moments, rare as they
vere in her line of work.

Safreed: There was more on that tape from Jeter, too. Play that one.

Jeter on tape): We've been losing for a few years. Every year it's a different group, and this group just didn't get it done.

Safreed: Translation. A-Rod sucks!

Halloran: That might be one of the general themes of the day. But this is supposed to be a day for celebration. Let's see if we can keep things more positive with Joan in South Yarmouth.

Joan: We believe! God, forgive us for ever doubting it could happen. We believe!

Halloran: It's amazing to see the attitude of Red Sox fans change from waiting for the rug to be pulled out from under them to now expecting good things.

Joan: It's all different now. And I have to say something. You guys said last week it wouldn't matter who we faced in the ALCS, Minnesota or the Yankees. But I think you were wrong. We wouldn't be celebrating today like this. It wouldn't be the same.

Halloran: You're right. Even if they had won four straight like they did. This is different because it's the Yankees, no doubt about it, because they've been the torturers for years.

Safreed: Do you think the Minnesota papers would have had headlines that were as much fun?

Halloran: Not a chance. Here's John in Victory, Vermont. Things must be wonderful in Victory today.

John: I just wanted to get a general sense of what it's like down there.

Safreed: Most people are hung-over, I think.

John: I have two Yankee fans as roommates, and they lost all confidence when Schilling was able to keep going in Game 6. Once they knew he was for real, they knew they were in trouble. And I can tell you this; Yankee fans had no confidence in Kevin Brown last night.

Safreed: He really did them in. Yankee fans must be having trouble figuring out who to hate the most today. A-Rod's a punk. The heart of their order crapped out. And Kevin Brown went out there with nothing, didn't even make it out of the second inning. He might just as well have printed up tickets to the World Series and handed them out to all the Red Sox.

Halloran: That might be a little forgotten good fortune for the Red Sox, the fact that he broke his hand a month ago when he punched a clubhouse wall. That really diminished the Yankee rotation.

Safreed: Tough luck for them.

"Yeah, tough luck for them," Jimmy echoed.

Halloran: Here's Kurt in Russell.

Kurt: What a day! What an escape from New York. I think I'm starting to bruise from the number of times I've pinched myself. These are the best of times! But here's what I don't like. Everybody's saying the Yankees choked. That's disrespecting what the Red Sox did.

Safreed: But it was the biggest choke job in the history of sports. You can't deny that.

Kurt: I think it's a combination of the Red Sox having outstanding heart and character, and the Yankees choking. You need both for something like this to happen. One team has to falter, and the other has to rise up. If both parts don't cooperate, you don't have this.

Halloran: What you have here is the Boston Massacre being replaced with the Boston Miracle. And yet isn't it strange that the Red Sox were really the favorites going into the series, and yet this became one of the greatest upsets in the history of sports?

Safreed: That's just a reflection of how things changed. After Game Three the Red Sox weren't the favorites any more, so then it can be an upset. But it's still an unprecedented choke. Look, I don't want to take anything away from the Red Sox, but c'mon, this is an easy one. Let me ask you, Harvey, how many times has a team come back from 3 games down?

Kurt: Zero before last night.

"He called him Harvey, and the guy didn't even correct him."

Safreed: Zero times. That makes this the biggest choke in baseball history. And I think you could argue it's the biggest choke in all of history. There's no question. Not only to be up 3-0, but to win Game Three 19-8, and then be up in the 9th inning on the verge of a sweep. It's a monumental choke.

Kurt: I think you're choosing to call it a choke instead of focusing on the Red Sox achievement, because you like saying the Yankees choked.

Safreed: Not gonna deny that.

Halloran: No matter how you look at it, it's just so immensely satisfying. I even think the satisfaction is enhanced, because we allowed Yankee fans to beat up on us for a few days. They were feeling really good. And they had a right to feel good. And then we get to just wallop them across the face. This is good.

Safreed: Real good.

Halloran: Joel's on the cell phone. Good afternoon, Joel.

Joel: Great afternoon! The best afternoon of my lifetime! My ex-wife is a Yankee fan. God, I hate her. And I'm absolutely loving this today.

Halloran: That's awfully big of you.

Joel: Man, if you only knew. This woman is pure evil. It should have tipped me off when I found out she rooted for the devil's team, but I married her anyway. The day I left is now the second best day of my life.

Halloran: Hell hath no fury like a Joel scorned. Daniel in Webster, you're next on "The Ted" with Bob and Fred.

Daniel: Everyone is smiling today. Everywhere you go, people are smiling. Suddenly, people who used to flip you off are waving you through intersections. 'No, you go ahead. No, you come on through.' The world is upside down.

Halloran: People don't know how to be themselves any more. It's like the Red Sox are guilty of some mass identity theft.

Daniel: I know who I am. I'm the guy who made up my mind yesterday to drive to Yankee Stadium. I just had to be there to witness the greatest comeback in sports history.

Safreed: Good man.

Daniel: It was absolutely fantastic. I had the day off, took a few hundred bucks out of an ATM, drove down there, paid 50 bucks to park, got a ticket for 200 dollars, walked in there, sat down and lived the glory that I've been waiting to see for 50 years. It was unbelievable!

Jimmy was still pacing, staring at his feet as he walked. He was ignoring Angela, but he knew she was still there. And it felt good to know that.

Halloran: What's that commercial? Beating the Yankees in a Game 7 at Yankee Stadium: priceless.

Daniel: Oh yeah, and the priceless part was when Mientkiewicz came out spraying the champagne, and a drop of it landed in my mouth. That was priceless!

Halloran: I wonder how many stories like that one are out there today. Annie's next from Lennox.

Annie: Sweet dreams are made of this. It's not just seeing a baseball team win a game. It's bringing families together. I've got three kids. One of them is out in L.A. He called me. Another son was on Lansdowne Street. He called. And my daughter is in New Jersey. She called. All of us – living the dream – together.

Halloran: That's true. Generations have been waiting for this. It's probably one of the happiest times a family will have, apart from a new baby or a wedding.

Annie: I've been watching this team since 1956. And I know he took some heat during the season, even during the playoffs, but I would never, ever, never question anything Terry Francona ever does with this team.

Halloran: You promise?

Safreed: Until the first inning of the World Series.

Annie: I'm telling you. He just knows. Everybody says you should take out Mark Bellhorn. But Bellhorn hits a homer. Everybody says Damon should come out. And then look at the game he has.

Halloran: Look, you know how the game works around here. Francona will never get an ounce of credit, even though he should. Because somehow the Red Sox beat the Yankees without an RBI from Manny Ramirez, without a win from Pedro Martinez, and after falling behind three-games to none.

Annie: I just think he is one of the best managers the Red Sox have ever had.

Safreed: He is prepared. I'll give him that. I knock him for plenty of his decisions, but he always has a reason for anything he does.

Halloran: So, what was Pedro doing out there in that game last night?

Jimmy had lost his train of thought and started thinking about Tom's physical appearance and the battle that was ahead for him. Then he looked up and said: "Yeah, why DID they bring Pedro in last night?"

Safreed: I'm scratching my head over that one. I think he just wanted Pedro to be a part of a big moment at Yankee Stadium, the place where he blew the lead last year and he had to listen to all that 'Who's your daddy' stuff. I don't think he expected Pedro to come in and almost let the Yankees back in the game.

Halloran: But that's what happened. No one will care and history won't even remember it, but that was bizarre bringing him in to an 8-1 game in the seventh. Just crazy! Joey's in Lawrence. Can you explain that move?

Joey: Not a chance. I couldn't understand why he took Lowe out in the first place. The guy had only thrown 69 pitches and he only gave up one hit in six innings. But I'll agree with the previous caller. I don't know anyone who would give the edge to Terry Francona over Joe Torre before the series started, but now what would you say? I mean, you have to give the manager credit when the team wins the series, because you know he'd get the blame if they lost.

Halloran: I don't think we're ready to say Francona's a better manager than Joe Torre just yet. That guy's got four World Series rings and Francona has none. But Francona got the better of him this time. That's for sure.

Joey: I do have to say though that a lot of people want to compare this to the U.S. Hockey team beating Russia in the 1980 Olympics. But I don't think so. Those were a bunch of college players taking on elite professionals. This was pros playing against pros and the Red Sox were favored to win.

Safreed: It's not winning the series that's like the Miracle on Ice. It's the being down to their last three outs, and being down in the series three-games-to-none. At that moment, the Red Sox became a bunch of college kids against elite professionals. And that's why the Cardinals just became Finland. Remember? After beating Russia, the U.S. still had to beat Finland to win the gold medal. Right now, the Red Sox have only assured themselves a silver medal.

Halloran: But if the 1980 hockey team only won the silver, they'd still be feeling pretty good about themselves.

Joey: I don't think so. I think they'd be kicking themselves for a missed opportunity. And I'm sure history would remember them very differently.

Safreed: Al Michaels would be saying: 'Do you believe in letdown games?'

(Herb Brooks from Miracle): One game. If we played them ten times, they might win nine, but not this game. Not tonight. Screw'em. This is our time. Now go out there and take it!

Halloran: You think Francona had one of those speeches for the boys in the clubhouse before last night's game?

Safreed: No, but I'll bet most of the Red Sox have seen the movie and felt the inspiration at one time or another.

Halloran: Douglas is in Adams. What's up, Doug?

Douglas: Hi! We were at the Stadium last night. Greatest night ever! I've never seen 55-thousand people run out of Yankee Stadium like that in my life. They all had that long, depressed glazed-over face on that we've had for years. It was so nice to see it on them for a change.

Halloran: Right you are, Taylor. So, does this reverse the curse, you think?

"Why do they keep messing up the callers' names today?"
"I'm sure they're a little sleep deprived. Nobody's brain is working quite right today."
Jimmy looked up acknowledging Angela's response. She tapped her temple a few

imes, and then blew Jimmy a kiss and got up to leave. She had other children to
visit.

Douglas: You're talking to the wrong guy. I hate the curse! I don't believe in it. And even if you proved it to me, I still won't believe in it. If I spoke of little fairies and gnomes in the outfield tripping up outfielders, or making fair balls go foul, people would fit me for a straight jacket. But the curse? That you can take seriously?

Safreed: Besides, even if the curse were real, it's not over. The curse is supposed to be about not winning the World Series. Beating the Yankees is nice, but all that silly talk about curses will live on if the Red Sox don't beat the Cardinals.

Halloran: Well, maybe beating the Yankees is how the curse gets broken. And that will enable the Red Sox to win the World Series.

Safreed: Curse schmurse! We've just had a reversal of fortune. The breaks started going the Red Sox way. Finally! You had the A-Rod hand slap getting over-ruled by the umpires, and there was the Mark Bellhorn home run that was initially called a double, but that got overturned as well. Those are the kinds of things that usually go against the Red Sox, but they started getting some breaks this time.

Halloran: Could be the curse being lifted. And talk about a reversal of fortune, the Red Sox spent a fortune to get this done.

Safreed: Money well spent.

Halloran: Good point by you. Let's rapid fire some of these calls today, so as many people get a chance to speak as possible. Don's in Sutton. How you doing, Don?

Don: Doing great guys. The House that Ruth built is the house that Curt tore down! Great, great pitching. That's what it takes. Murderers Row was reduced to Skid Row.

Safreed: The guy writes bumper stickers for a living.

Don: This is monumental, and you can't underplay it at all. It's just a remarkable seven games that we just witnessed. I just can't believe we saw all those amazing games, even the first three. Without them it's not a perfect script. Even last night was perfect because it was over so quickly. It gave us an opportunity to enjoy what was happening, instead of sweating out another one.

Safreed: I will say that it was fun feeling so confident for a change. The minute Johnny Damon's grand slam cleared the fence, I knew it was over. I sat back and relaxed for the rest of the night.

Halloran: The edge of your seat thanks you. Sean's in Salisbury now. What do you have, Sean?

Sean: I've got a newfound respect for athletes in general, and this Red Sox team specifically. I couldn't believe it when the Red Sox players said after Game 3 that they still believed in themselves. I figured it was just lip service. But now I'm thinking they must have meant it. They followed through with their words, and that is the ultimate vindication for them. The players kept saying that people lost faith in them, but they believed in themselves. That's terrific.

"I don't understand why people have so much trouble believing in believing," Jimmy said out loud to an empty room. "Bunch of quitters, that's all."

Halloran: Even Joe Torre said after Game Three that it was important they go and win Game Four, because he didn't want to let the Red Sox get up off the mat.

Safreed: And they couldn't deliver the knockout punch.

Halloran: Joe's in Johnston, Rhode Island. Go, Joe!

Joe: The best part for me is just shutting up those people who think being a Yankee fan guarantees them a championship, or at least if nothing else a victory over the Red Sox. The Yankee fans who had to watch the horror of their team going down in flames in four straight, what are they feeling like today?

Safreed: They can't hurt enough to suit me. They can't feel enough pain. FOX couldn't show enough suffering Yankee fans last night to satisfy me. They should have just skipped pitches. Just show me more suffering Yankee fans.

Halloran: I listened this morning to one of our diehard Yankee fans who calls regularly, and he left a message. And he sounded almost suicidal. I have to admit; it made me feel real good. I hope nothing tragic happens, but as long as he only feels like dirt, then I'm all right with that. Let's go to Red from Auburn now.

Red: Here's what I've been thinking. I think the Red Sox are like Jason from Friday The 13th. They were beaten, shot, stabbed, run over and kicked in the nuts. Yet they still managed to rise up, stumble around, and kill their enemy. They terrorized their victims until they realized there's no way to kill the undead.

Safreed: Red scares me a little bit.

Halloran: I know who really scares you. It's Jimmy from Boston. Hey, Jimmy, you must be feeling better than you have in your whole life today.

Jimmy: I have to admit I haven't felt this good in a long time.

Safreed: Are you here to throw a little 'I told you so' our way? As I recall, you were one of the rare breed of true believers.

Jimmy: Oh, I had my doubts. Believe me, I did. If I didn't I wouldn't have nearly passed out a bunch of times during those last four games.

Halloran: No doubt that series took a toll on a lot of people. It's like during the winter when newscasts remind you to check on the elderly when it gets especially cold. I think we needed to check on the elderly during the series, just to make sure everyone was all right. Even kids like Jimmy here, they need their sleep and the Red Sox sure didn't help.

Safreed: Ah, I'll sleep when I'm dead.

Jimmy: Yeah. Anyway, I just wanted to tell you guys, that if this series teaches us anything, it's that none of us knows what we're talking about.

Halloran: What's he mean by that?

Jimmy: We all love to guess, and predict, and um, postulate I think is the right word...

Safreed: This kid really affects my self-esteem.

Jimmy: But other than being entertaining, all the talk doesn't mean a whole lot, because they still have to play the games. And the Red Sox weren't interested in talking about how close it was to being over. They just wanted to play the next game. They had the right attitude all along. They knew that being close to the end didn't mean they were at the end.

Halloran: So, they fought, and they kept fighting, and the end never really came, did it?

Safreed: It came for the Yankees.

Halloran: And they fought, too. So, it becomes another example of how life and sports operate. Sometimes you put up a valiant fight and win, and other times you fight as hard as you can, but you end up losing anyway.

Safreed: Sometimes life sucks. But not today. Definitely not today.

Jimmy: Nope. Life is good – today – because an awful lot of people have been trying to live long enough to see the Sox win it all, and now we all might get that chance. Talk to you guys later.

Safreed: We?

Halloran: Terrific kid. And he's right. It sure would be nice for the Red Sox to win the darn thing for the first time since 1918.

Safreed: Do it for all the old-timers. And anyone else who's been down on their luck and could use a little pick-me-up. If the Red Sox even thought for one minute how much joy it would bring to so many people, it would just add so much pressure. Imagine knowing you have the power to affect that many people.

Halloran: It's true. Let's see if anyone's left that kind of sentiment in our Mixed Messages.

Recorded Voice: You have eleven unheard messages. First message:

Message One: Hey I was at Yankee stadium yesterday and I went to the bathroom around the 7th inning, and I saw Yogi Berra, and he was saying, 'It's over. It's over.'

Message Two: I saw Yogi leaving in the 5th inning. He was in the elevator ripping the Yankee pitching to the attendant.

Halloran: Have you seen Yogi lately? He's about three feet tall.

Safreed: I guess it's never over until the midget goes to the men's room.

Halloran: Did you notice we had two conflicting stories there? One said he left in the fifth inning, and the other said he was in the bathroom in the seventh.

Safreed: What does a bathroom attendant do anyway? Like I can't get my own towel and grab a mint on the way out.

Halloran: I think they're there just to keep you company.

Safreed: I'm at my best when I go solo.

Message Three: Lord, thank you for crapping in the Yankees corn flakes, but do you think you could stick around for another week or so?

Halloran: Interesting prayer.

Message Four: I couldn't believe it when I saw A-Rod trying to slap the American League trophy out of John Henry's hand.

Halloran: That was really uncalled for.

Message Five: Hey, that was a great picture in the Herald today of the fans carrying Jim Lonborg off the field in 1967. What would the fans do to him nowadays, flip him over and set him on fire?

Safreed: My God, when did all that start? I mean, how long have fans been so happy they had to celebrate by flipping over cars?

Halloran: Probably for as long as they've had cars and beer.

Message Six: (voice of Pedro Martinez) The Bambino was a good man. He was good in the community and to his family. And I don't believe he was a bad man. So, he should not be doing any curses. Right now, he should be drunk around here.

Halloran: Nice of Pedro to call, kind of work us into his busy schedule.

Safreed: Well, he better answer the call when it's his turn to pitch in the World Series.

Halloran: Nicely done there, Fred.

Message Seven: All my life I've hated the Yankees with the white-hot intensity of a thousand suns. I always thought nothing would give me more pleasure than the day the Red Sox really stuck it to them. And it turns out I was right.

Message Eight: I hear a lot of bozos talking about if the Red Sox go on to win the World Series, their fans will end up having some kind of identity crisis, like they won't know how to react to everything being different. Well, if this is the beginning of an identity crisis, slap a dress on me and sign me up for therapy, because I love it!

Safreed: Yeah, I hate that identity crisis garbage! How are fans going to react if the Red Sox win the World Series? They're going to act like champions. And it's gonna feel real good, too.

Message Nine: I know it's possible that we take sports too seriously sometimes. But is it O.K. if I paint a mural of David Ortiz on my bedroom ceiling so that Big Papi is always looking down on me in my times of need.

Halloran: It's O.K. with me.

Safreed: I think we could have another candidate for therapy right there.

Message Ten: Hey, stick a fork in those Yankees. And then pull the fork out, and stick it back in again. And then just keep sticking and stabbing, and sticking and stabbing until you rip the heart right out of them. They're done!

Halloran: Even more therapy. And he goes to the front of the line.

Message Eleven: I was on a plane last night, and as we flew over New York City, the pilot came on and said: 'Ladies and gentlemen of Red Sox Nation, we're flying over New York City. If you look down to your left very closely, you can see Derek Jeter helping Alex Rodriguez load his golf bag into the car.'

Halloran: And that's going to do it for this American League Championship edition of "Sports Overtime". Tomorrow? Meet me in St. Louis! The Red Sox are going to the World Series!

(*Sweet Caroline* begins playing as Red Sox radio announcer Joe Castiglione makes the call): 1-0 pitch. Swing and a ground ball to second base. Pokey Reese has it. He throws to first, and the Red Sox have won the American League pennant! They mob Alan Embree on the mound. The Boston Red Sox have pulled the greatest victory in team history.

(voice of Sox president, Larry Lucchino): All empires fall sooner or later. This is a great moment for Red Sox nation.

Announcer: Can I get an Amen!

CHAPTER TWELVE
Miracles Do Happen

"It's just so wonderful having you home again," Eileen repeated for what Jimmy thought was the millionth time. Jimmy knew that being home meant that his mom could worry about him a little less, and check in on him a little more. What he didn't know, or didn't consider, was that having her son home meant a return to normalcy for Eileen and for Glenn.

Nearly every day for the past nine months, Eileen made the thirty-minute trip into the city, and the hour trip home. It seemed no matter when she left the clinic, there was always more traffic than she had encountered on her way in. By the time she returned home, it was time to start dinner, get the laundry done, run to the supermarket, sort the mail, and take care of an endless list of life's small details. And in truth, she never had enough time to keep things straight at home, and she rarely spent any time with her husband.

It was important that one of them be with Jimmy at all times which meant they were almost never alone with each other. Glenn usually visited at night, after he got off work from the bank. A few minutes were all he shared with Eileen before she raced off. The visits were often frustrating for him, because he would arrive around 6:00, and Jimmy would invariably be sleeping. Jimmy liked to nap in the middle of the afternoon, so he could watch the Red Sox games at night. Glenn watched along with him, but invariably fell asleep, and stayed that way until Eileen returned to send him back off to work.

Now, while there was still a significant amount of time devoted to keeping a watchful eye over Jimmy, Glenn could come straight home from work. Eileen could get chores and errands done during the time she used to spend at the clinic. And when Jimmy was up to it, they could all sit down and enjoy a dinner together. It made Eileen feel like they were a normal family, instead of a cancer family.

Evidence that they were, indeed, still a cancer family was Jimmy's central line. The tubes sticking out of Jimmy's chest remained, so that medicine, blood and platelets could be inserted during his weekly clinic visits. While at home, Jimmy was in charge of cleaning the catheter on an almost daily basis. He swabbed the skin with alcohol and povidone-iodine before applying a sterile dressing. He used heparin to flush the catheter, and he left it to the nurses at the hospital to clamp the catheter and change the injection cap.

In fact, Jimmy was able to take such good care of himself, there were sometimes hours at a time in which Eileen didn't think about her son's illness. She relaxed, even going so far as to let her guard down, which is something she had refused to do for such a long time. Rather, she was determined to always be ready for the next turn, whether it was for the worse or the better. She had been less guarded when Jimmy was in remission, and his relapse had been like a hard kick to the stomach. It seemed so much worse than the initial diagnosis.

When she first heard Jimmy had leukemia, she was stunned, but she quickly turned optimistic. After all, so many wonderful advances had been made in treating all types of cancers, especially leukemia. Jimmy would be well taken care of. That confidence was validated when the disease went into remission. It's return, however, indicated something far more insidious. Now, since the bone marrow transplant, the roller coaster ride of emotions had been sickening and exhausting. Just 39-years-old, Eileen was haggard and graying.

Now, the family was better rested. It was less of an effort to smile. There was a bounce in Glenn's step as he raced through the door each evening. Eileen had begun napping when Jimmy napped, so they could watch the World Series games together.

"Why do they have to put these games on so late?" she lamented.

"It's not supposed to be easy to be a Red Sox fan, Mom."

"No, but it's getting easier," Glenn said.

Mark joined them each night during the World Series, and the four of them squeezed together on the couch as the Red Sox reeled off four straight wins against the St. Louis Cardinals. By the time Keith Foulke had the ball in his glove, Jimmy was two feet off the ground, hands raised high in triumph. And as Foulke flipped the ball over to first base for the final out, Mark gave his little brother a big high five. Glenn leaped up a moment later and gave his boys a hug, and Eileen started to cry. She intermittently looked at the celebration on the field and the celebration in front of her. Jimmy had shot down to his knees like a Wimbledon champion, and repeatedly pumped his fists while yelling out: "Yes! Yes! They did it! I can't believe it! This is the best day of my life!"

Eileen saw the beaming smile on Jimmy's face and the tears in his eyes, and she couldn't help but cry. Glenn had his arm draped around Mark and the two men stared at the television, soaking in every moment as the Red Sox players pig-piled on the field and sprayed each other with beer and champagne in the locker room. They watched the presentation of the World Series trophy, and they told each other, "We have to remember this. We have to remember every moment of it, every detail."

The Macombers were doing exactly what families across Red Sox Nation were doing. They were laughing, jumping, dancing, singing, and crying. When things began to settle down, Glenn looked at his wife who was still in tears. He bent down and kissed her on the lips. Then he pulled back, holding her face in both his hands, and said: "You see, honey, miracles do happen."

"Sports Overtime", Show Open, October 28, 2004

Joe Castiglione, (call of the final out of the World Series): Swing and a ground ball. Stabbed by Foulke. He has it. He underhands to first. And the Boston Red Sox are the World Champions! For the first time in 86 years, the Red Sox have won baseball's world championship! Can you believe it?

Announcer: Never doubted it for a second.

(John Hiatt sings *Have A Little Faith In Me*)

Announcer: All it took was 31,458 days of waiting, a bunch of idiots, a lunar eclipse, and a bloody sock, and the Red Sox are Champions of the World!

Police Chief Hubbard from *Beverly Hills Cop:* What's this man doing here?
Axel Foley: Bleeding, sir.

Announcer: Curt Schilling bled again for his team. Señor October came up huge. Manny was just being Manny when he won the World Series MVP Award. And the Red Sox made 86 years of blood, sweat and tears look easy. I'd say it's time to party like a rock star.

Westley from *The Princess Bride:* I do not envy you the headache you will have when you awake. But for now, rest well and dream of large women.

Announcer: The Red Sox swept the St. Louis Cardinals as Derek Lowe becomes the first pitcher to ever win all three series clinching games in one post-season. How's that guy who was kicked out of the starting rotation look to you now, huh?

Frank from *Old School:* He looks GLORIOUS!

Announcer: The Boston Glee Party gets going right here on "Sports Overtime" with Bob Halloran and Fred "Freddie the Fredderman" Safreed. They've got a smile above every chin. Today, they'll be taking your calls so you can bask in the glow of the 2004 World Series Champion Boston Red Sox. Hey, that's got a nice ring to it, like a World Series ring.

Jack Dawson from *Titanic:* I'm king of the world!

Joe Castiglione: The Boston Red Sox have forever put that 1918 chant to rest as this band of characters who showed great character all season have come through and won their first World Series since 1918. Maybe after all the pain of '78 and '86 and '03, this one's even sweeter.

Announcer: If it were any sweeter, you could pour it on your pancakes. And we're going to lay it on thick with the sappy stuff today. The Red Sox have just won the World Series. It's O.K. to cry.

Sox G.M. Theo Epstein: That's beer coming from my head. I do not cry. I'm a true modern American male.

Announcer: We know what most of you are thinking. 'Holy crap! We won! Now what do we do?'

Bob Wiley from *What about Bob:* Roses are red. Violets are blue. I'm a schizophrenic and so am I.

Announcer: Well, undertakers better get ready to begin undertaking. A lot of people just wanted to hang on long enough to see the Red Sox win the World Series. Now, what are they living for?

Lloyd from *Dumb and Dumber:* Hey, I guess they're right. Senior citizens, although slow and dangerous behind the wheel, can still serve a purpose. Now, don't you go dying on me!

Announcer: For every Red Sox fan who kept hope alive, and for everyone who wondered 'Why not us', this is your moment, you're once in a lifetime moment. Share it with Bob and Fred, right now on WTED's "The Red Sox Are World Series Champions Sports Overtime Spectacular"!

Willy Wonka from *Willy Wonka:* And Charlie, don't forget what happened to the man who suddenly got everything he'd ever wished for.
Charlie Bucket: What happened?
Willy Wonka: He lived happily ever after.

Halloran: I gotta tell you, all the positivity in this town sucks, and it stinks, and it sucks.

Safreed: The fellowship is no longer miserable. Every time the Red Sox get a ring, an angel gets its wings.

Halloran: Sox fans are going to enjoy this for the rest of their lives, but you know, it's like an amusement park ride. It was so scary and thrilling and wonderful that as soon as you get off, you want to get right back on again. You know?

Safreed: Uh-huh.

Halloran: Are you all right today, Fred?

Safreed: I feel great.

Halloran: Just have the EMT's on alert today. I'm a little bit concerned about my big friend.

Safreed: I'll be fine. I'm getting my second wind, Mr. Fakes Concern For My Well-being.

Glenn walked into the kitchen to find Eileen enjoying her morning coffee and listening to the radio. He thought he heard her say something before he entered the room, and assumed she was talking to Jimmy, but it turned out she was alone.
"Did you say something, honey?"
"Oh, hi. Good morning. No, I mean, yes, I probably said something to the radio. I don't know. I think I was lost in thought."

Halloran: I'm sure all of Red Sox Nation is a little tired today. Hard to get to sleep after a night like that. That was just a wild scene at the ballpark last night, wasn't it? I think the only thing that could have made it better is if the Red Sox won it at home.

"What are you thinking about?" Glenn asked as he sat down with his own cup of coffee.
"Just how lucky we all are and how things have turned out. Jimmy's home. He's never been happier. And good things are starting to happen again."
"I know. It's about time."
Glenn wanted to caution his wife about assuming too much good fortune, and to re-mind her that Jimmy's situation remained unpredictable, but he chose not to impair the moment.

Safreed: It was a bit surreal celebrating at Busch Stadium, but it's probably for the best. I heard there were a lot of people dancing in the streets of Boston last night. But I'm guessing some of those so-called dancers were really having convulsions from being pepper sprayed.

Halloran: Nothing like that around here. In fact, you really have to hand it to the fans of St. Louis. They were applauding the Red Sox last night, joining right in with the Sox fans who made their way down toward the dugouts.

Safreed: Very classy. They're not very bright, but they're very nice people here in St. Louis.

Halloran: I heard a great story about a guy who owns a bar in Cambridge and drove with three people overnight, got there in the sixth inning, went to the box office and gave them his tale of woe, and the guy says 'Let's see your drivers' licenses', just to make sure they weren't slinging bull. And it all checked out, and the guy says 'Come with me', and he let them in, and they sat there and watched the last three innings.

Safreed: And I heard a lot of the Cardinal fans saying that if they couldn't win it, they were glad it was the Red Sox.

Halloran: The world is united by its love of the underdog.

Safreed: And its hatred of the Yankees.

Halloran: And speaking of the Yankees, didn't you think this whole thing was just a bit anti-climactic? I mean, it was great and everything. But almost because of what they did in the Yankee series, last night and this whole series just didn't have the same kind of appeal.

Safreed: To me it did, because of the finality of it. They needed to take this step. They needed to win the World Series. Beating the Yankees was such a relief, and there may have been more pure joy then. But last night, I don't mind telling you, I got a little misty-eyed.

Halloran: It's probably not worth trying to rank your emotions, but on a scale of one to ten, the Yankee series was an eleven, and the Cardinals was a 10.9.

Safreed: The whole experience was a fourteen! It's off the charts good. And I'm not coming down from this high for a long time.

Halloran: And I'm sure you're not alone in feeling that way. We'll get to the phone calls on this wild, amazing, super "Sports Overtime". And we'll start with Lance in Boylston.

Lance: Hi guys! Great day! I was just wondering, now that the World Series is over, has anyone seen my wife and kids?

Halloran: Been a little negligent, have you?

Lance: Yeah, I'm just kidding. But I do wish I could share this with them. My wife isn't really into baseball. I mean she watched most of it with me because she

186

understood the magnitude of the event, like landing on the moon. But she'll never be able to grasp the depth of what this truly means to nut jobs like me. And my kids are just too young.

Halloran: You know, strangely, a part of the New England experience has been robbed from an entire generation. For years, every kid growing up learned about, and came to understand what it meant to be a Red Sox fan. They lived the futility and frustration, and they shared that with their parents, and their grandparents. Now, all those kids, the ones under the age of say, twelve, are going to grow up feeling very differently about the Red Sox.

"Kids around the age of fifteen feel pretty differently about them today, too," Jimmy said as he traipsed sleepy-eyed into the kitchen. Eileen stood up and gave him a hug. She then reached into the refrigerator and pulled out his breakfast she had prepared an hour earlier. Jimmy went straight to the phone, dialed the radio station, and proceeded to eat his breakfast while on hold.

Lance: I know. And if the Red Sox win another one in their lifetimes, it won't mean nearly as much to them as this one did to us.

Safreed: If I might interject something here… who cares? You guys are like women. All you want to do is express how you're feeling. Why don't you just feel it for a while instead?

Halloran: Fred's not fully developed yet, Lance. Still not in touch with his feminine side. Thanks for the call. Here's Deion from Warwick, Rhode Island.

Deion: That guy's wife just doesn't get it. My wife and I high-fived after every one of the Cardinals' outs. We missed a few when she was out of the room making dip, but we'd catch up as soon as she got back. We were in this thing together. And finally, when Doug Mientkiewicz caught that ball for the final out, I turned to her and said, 'I've been waiting for this moment all my life.' We hugged for a long time. And then she left to go watch Lifetime television, and I muted Tim McCarver for the last time this year.

(Homer Simpson: I like stories!)

Halloran: I'm sure that moment was played out in living rooms all across New England. Bee from Dalton, can you top that?

Bee: Well, I am a wife, and I'm a mother. And I can tell you getting married and giving birth to my children were the biggest thrills in my life. But this one might top them all, because I wasn't nearly as medicated.

Halloran: Medicated for the wedding, too, were you?

Bee: In a manner of speaking. If you met my ex-husband, you'd know why. I used to tell him that anybody who watched 500 hours of baseball every year was an idiot. And he'd say, 'Well then, I guess you married a dumb ass'. And he was right. So, I threw him out, and started watching 500 hours of baseball. Maybe that makes me a dumb ass, too. But at least I got rid of one.

Safreed: Another fine testimonial of how the Red Sox World Series is bringing families together.

Halloran: Hey, have you seen this press release issued by Steinbrenner? He says: 'Congratulations to the Boston Red Sox, to their ownership and to the people of Boston.'

Safreed: That's a nice start.

Halloran: 'The Red Sox deserve all the credit for what they have accomplished. But make no mistake about it. We are hard at work and will be back with a strong team for our loyal New York Yankee fans.'

Safreed: You know what? Shut up. Recognize the moment, and just leave it at 'Congratulations'. Now is not the time to turn the spotlight around to see what the Yankees are doing. The Yankees aren't doing anything right now, except licking their wounds.

Halloran: I had a guy ask me last night if the reality is as good as the dream, and I was like, I can't really tell the difference. This feels like a dream. Except that my dreams are usually in black and white and I'm a lot taller.

Safreed: Then let me clue you in. This is reality, and you're still short.

"How are you feeling today, Jimmy?" Glenn asked as a matter of routine. "Great," Jimmy replied, which was almost true.

Halloran: Hal from Sutton, you're up!

Hal: What an honor and a privilege it is to talk to you on the third best day of my life.

Halloran: Got two kids?

Hal: No, but I made it out of the Gulf War with all my limbs still attached, and I married a beautiful woman just over a year ago. But from a sports perspective, this can never be topped. I was trying to think of a scenario that could possibly be sweeter.

Halloran: Well, they could go the next 87 years without winning another one.

Hal: Yeah, but would it be as perfect as this? A guy like Schilling having two surgical procedures within a week of each other and going out there bleeding and grimacing and gutting it out. The Yankees trotted Bucky "bleeping" Dent out there for Game Seven, and we danced on their field. I think you could play the Yankees again next year and sweep them in four straight by crazy, lopsided scores, and it wouldn't be as good. As the commercial says, 'It doesn't get any better than this'.

Safreed: How did you celebrate last night?

Hal: I had to get out of the house. I wanted to come full circle. I remember walking out into the streets after the Red Sox lost Game Six of the 1986 World Series. There were a lot of us out there, just walking around like zombies, and one guy walked by and said to me, 'This is the worst day in this town since JFK was shot'. I was really hoping to see that guy again. I hope he lived to see it.

Halloran: Thanks, Hal. And thanks for your service to the country. Chris from Palmer, what's on your mind?

Chris: Well, I've heard a lot of people talking today like that last guy, about how much they wished some long-time Red Sox fans had lived to see this day. And I do, too. But I really wish there were some long-time Yankee fans who didn't die too soon, because I'd love to shove this in their face. Instead, all I can do is laugh in the general direction of hell, and say 'I wish you were alive today, you Yankee fans, because this would absolutely kill you'!

Halloran: Well, Red Sox fans are passionate, but nobody ever said they were compassionate. Tom from Becket, Mass. Welcome to "Sports Overtime"!

Tom: I just thought the Red Sox were amazing. Nobody rips Pedro Martinez more than me, and D-Lowe was my new whipping boy late in the season. But those two guys, I mean, both of them throwing seven shutout innings in Games Three and Four, they were huge!

Safreed: And Schilling only gave up one run in six innings. That supposedly great Cardinal offense only scored a total of three runs in the last three games.

Tom: Schilling gets most of the credit, and it's well deserved. But it was Bellhorn who hit the game wining home run in Game One. Manny was the MVP, and Foulke pitched in eleven of the fourteen playoff games and only gave up one run.

Safreed: I don't even know if this is a lot or not, but it shocked me to see that he threw 257 pitches in the post-season. That seems like an awful lot to me for a relief pitcher. And it could very easily have been more if the Red Sox hadn't swept the Cards in four straight.

Halloran: It was the starting pitching and Foulke at the end that got it done. You can say all you want about the affect of the Nomar trade, but the two moves that put the Red Sox over the hump were the acquisitions of Schilling and Foulke. Without them, they don't win this thing.

Safreed: And with Nomar, they don't either.

Halloran: I don't know if I'm buying that. Beyond the chemistry and the cancer bologna, the trade was supposed to work because it would improve the Sox defense. Well, they committed EIGHT errors in the first two games and won them both anyway. They won them because in Game One they scored eleven runs, and in Game Two, they had Schilling and Foulke starting and closing.

Safreed: I think it was all the moves. It was everything Theo did, and it was everything Francona did throughout the playoffs. All the planets had to align properly for this to happen. We even had that lunar eclipse as the Red Sox were winning it all.

Halloran: A Red Moon, also known as a Blood Moon. Don't think the irony is lost on me. And you're right about Francona. Think about this, he just out-managed Mike Sciosca, Joe Torre, and Tony LaRussa, and all three of those guys have won at least one World Series.

Safreed: I didn't see it coming, I can tell you that. And you know we'd be calling this guy a bum, and a failure if Dave Roberts doesn't steal that base. But everything worked out, so Francona comes out smelling like a rose.

Halloran: This is the same guy we watched rocking back and forth in the dugout like some sort of *Rainman* during the regular season. Then he starts going to the bullpen at the right time, saying all the right things, keeping his team loose. And he stuck with his guys even when they were going bad. And in the end, he was vindicated.

Safreed: That may be the first time we've ever praised him.

Halloran: And it may be the last time, too. Earl from Monroe, you're on "The Ted" with Bob and Fred.

Jimmy tried not to sniffle, but the mucous was dripping from his left nostril. Occasionally during breakfast, he would attempt to reverse the post-nasal drip by tipping his head way back while he drank his milk. He was torn between telling his parents what had happened upstairs and knowing that if he did, they'd be headed back to the hospital. He knew what the right thing to do was. He knew what the smart thing to do was. But for a little while longer, he tipped his head back.

Earl: I'm just amazed at how easy it all was. An eight game winning streak in the playoffs! Are you kidding me? The Yankees choked, and the Cardinals barely showed up. Are the Red Sox really that much better than St. Louis?

Safreed: Yes, I think they are. Don't you get the feeling that if they played them again tonight, they'd win again, and again, and again.

Halloran: Look at it this way, Manny Ramirez was the MVP, and he hit .412 in the series, which was 412 points higher than Scott Rolen.

Earl: That's just it. The Cardinals were putrid. Their hitters pooped at the plate. I was looking at some of the stats from the series. The Cardinals only hit .190, and their ERA was 6.09. How did they manage to win 105 games during the regular season?

Halloran: You just can't explain how cold their stars went. Scott Rolen drove in 124 runs during the regular season, and he was 0-for-15. Jim Edmunds had 42 home runs, and the only hit he got was that little bunt in the first game against an overshift in the infield. Albert Pujols had 6 homers and 14 RBI in the first two playoff series, but against the Red Sox, zero homers, zero RBI. Was the Red Sox pitching that good? I don't know. But those guys are lucky to be playing in St. Louis, because if they played like that in Boston, they'd be run out of town on the Grady Express.

Earl: I'm actually a little disappointed in the Cardinals. I thought they might actually score a few runs or something, maybe create a little suspense. But the team from the Show Me state showed me nothing.

Safreed: They turned into the St. Louis Devil Rays. Not a worthy opponent at all. Did you know the Cardinals threw 679 pitches in the series, and the Red Sox only swung and missed 37 times?

Halloran: Wow! That's some real digging there, Fred.

Safreed: I read it somewhere. Hope it's accurate.

Halloran: Well, it sounds good. And it helps explain how the Red Sox managed to hold the lead in 34 of the 36 innings. They never trailed. Just total domination by the World Champions!

Safreed: Keep saying it.

Halloran: World Champions. Now here's Abe in Lincoln.

Abe: The world will long remember what the Red Sox did here. And I'm so glad they won the World Series, because without it, there'd be no way to really stick it to the Yankees.

Halloran: That's right, because if we called them chokers, they'd just chant '1918'. Now, they've got nothing.

Safreed: Except 26 rings.

Halloran: Almost nothing.

Abe: Well, now we'll always be able to take that stamp out that says 'biggest chokers in baseball history' and press it to the foreheads of A-Rod and Sheffield and Matsui. They were feeling pretty good about themselves after going three games up, and now they're the laughingstock of baseball. And if that doesn't make you smile, then you're just not evil or vindictive enough.

Halloran: Oh, we are plenty vindictive here today. Don't worry about that. Rick's in Carlisle. How's it going, Rick?

Rick: Great! This is the day I told my Dad that he's forgiven. He's the one who made me a Red Sox fan. It's his fault I suffered so long. When you're a kid, you don't know any better. You're just born, and they tell you you're Jewish or Catholic, or Irish or Italian, or a Red Sox fan or someone who's going to be happy and well adjusted. It's like being brainwashed. But Dad, again I say, you're forgiven. And thank you for leading me to this day.

Halloran: Do you have a favorite moment you're going to hold on to, Rick?

Rick: I think I'll remember every moment of both Game Seven against the Yankees, and Game Four against the Cardinals. They were both so easy. They were like getting to the top of the mountain. Even though you're not quite there yet, you can see it and you know you're going to get there. It gives you time to take a breath and look back upon where you've been. I sat there thinking about all the years, and all the near misses, and I relaxed while the Red Sox forged ahead and got to the top of that mountain.

Eileen was the first to notice the trickle coming from Jimmy's nose. But it wasn't mucous. It was much redder than that. Jimmy's nose was bleeding!

Halloran: Why not them? That's the question they asked, 'Why not us?' And nobody could answer the question other than to say, 'Because you're the Red Sox, and the Red Sox never win'.

Safreed: But this group wouldn't accept that answer. If you think about it, they were the perfect group to get this done. You needed guys like Millar, who keeps things loose, and Damon with the hair, or Manny who didn't let being placed on waivers and nearly traded affect him. You needed a guy like Bellhorn who barely has a pulse, and Varitek who's such a strong leader. You needed all these different types of personalities to mesh perfectly, to believe in one another, and it helped that they're really talented.

Halloran: Yeah, they had that going for them, which is nice. But while they really had a wide range of personalities ranging from the free-spirited guys to the born again Christian types, the one thing all those personalities had in common is that they wouldn't let the pressures of playing in Boston get to them. If you're answering to God, you're not going to worry about what the media is saying. And if you just don't care, like Manny, then you can go out and be a World Series MVP. Manny said as much when he said: 'We're just a bunch of idiots who go out there and have fun. We don't think. We eliminate thinking." You see that? Eliminate thinking That's the secret. When you put on a Red Sox uniform you feel the heaviness of what that represents. And how do you get rid of that? You do it without thinking about the curse, about the pressure, about the fans, about the boos.

Safreed: And they're really talented.

Eileen looked at Glenn to get his attention, and then looked at Jimmy. Glenn immediately recognized what was wrong. Eileen pushed her chair back from the table and dampened a cloth at the kitchen sink. Glenn coughed and when Jimmy looked up, Glenn tapped his nose and nodded at Jimmy. Jimmy realized the blood was coming out, and soon, so would the truth.

Halloran: Understood, Fred. Now, let's go to Ty from Warren.

Ty: Am I on?

Halloran: On, and off to a great start.

Ty: Oh, sorry. Anyway, first time caller, long time listener.

Safreed: Not getting any better, Ty.

Ty: O.K. I mean, I've just been so excited, and exhausted. But did you guys happen to notice how people were reacting last night to the lunar eclipse and the Red Sox game. I was outside looking at the moon with my daughter and you could hear people screaming. I mean it was red. It was amazing to see. And people were yelling, 'Hey, look at the moon.' And other people were inside their homes yelling, 'David Ortiz just hit a double!' And one group would say, 'Shut up! Don't you know something like this won't happen again for like 50 years?' And the other group would say, 'Yeah, I know. That's why I'm watching it.'

Halloran: A bizarre convergence of two extremely rare occurrences. Could be a sign of the apocalypse. Or as we said already, the stars were aligned for the Red Sox to make history. Hugh from Douglas, what do you have for us today?

Hugh: Nothing but love, Bob. I feel like the Grinch. First my heart was two sizes too small due to the beatings it's taken over the years. And now it's grown to its rightful size, and it's filled with the warm fuzzies. Now, I walk around and spontaneously start to cry. I feel like a woman!

Halloran: You're evolving, Hugh. Don't fight it.

Safreed: Yeah, but quit crying, you little girl!

Hugh: I'm trying, but this is just more than I can handle emotionally. Can you guys play that thing that Curt Schilling said about A-Rod?

Halloran: About not getting him during last off-season being a good thing?

Hugh: Not just a good thing – the best thing.

Halloran: Yeah, he said it last night. Go ahead and play that.

(Schilling on tape): The biggest move, when all was said and done, was the non-move. I think if we get A-Rod, we don't get here. I don't question that for a second. He's a Hall of Famer, sure. But after getting to know people who, A, play with him and, B, have played with him, I don't think it would have worked here. I think this clubhouse would have been a much different place, and I don't think it would have been better, given the personalities involved.

Safreed: Powerful stuff. Damning stuff, actually. That's coming from a guy who, A, doesn't mind stirring up the rivalry a little bit, and B, knows he'll never be A-Rod's teammate.

Halloran: And Schilling can pretty much say anything he wants to from now on. He's walking in that pantheon with A, Larry Bird, B, Ted Williams and C, Bobby Orr. That guy gets his own wing in the Boston Sports Hall of Fame. Andre's in Ware, Massachusetts.

Safreed: Where's Ware?

Andre: Between Worcester and Springfield.

Safreed: I didn't really care, but thanks.

While Eileen pinched Jimmy's nose with the wet cloth and held his head back, Jimmy explained that he had blown his nose upstairs.
"I guess I blew too hard and my nose started to bleed," he explained. "And then I couldn't get it to stop."

Andre: Well, I'm calling to talk about the loved ones who didn't get to see this, like my dad. He died just about two years ago to the day, and I remember thinking last year that I was glad he didn't have to live through that disappointment. Today, I'm feeling just a twinge of sadness that he isn't here to enjoy this with me. He would have loved this.

Halloran: I'll bet the news got to heaven pretty quickly.

Andre: If it didn't, he knows now. I went out to his grave this morning and toasted the Red Sox. Instead of flowers, I stuck a little Red Sox pennant in the ground. Like I said, it was a bittersweet moment for me.

Halloran: I can honestly say, going to the cemetery was not on my "to do" list today, but I know it's an important part of the process for a lot of people. Simon from Bridgewater, it's your turn to speak.

Simon: I don't want to be insensitive here, but as I listened to the last caller, all I could think of was I must be the most selfish person on earth. I know some Red Sox fans who passed on without ever seeing this moment, and maybe I'll feel for them tomorrow, but right now, this moment is all about me. I felt all the pain all those years. I was the one who committed so much of my time and energy into a team that consistently let me down. This is my moment! And I'm feeling too good to feel bad for anyone else, especially a dead person.

Safreed: You're right. You may be the most selfish person on earth.

Halloran: Eddie's in Belmont. Eddie?

Eddie: I've decided my wife's a jerk.

Halloran: Nice opening.

Eddie: Well, listen to this. When we got married, she didn't even really like baseball. Then, she decides to become this dyed in the wool Yankees fan. She watches them win four World Series titles, needling me all the while. So, then after last year's debacle nearly put me in a straight jacket, she finally understood what it meant to me to see the Red Sox win it. So, boom! Just like that she changes her allegiance and becomes a Red Sox fan.

Safreed: She's not allowed to do that.

Eddie: She did it. And she's watching every pitch, really pulling for them, you know. And now she thinks she's earned the right to enjoy this as much as me.

Safreed: No way! She hasn't earned it. She's not even close to truly appreciating what this means.

Eddie: I can't even bring myself to share this with her. I don't want to see her celebrating. Maybe I'm petty, but I was jealous of her when she was a Yankee fan, and now I'm jealous of her as a Red Sox fan.

Halloran: It'd be easier if she'd just cheat on you, though it might be fun to see you explaining this story to a judge in divorce court. 'We have irreconcilable differences, because that woman over there didn't have the decency to let me rub a Red Sox win over the Yankees in her face.'

Eddie: She owed me that.

Safreed: Split the assets and move on.

Halloran: We're moving on to talk with Mike in Lowell. He's been waiting a long, long time.

Mike: I am absolutely speechless!

Halloran: Well, thanks for the call, but this is talk radio. No room for speechless. Larry in Lawrence, you're next. What's on your mind today?

Glenn called the hospital from his cell phone and explained what was happening. Everyone agreed it would be best for Jimmy to come in today, rather than to wait for his next appointment on Tuesday. Once the bleeding had stopped again, Eileen sent Jimmy upstairs to pack an overnight bag. Chances were pretty good that he wouldn't be sleeping in his own bed tonight.

Larry: I just feel so vindicated. After all these years of having to explain why I'm a Red Sox fan to people who look down on us, and pity us, I hope they finally understand. There is honor in being a Sox fan. We certainly don't choose this life because it's easy. But there has always been the promise that this day would come eventually. And now what those on the outside looking in can finally see is that we are now feeling the kind of joy that only comes after years of despair. What I know is that my love for this team has always been unconditional. I've laughed and I've cried, and today I'm doing both. This team has always been more about the ride than the destination, and the ride, after all, is what life is all about.

(pause)

Safreed: What do you have there, Mr. Ignores The Phone Callers?

Halloran: I'm just looking at a couple of quotes here from Lucchino and a few others. Sorry about that, Larry was it? Thanks for the call.

Safreed: I really wasn't listening either.

Halloran: No matter. I like this one from Schilling who, right in the middle of the pandemonium says: 'I'm happiest for guys like Bill Buckner, Calvin Schiraldi, Rich Gedman, Bob Stanley, Johnny Pesky, Ted Williams, all of the Red Sox who played before us, who will now be remembered for the great players they were instead of all the other crap.'

Safreed: I hope he's right about that.

Eileen was happiest for Jimmy. But right now she was silently berating herself for letting herself get too happy. "When will this cloud over us finally disappear?" she thought.

Halloran: And here's John Henry talking about the fans, 'They waited their entire lives and they never gave up. They never gave up even after that terrible, horrible loss last year in New York. I feel like all the Red Sox fans. That's what they're saying now. We are world champions.' You think they never gave up? I'm not so sure about that.

Safreed: I think most of them give up at least a few times a year, but just think back to how the crowd was going wild when Roberts stole second against the Yankees. What were those people thinking, if not that the Sox still had a chance? Those are the people that Henry's talking about. They're the ones who bring honor to being a Red Sox fan.

Halloran: Being a Red Sox fan is honorable, hmm. I never heard it put that way. Not bad, Fred. I always thought being a Red Sox fan was more of a psychosis than anything else.

Safreed: It's that, too.

Halloran: Andrew's in Spencer, what say you, Andy?

Andrew: I had a Yankee fan try to tell me the Red Sox were lucky this year.

Safreed: Lucky the Yankees choked.

Andrew: Nah, he was getting into all the things that happened long before the playoffs, telling me there were forces at play when the Sox put Manny on waivers and nobody claimed him. He says, if the A-Rod deal happens, then we end up with Magglio Ordonez in left and A-Rod at short, and Nomar's off to Chicago. Not getting Jose Contreras the year before, things like that he says all mean the Red Sox were just dumb lucky.

Safreed: That is such total bull!

Halloran: Now wait a minute, Fred. There was a degree of luck in all of that. The problem is that when people start talking about random luck and destiny, some fans will think you're demeaning the team. But we should embrace luck. It's part of life. Why fight it?

Safreed: I just don't like to use the word luck. It wasn't bad luck that caused the Sox to lose all those other years. So, why does it have to be good luck that they won this year? I mean, just as long as we don't sum it up with, 'The Red Sox won, because they were lucky'. The Red Sox are not lucky. Who the heck would ever accuse them of that? It took a lot of talent and smarts from the front office to get this done.

Halloran: Talent, smarts, and good luck. When you succeed because so many of your plans failed, you have to admit, that's a little bit lucky – combined with the intelligence to have solid back-up plans.

Andrew: Well, it wasn't luck. It was pitching. Period. We had two horses at the front of the rotation, and we had the bullpen.

Safreed: That's exactly right. And that's what separates this Red Sox team from all the others. Finally, they got it figured out. No matter what moves did or didn't happen. If you do not have great pitching you cannot win the World Series!

Halloran: And it's not just the top two guys. The Red Sox have been close to the Yankees over the past 10 years, but the Yankees have had a guy who comes out of the bullpen every night and closes out games. And now the Red Sox have one of those guys.

Safreed: Their guy blew it – twice – and our guy was spectacular.

Halloran: Lonnie's on the car phone. What do you have for us, Lonnie?

Lonnie: Just 'living la vida loca' guys! I can't get over how quickly the Red Sox were on the verge of writing another Shakespearean tragedy, and then Bing, Bang, Boom, they run off eight straight wins. They were a juggernaut! There's inspiration here, guys. Anyone facing nearly impossible odds should be able to look at what just transpired and never stop believing that things can get better.

Eileen heard those words and thought about her son upstairs. She looked at Glenn who was suddenly rushing to get ready. He was supposed to have this day off. Instead, he was wolfing down the final bites of an English muffin, and gulping his coffee. They'd be leaving for the hospital soon, and there was no telling when he'd be able to eat again.

Halloran: Yup, all they need is 125-million dollars, and their lives can be as good as the Red Sox. I feel inspired already.

Lonnie: You know what I mean. Forget the money involved. Just pay attention to the circumstances. This Red Sox story is ours, but it's not ours alone. People every-where can take something out of it. You know, I may have over-stated it a little bit, but I woke my 6-year-old up so he could see the final few outs last night. And when I put him back to bed I said, 'You're going to wake up in a better world tomorrow'.

Halloran: Because the Red Sox won the world is a better place? How do you figure that?

Lonnie: Because hope was rewarded. And people will see that, and they'll change the way they approach their lives.

Halloran: Nobody's changing over this, Lonnie. I hate to break it to you, but no-body's changing. They're going to smile around New England for a few days, and then they're going right back to the way things were.

Safreed: I don't know about that, Bob. There's an edge that's missing, and I think it's gone for good. What happens if in like 50 years, the Red Sox haven't won another World Series, and Yankee fans start chanting '2004' like they used to chant '1918'? Don't you think you'd be O.K. with that, you know, because of what just happened?

Halloran: Short answer, no. In fact, if the Yankees win next year and then they start chanting '2004', it's gonna bother me. Nothing's changed. Our need to beat the Yankees remains pathological. We're up on them right now, but if we don't stay here, you'll hear the criticisms and the boos and the dissatisfaction start all over again. Chad in Everett, welcome to "Sports Overtime".

Chad: Hey, guys. I've been a fan all my life, and I could have lived with just be-ing able to shove it down New York Chokees fans' throats. But getting the whole enchilada is just the icing on the cake. You know what I mean?

Safreed: You're happy. I get it.

Chad: Not just happy. I was so happy I almost kissed my sister-in-law. I'm going to enjoy the rest of this day. Good luck to you guys, and thank you.

Jimmy wasn't surprised. In fact, he hadn't even completely unpacked his travel bag since he'd been home. In the back of his mind he always assumed he'd be heading back to the hospital at some point. He just didn't think it would be this soon, and he hated that it was impinging on his World Series moment. "Oh well, at least I was home when it happened."

Halloran: I can't believe this. Have you seen this, Fred?

Safreed: Seen what?

Halloran: There were 10,021 fans at the Celtics pre-season game last night at the FleetCenter. These people actually went to a pre-season game instead of watching the World Series? Unbelievable!

Safreed: Maybe that's how many bought tickets, but maybe only about a hundred people actually showed up.

Halloran: They should have just canceled the thing due to lack of interest. Karl in Malden?

Karl: Hey guys! Can you do me a favor and deliver a message to Grady Little? Tell him the lesson's over!

Halloran: You think he learned anything the past couple of weeks?

Karl: Probably not, but that's all right. All is forgiven. The only thing I wish I could change now is my big moment when the Sox won. All I did was clap my hands and pump my fist. I should have been running around the house buck-naked screaming, 'Free at last. Thank God almighty, I'm free at last!'

Safreed: If it's any consolation, I think you made the right choice.

Halloran: Yeah, you never want to run with scissors or when you're naked. You don't want the paramedics showing up and wondering what the heck was going on.

Safreed: And all this begs the question, you watch the games naked?

Karl: No, it's just that I've got a friend who's doing a lot of cleaning up today. He celebrated like the Red Sox did by pouring beer and champagne over all his guests. But unlike the Red Sox, he forgot to put up all that plastic to protect his furniture and rugs. He says his house smells like a fraternity right now, but he wouldn't change it for the world. I wish I had done something like that to have that moment to remember.

Safreed: You'll always remember. We will all always remember where we were when the Red Sox won their first World Series in 86 years.

Halloran: So, keep that in mind, and keep your clothes on. O.K., Karl? Whitey's next from South Boston.

Whitey: I thought the Red Sox left too many men on base, and they definitely could have won by more if they started Mientkiewicz.

Safreed: Are you kidding me?

Whitey: Yes, I'm only kidding. Just didn't want all the negativity to go away over night.

Safreed: Good, because anyone who whines today ain't got no soul!

Whitey: Agreed. In fact, I just wanted to say thanks to the Red Sox for not making my kids suffer as long as I did. There is a whole new generation that will grow up as optimists.

Halloran: We can hope.

Whitey: That's what I mean. You're talking to a guy who found out the day after last year's Game Seven that his wife had breast cancer. Friends found out and they came over and saw how depressed we were, and they couldn't believe it when we said we were more bummed about the Red Sox than the diagnosis. We knew my wife would be fine, and she is, but we didn't know if the Red Sox would ever be fine. It's a great day! Hey, Curt, thanks for playing 'wicked haaahd when you come to the paaaahk'. And Bucky Dent can kiss my hairy ass!

Safreed: Mine, too.

Halloran: Might as well pucker up for mine, too.

Eileen had finished cleaning up the kitchen and turned the radio off.

Whitey: Isn't this just the best. When Foulke grabbed the ball, I jumped up from my seat. And then when Mientkiewicz caught it, I fell to my knees, and I just had no idea how to react. Finally, it hit me. I went outside and heard the celebrations beginning to pour into the streets. So, I pulled my car into the driveway.

She could still hear the radio program, though just faintly, and wondered where it was coming from.

Halloran: Ha! Good move. Any car on the street is just ripe for the tipping.

Whitey: I've been trying to figure out how much money I've spent over the years on the Red Sox. It's got to be into the thousands for parking alone. Then you add up the tickets, and beer, and sweatshirts and everything, it's like a college tuition. So, I'm pretty happy today, but I didn't want to lose my car over it.

Suddenly, she remembered Jimmy was on hold. The radio was still coming through the phone.

Halloran: I know it. Red Sox fans were out there acting like they hadn't won anything in a while. Can you imagine? We've only got time for one or two more calls. We haven't heard from Ben from Franklin in a while. Ben, what's up?

Ben: I thought the only things certain in this world were death and taxes, and a Red Sox collapse. I'm glad the Red Sox won, but if one certainty had to be crossed off the list, I wouldn't have minded if it were taxes.

Safreed: Not death?

Ben: No, who wants to live forever, especially now that the Red Sox have won the World Series. Now, it's O.K. to die.

She heard the words in the receiver, and was just about to hang up...

Halloran: Not that we're recommending it. Jimmy from Boston, it's your turn at the plate.

(pause)

Safreed: C'mon, kid. Speak up. We're up against the clock.

Eileen: Oh, hi. Um, this is Jimmy's mother, Eileen. He can't come to the phone right now.

Halloran: Mother Nature calling, huh?

Eileen: Not exactly. To be honest with you he's packing to go to the hospital.

Halloran: What's wrong? I hope it's nothing serious.

Eileen: Oh, it's very serious. He's been battling leukemia for a few years, and this year he had a bone marrow transplant. It's been just awful for him. He was so sick we almost lost him a couple of times. Jimmy might not want you to know, but I'm telling you this, because I want you guys to know how much you've meant to him. He listened to you every day, and some days it was the only thing that made him truly happy. So, I want to thank you for that.

Safreed: Wow! We had no idea. Is he going to be all right?

Eileen: We believe he will. Nobody's giving up, I can tell you that. The doctors can't give us any guarantees that he's going to be around to see a lot of his dreams come true, but one of his dreams came true last night, and we're so thankful for that. Pulling for the Red Sox gave him something to live for, and to fight for. And watching them do something against such improbable odds, well, I just know it has to help him believe in his own possibilities.

Halloran: I really don't know what to say. I mean, we've really grown fond of Jimmy, and we just never had a clue. Now, I'm thinking instead of just being a smart kid, he's an amazing kid.

Eileen: Yes, he is.

Safreed: Hey, you tell Jimmy that if the Red Sox can win the World Series, then anything can happen. And his goal should be to see them win it again.

204

Halloran: Even if it takes another 86 years.

Eileen: That's what we pray for; another miracle.

Halloran: They do happen. We've all seen it with our own eyes.

Eileen: Jimmy's proof of that. Again, thanks to the both of you for letting Jimmy be part of your show. He walked on air after he was on with you.

Halloran: It was our pleasure. And Eileen, I'm sorry. Please give our best to Jimmy, and let us know if there's anything we can do. And you tell that kid we expect to hear from him when spring training rolls around. I like as many callers as possible to pummel Fred in an argument.

Safreed: I'll be ready for him next year.

Eileen: Thanks very much. We can't wait till next year!

Jimmy dropped his bag in the kitchen. He had been listening to the tail end of his mother's conversation. He didn't hear her tell Bob and Fred about his illness, but he could quickly discern whom she was speaking with. "So, you're the radio star now. Is that it?" he said.
"No, just a stand in. They'd much rather talk to you."

Halloran: Isn't that funny. Red Sox fans have been saying 'Wait till next year' for years and years. And now it's going to be 'We can't wait till next year'.

Safreed: And we'll always have last year. It's remarkable. The World Series itself is relatively forgettable. There were just these four quick drama free games. What happened during those games, I don't know if anyone will remember. Instead, we'l remember only THAT they won, and we'll remember how it affected us each individually, and Red Sox Nation as a whole.

Halloran: In the end, that's what this has all been about, the Holy Grail. It was a quest for so many. And some people lived to see it, experience it, to taste it. And some people didn't. And I guess some of the people who lived to see it, won't live to tell about it either. But it was a dream for people like Jimmy, and it was a dream for millions more. And on this day, for all of them, life is good. The Red Sox are World Series Champions. And maybe the fellowship is a little less miserable.

Safreed: I can attest to that. I didn't get flipped off once on my way to work today.

Halloran: And that's all the proof you need. We'll be back with more on the "Red Sox Are Champions" special edition of "Sports Overtime" right after this.

(President Thomas Whitmore from *Independence Day*): We are fighting for our right to live. To exist. And should we win the day, the Fourth of July will no longer be known as an American holiday, but as the day the world declared in one voice: 'We will not go quietly into the night! We will not vanish without a fight!' We're going to live on! We're going to survive! Today we celebrate our Independence Day!

CHAPTER THIRTEEN
Platelets and Patriots

On the way to the hospital, Jimmy was thinking about a water hose. More precisely, he was thinking about the especially hot summer days when he and Mark would play in the backyard. It was a long time ago, but the memory was still fresh.

While Jimmy stood in his bathing suit waiting to be showered with freezing cold water, Mark would intermittently squeeze and release the hose. There were long durations when Jimmy waited and begged for the beautiful torture of a cold blast of water on a humid New England day. Mark took his time, bending the hose in half, preventing the flow of relief that his brother craved. There was no cruel intent in this exercise, only the mildly excruciating delay of the desired affect. That was part of the game. Finally, Mark would release his pinch on the hose, and the cascade of water would nearly knock Jimmy to the ground. This would continue until large puddles of mud formed in the yard, and the boys were called in for lunch or supper.

The reason that memory flashed so vividly in Jimmy's mind was because his nose was bleeding like the water hose. There was nothing, then a large gush followed by nothing again. His bleeding was of frightening concern to the Macombers. Over the years, they had become quite adept at recognizing when it was the right time to worry. They were worried.

Dr. Fitzpatrick was, too. The Macombers could see it in his face, and they could hear it in his words.

"There's an awful lot that we have to rule out first," he said. "Right now, I'm happy that you haven't reported any blood in your urine. So, we're not thinking about hemorrhagic cystitis. You're also not showing any obvious signs of diffuse alveolar hemorrhage. Both of these are life threatening complications of excessive bleeding."

The words were meant to be a relief, but the Macombers had come to know how Dr. Fitzpatrick presented his information. He liked to first tell them all the bad things it wasn't, and then tell them the bad thing that it was. They were still waiting to find out what the bad thing was this time.

"Thrombocytopenia," he blurted out. "I know you're waiting to hear what the trouble is, and while we're waiting for your blood tests to come back to confirm it, I feel pretty confident that it's thrombocytopenia."

"Platelets, huh, Doc," Jimmy said.

"Exactly. As you know, platelets help with the clotting process, and if you don't have enough of them, you're likely to start bleeding. That's what brought you in here today."

Dr. Fitzpatrick went on to explain that the platelet count in the circulating blood is normally between 150,000 and 400,000 per microliter of blood. Bleeding doesn't usually occur until there are less than 100,000 platelets per microliter. The way Jimmy's nose was hemorrhaging, the doctor anticipated his platelet count might be as low as 10,000. Dr. Fitzpatrick also noted the tiny red dots on Jimmy's skin. That was petechiae caused by broken blood vessels and leaks in the capillary wall. Jimmy didn't have any noticeable bruising, and since Immune Thrombocy-topenic Purpura (ITP) is a diagnosis of elimination, Dr. Fitzpatrick had to order a series of tests to rule out all other causes of low platelets.

Among those tests would be a bone marrow aspiration. Platelets are produced in the bone marrow, so the aspiration is done to confirm that the platelet production process is working properly. Jimmy was asleep before a needle was pushed through his hip bone and into the marrow. Once again, some of his marrow was suctioned out and examined.

Within a few days, Dr. Fitzpatrick diagnosed Jimmy's condition as ITP. He explained to the Macombers that ITP is commonly associated with chemotherapy drugs, and occasionally associated with chronic graft versus host disease. He didn't yet know the severity of the problem.

"I'm sorry to say it, Jimmy, but welcome back to the hospital. Get comfortable and we'll get you back home as soon as possible."

His words fell a little short of being reassuring. Glenn and Eileen had heard from other parents about ITP. Low platelets can cause dangerous bleeding in the lungs, the intestines and the brain. They knew that multiple blood transfusions combined with assorted IV fluids and medications could lead to fluid overload. They believed that's what caused Jimmy's bouts with pneumonia, and they feared that another onset of pneumonia along with ITP could be fatal. They also knew that his many complications, and the insane amount of drugs Jimmy had taken over the past 9 months would likely lead to further complications down the road. There was nothing reassuring about being back in the hospital.

The reason Jimmy had a low platelet count is that the platelets were being destroyed by either his liver or his spleen. Once it was determined Jimmy's spleen was functioning properly and that a splenectomy would not be required, Dr. Fitz-patrick considered starting Jimmy on prednisone. It's a steroid that suppresses the immune system and has been beneficial to many people in treating ITP. But predni-sone can also cause weight gain, joint aches, and gastritis. Long term it can contrib-ute to osteoporosis, high blood pressure and diabetes. Ultimately, Dr. Fitzpatrick felt Jimmy's ITP could be successfully treated with a small dose of prednisone and other steroids along with intravenous gamma globulin. The steroids prevent bleed-ing by decreasing the rate of platelet destruction, and often produce an increase in platelet counts within two to three weeks. The IV gamma globulin is a protein that also slows the destruction of platelets. It can work even more quickly.

The treatments worked well and with limited side effects. His platelet count continued to rise, but very slowly. Jimmy was in the hospital for six weeks. And during his month and a half in the hospital, Jimmy listened to the radio, surfed the Internet, and tried to keep up with a school curriculum geared toward a high school freshman or sophomore. He also learned that his friend, Tom, had died.

Tom had engrafted successfully, but developed acute graft versus host disease. The complications were sudden and severe and he died on day 57. News spread around the hospital quickly. Every child there was forced to confront what could be their future as well. Every family battled the guilt of feeling just a little bit relieved that it wasn't their child. Every doctor, nurse, and hospital employee was forced to deal with the loss of another special child. It was especially tough on them. The patients were resilient.

Jimmy was at his strongest at times like this. His resolve magnified. His determination intensified. He was unfaltering in his resoluteness to make sure that didn't happen to him. He had come too far, suffered too much. His parents needed him too much. If he died now, what was it all for?

Jimmy mourned briefly and then looked forward. The days passed, and while he spent Thanksgiving in the hospital, he was home in time for Christmas. He was there to celebrate New Year's Eve and New Year's Day, and on the very next day, he watched the Patriots wrap up a wonderful 14-2 season. He enjoyed a healthy January and celebrated the Patriots playoff victories over the Indianapolis Colts and Pittsburgh Steelers. And just as he had done a year ago, he sat with his family and watched the Patriots play in the Super Bowl. This time the Patriots would face the Philadelphia Eagles. And this time, Jimmy watched the entire game, including an uneventful, family friendly half-time show.

It was almost a year since his bone marrow transplant, and Jimmy was still around, still smiling. His favorite teams were winners, and so was he.

"Sports Overtime" Show Open, February 7, 2005

Announcer: This is "Sports Overtime" on WTED, the best sports radio station in America. And we've got the best football team to go along with our number one baseball team. Loserville has been re-named. We're Title Town now!

Galadriel from *Lord of the Rings*: The world is changed. I feel it in the water. I feel it in the earth. I smell it in the air. Much that once was, is lost, for none now live who remember it.

Fred Venkman from *Ghost Busters*: We came. We saw. We kicked its ass!

Announcer: The Patriots have won back-to-back Super Bowls. That's three championships in four years if you're counting, and we are. And that means you can start using that word that begins with a "D" and has a little "nasty" in it. The Patriots are a dynasty!

Earl Keese from *Neighbors*: You're really wonderful!

Ramona: That's what I've been trying to tell you. Is it so hard having your fantasies come to life?

Announcer: While the Eagles quarterback was choking – literally. He was dry heaving in the huddle....

Homer from *The Simpsons:* Uh-oh, here comes the gospel according to puke!

Announcer: ...the Patriots quarterback was winning his third Super Bowl. Tom Brady is the Lord of the Rings!

Gandalf from *Lord of the Rings:* One ring to rule them all; one ring to find them. One ring to keep them all, and in the darkness bind them.

Announcer: Yeah, well, whatever! If that means we're the center of the sports universe now, then it sounds good to me. We're the best! Let some other fans in some other city whine and complain. We've had an extreme makeover, and it was long overdue.

Frasier from *Frasier:* I know how bleak these times can be, but believe me, they will come to an end sometime or later. I remember a time back in Boston I was going through exactly what you're going through now.

Announcer: We've got Bob Halloran and Fred "Freddie the Fredderman" Safreed sitting up properly in our studio once again.

Ray Barone from *Everybody Loves Raymond:* Uhh! It smells like a skunk that came out of the ass of another skunk.

Announcer: Our big fellas are back from their luxurious confines in Jacksonville, Florida, where they just witnessed the coronation of the Patriots as the newest football royalty. They also had a chance to sit down for a chat with Tom Brady, and they were smart enough to tape the interview so you'll be able to hear what he said.

Frank Barone from *Everybody Loves Raymond:* I could have eaten a box of Alpha-Bits and crapped a better interview.

Announcer: And of course, we want to hear from all of you. It's another day of celebration in New England, and we're assuming that will bring the best out of our happy and dignified listeners. Of course, we've been wrong before.

Lilith from *Cheers*: Incidentally, I've taken your little wisecracks for a few years now, you hideous gargoyle, and if you ever open that gateway to hell you call a mouth in my direction again, I'll snap off your extremities like dead branches and feed them to you at gunpoint.

Announcer: Anyway, there was a time when the Red Sox were flotsam, and the Patriots were jetsam. But our bottom feeders are now at the top of the sports food chain. Kinda makes you wonder how New England climbed up from the bottom rung of society.

Homer from *The Simpsons*: I think it was when that cold snap killed off all the hoboes.

Announcer: However it happened, it's a whole new world. And it feels good, don't it?

Bilbo from *Lord of the Rings: Fellowship of the Ring*: I've thought of an ending for my book – "And he lived happily ever after... to the end of his days."

Announcer: Here now, it's "Sports Overtime" with Bob...

Norm from *Cheers*: It's a dog eat dog world, and I'm wearing Milkbone underwear.

Announcer: ... and Fred.

Homer from *The Simpsons*: How come they can put a man on the moon, but can't make my shoes smell good?

Halloran: Quite an introduction there today, Fred. They had you smelling twice.

Safreed: I don't think I smell.

Halloran: Strong defense. Just keep your shoes on, all right? Hey, this is some pretty amazing stuff that's been happening around here. First it was the Patriots, then the Red Sox, and now the Patriots again. Three championships in twelve months.

Safreed: It's like a championship sandwich.

Halloran: Yes, an Oreo cookie of success, if you will.

Safreed: Who else is getting hungry?

Halloran: I doubt Donovan McNabb is hungry. He certainly wouldn't be able to hold his cookies the way he was choking yesterday. Have you seen some of the reports that say he was dry-heaving in the huddle? I mean, we've heard of guys that get nervous and maybe throw up BEFORE a game, but usually once the game starts they calm down and get to work. Not McNabb apparently. He's bringing a whole new meaning to the term "choke job".

Safreed: They must really be throwing him under the bus in Philly today. He looked awful in that game, didn't he? I mean, even in the first half. By the time the game's over people forget that interception he threw around the goal line in the first quarter. The Eagles were looking at at least three points there, and he just lobbed it up for Rodney Harrison to run under it. Look at the final score. That pick was big.

Halloran: And he apparently didn't start literally gagging until the fourth quarter.

Safreed: Makes me glad for the umpteenth time that we've got Brady as our quarterback. First there was "Joe Cool", and now there's "Tom Cool".

Halloran: He just finds a way to win. Let's find out what's on the minds of our listeners today. We'll start with Martin in Lawrence.

Martin: Man, these are some bad boys all right. Last year, they were bad boys for sure. And this year they were bad boys, too.

Halloran: Whatcha gonna do?

Jimmy heard the opening minutes of the show from the backseat of his father's car. He was on his way back to the Dana Farber clinic.

Martin: I mean those guys play like they've got nothing to lose. They do the right things, and I'm sure they're thinking, what's the worst that could happen? That's the way to do it. They are the perfect team with a capital "T" little "-eam".

Safreed: No doubt they're the most balanced team in the NFL. They can run and throw on offense. They stop the run and the pass on defense. They've got great special teams, and the best clutch kicker in the history of the game. Simply the best, that's what they are.

Jimmy was fine, great actually. But when the Patriots won the Super Bowl, their

212

victory parade was scheduled for Tuesday, which just happened to be when Jimmy's regularly scheduled check-ups were. He was a Tuesday kid now. Glenn wanted nothing to do with trying to drive into the city with millions of football fans lining the streets and making it nearly impossible to get around. So, he called and had Jimmy's visit switched to today.

Martin: But that's why I don't much like you guys talking about McNabb and the Eagles choking. That sort of takes credit away from the Patriots, you know? If the other team gags, it's like any team could have beaten them. You guys did the same thing with Peyton Manning in the first round of the playoffs, and you did it with the Red Sox in October. You think it's funny, and I guess it is to some extent, that the Yankees were guilty of the baseball's biggest choke. But...

Safreed: Not just baseball's biggest choke. It was the biggest choke in the history of all sports.

Martin: Yeah, but I like to think the Red Sox dug down deep and willed themselves to victory. I say give credit to the other team and it makes your team that much more impressive.

Safreed: Hey, all we can do is analyze the game honestly. And if it's obvious the Patriots played great, we'll say it. But they didn't really have their best game. So, how'd they win? Well, the defense kept them in it long enough for the offense to come around, AND the Eagles made critical mistakes in key situations.

Halloran: Or to put it another way, they choked!

Safreed: It happens to a lot of teams, and again, that's why you need a quarterback who can be a rock solid steadying force like Brady. The guy's Joe Montana. That's all there is to it.

Halloran: All right, Fred. If you're through with the ball washing for a minute, we'll talk to Don in Adams.

Don: You've got to get smart, Fred. Brady's a great quarterback, but he's no Montana, not yet anyway.

"This is what has always bothered me about talk radio," Glenn asserted. "This guy's gonna end up ripping Brady by proving he's not as good as Montana. Why can't they say both quarterbacks are great, and just leave it as a positive?"
"Yeah, especially today," Jimmy concurred.

Safreed: But he's well on his way. He's only 27 and he only needs one more Super Bowl, and one more Super Bowl MVP to tie Montana. And you're crazy if you don't think he can get that done, and maybe even surpass it.

Don: He's got a chance. I'll admit that. But Montana threw eleven touchdown passes with zero interceptions in his four Super Bowls. Brady's got six touchdowns and one interception, not to mention the fumble yesterday, in his three Super Bowls. It's no knock on Brady, but it's pretty hard to match the Super Bowl performances of Montana.

Safreed: Another guy who likes to come at you with meaningless stats. Montana led his team to victory, and that's what Brady's doing. Case closed. If Brady does it again, he's right there with the greatest quarterbacks who ever played the game.

Don: Hey, I'm a huge fan, too. I'm just saying that Montana's a pretty tough comparison. Did you know that during 1988, '89, and '90, Montana won seven straight playoff games, and that during those games he threw 20 touchdown passes and only two interceptions?

Safreed: Seven wins in a row is nice, but it's not nine in a row like Brady, is it?

Don: Nope, but Brady's performances seem more like Troy Aikman's who also won three Super Bowls in four years, and was what you might call an efficient quarterback like Brady.

Halloran: Can you handle that for now, Fred? Can Brady be Aikman for a while and then be Montana some time later? Would that be all right?

Safreed: Yeah, that would be O.K., I guess.

"Well, that wasn't so bad after all," Glenn affirmed. "Are you going to call in today?"

Timmy shook his head and left it at that.

Halloran: There does seem to be an awful rush to put players and teams in a category for the best of all time. Tiger Woods was going to break all of Jack Nicklaus's records, but he's slowed down a lot in that quest. Brady's Montana. Belichick is Lombardi. The Patriots are a dynasty. I mean, c'mon, the requirements for being a dynasty keep getting easier and easier.

Safreed: The Cowboys of the 90's were a dynasty, so that makes the Patriots one, too.

Halloran: That's right. But the Niners won five Super Bowls in thirteen years. The Steelers won four Super Bowls in six years. The Celtics won 11 championships in thirteen years. The Yankees won 26 championships in the 1900's. Those were some of the first teams to be considered dynasties. Now, you can get it done in four years. I mean what if the Patriots lost the Super Bowl this year, but won it next year. Is three in five years a dynasty? How about three in six? It's all so arbitrary. And why is that label so important?

Safreed: Because fans want their team to be considered one of the greats. The Patriots have done that. Brady's done it. And Belichick has done it. They're all reaching the bar that was set by the greats of the past.

Halloran: But are they? It looks like they're approaching the bar, maybe bellying up to it, but they're not quite there. Yet it seems like everyone around here wants to grant them admission into the club for greatest team ever maybe a few years too soon. People who watched Ted Williams play like to think they saw the greatest hitter ever. And they feel connected to that time. Today, some kid's gonna think Barry Bonds is the greatest hitter ever, and maybe he feels that way just because he wants it to be true that he's living in some fabulous period of baseball history. I don't know. Walt's in Whitman. Good afternoon, Walt.

Walt: O Captain! My Captain! Our fearful trip is done. Sorry to wax poetic for a moment. Gentleman, how are you? I celebrate myself on this great, great day. It never gets old.

Safreed: Losing got old, not winning.

Walt: Right you are. And you know, I'm originally from Long Island, and we had a nice little dynasty going with the Islanders there for a while. They won four Stanley Cups in a row in the early 80's. So, naturally, I'd compare this Patriot dynasty to that one. And while by today's standards, the Patriots are a dynasty, I don't think three titles really gets it done.

Halloran: So, you don't think if the Islanders had stopped at three in a row that they would have been a dynasty?

Walt: I don't know. It's hard to say. I think I'd say it was.

Halloran: Well, which is it? Does three make a dynasty, or not?

Walt: I'm not sure. Do I contradict myself? Very well then I contradict myself.

Halloran: You see, Fred, that's the problem. Nobody really knows how to define what a dynasty is. So, whenever a team gets close, its fans want to grab hold of the word and coronate their team.

Safreed: What's wrong with that?

Halloran: Well, it cheapens it. We used to have dynasties like the Islanders, or the Bulls who won six NBA titles in eight years. Then it was the Cowboys who won three in four years. You can't keep lowering the bar, lowering the standards, for what constitutes a dynasty, or else you'll end up watering it down.

Safreed: But it's almost impossible to have a run like the Celtics or the Montreal Canadiens had. Free agency changed the whole landscape in sports, and especially in the NFL where the whole system is built around having parity. They try to prevent dynasties. That's what makes what the Patriots have done so remarkable.

Halloran: Yeah, we say that about free agency, yet the Broncos won back-to-back. The Packers went to the Super Bowl in back-to-back years. The Rams went twice in three years. And even the Eagles have gone to the NFC Championship game four years in a row. Certainly, what the Patriots have done in winning three titles is remarkable, but a lot of other teams have sustained a high level of play for several years in a row. Maybe it's not so much harder today than it was way back when after all.

Safreed: Maybe not. I can see that, especially when you consider the Patriots won the Super Bowl last year, and then they were able to go out and get a Pro Bowl caliber running back like Corey Dillon.

Jimmy had taken a moment to consider his words and then decided to tell his father: "I don't really feel the need to call in anymore," he confessed. "When I was afraid of dying, I think I wanted to be a part of something big. I wanted to make an impact in the time I had. You know what I mean?"
This time it was Glenn who shook his head 'no'.

Halloran: That's right. Free agency may cause you to lose some players, but it also allows you to restock. Howie in the car, you're next on "The Ted" with Bob and Fred.

Howie: Hey Bob. Hey Fred. Usually, I'm the one taking calls. So, this is kind of nice. Anyway, I'd like to herald the accomplishments of the head coach. You call Brady a modern day Montana. I call Belichick a modern day Vince Lombardi.

Safreed: That comparison's already out there, especially now that Belichick's post-season record is 10-and-1, compared to Lombardi's 9-and-1.

Halloran: But because of the extra rounds in the playoffs, Belichick only has three titles, while Lombardi won five.

Howie: I thought Lombardi only won the first two Super Bowls.

Halloran: Yes, but he won three NFL titles before they started playing Super Bowls. And there's no doubt that Belichick is the best coach in the NFL today, but his playoff record is a little deceiving, because ostensibly he gets to play a couple of games against Wild Card teams or non-championship caliber teams before he gets to the Super Bowl. Lombardi's first three titles only included a total of four games, so he went right up against the very best. This was all in the paper today, Howie.

Howie: I guess I'll have to start reading the paper a little more. Thanks for the call.

Safreed: You called us, remember?

"I guess I just never got the impression you were afraid of dying," Glenn said. "We were afraid of losing you, but you always took everything in stride. You've been incredible that way."
"I was afraid, Dad. I still am sometimes. But now it feels just like it did when I was in remission. Things are starting to normalize. You can tell when the doctors and nurses come around. They're not pretending to be upbeat anymore. They really are."

Halloran: Robert in Palmer is calling us now. What's up, Robert?

Robert: I think this Patriot team is simply irresistible! They've got every kinda people on both sides of the ball. Everyone flying around doing whatever they can to help the team. It's like they just strap on the helmets and say 'Let's get it on'.

Safreed: I know, you can tell a lot about certain teams when the heat gets turned up come playoff time. Some like it hot, and then there's Peyton Manning and the Colts.

"Anyway," Jimmy added, *"this show gave me what I needed most. It was always tomorrow. No matter what I was going through, I knew that these guys would be there the next day, and I wanted to be there, too. And when I started calling in, it was just that much better. Looking forward to this show made me forget about looking back and made it easier to live in the present. You know what I mean?"*
This time Glenn nodded.

Halloran: Manning can't seem to handle it when the heat's right up in his face, but he doesn't like to play in the cold weather either. He's like Goldie Locks. Not too hot, and not too cold. Everything has to be just right.

Robert: I agree with you there. But it's not just Manning. It's all of the Colts. And all of the Patriots are just the opposite. They're just the model team in all of sports right now. Look at what happened early in that game yesterday. The Patriots offense only got one first down in their first four possessions. If Manning was that ineffective, he might find himself down by a couple of touchdowns, because his defense is so bad. But the Patriot defense forced two Philly turnovers, and the Patriots had time to get it together on offense and win the game.

Safreed: Well, that's Brady being able to figure things out, and then make the plays he has to make. That's the difference between him and Manning.

Robert: Fred, we all know you sleep with a Brady doll, but that's not my point at all. Brady's a great player on a great team. Manning's a great player on the Colts. There's a big difference. The Patriots only scoring drive in the first half was 37-yards because the Eagle punter crapped the bed. But the score at the half was 7-7 because the Patriots defense and their punter kept the Patriots in the game. THEN Brady turned it on. But it took the entire team. And that's why I'm addicted to love when it comes to all of the Patriots. They're simply irresistible!

Halloran: So, you've said. Turn the record over, Robert. Now here's Willie in Sutton.

Willie: It's almost criminal the way you guys have ignored Deion Branch and the wide receivers today. That group of receivers is the most under-rated and under-appreciated group I've ever seen.

Halloran: That's probably because Brady spreads the ball around so much. No one gets to put up big numbers week after week.

Willie: Yeah, but if Branch didn't win the MVP this year, that would have been

218

robbery. In last year's Super Bowl, he caught 10 passes for 143 yards. This year it was 11 catches for 133 yards. That's incredible coming from a guy who only had one 100-yard game all season. These guys have come up huge on the biggest stage.

Halloran: Branch certainly has.

Willie: And what about David Givens. He only caught three touchdown passes all year, but now he's got the post-season record with touchdown catches in five straight games. That's what it's all about. They definitely raise the level of their game.

Safreed: And what nobody seems to notice about these guys is that they never seem to drop a catchable ball. They make plenty of spectacular catches, but they never just drop one where you're like, 'Oh, what was that!'

Halloran: And one of them is always open. Brady almost never throws to a covered receiver. And that's a testament to him and his ability to read the defenses and find the open man, but the fact remains, there's almost always an open man which means these receivers are very good at finding a seam or sitting down in front of zone coverage.

Safreed: Yeah, but Brady's still the guy delivering the ball.

Halloran: Yes, Fred. You can have your binkie. Brady is a golden god.

Safreed: Thank you, Bob. I always knew you'd come around.

"So, what are you going to do tomorrow?" Glenn asked.
"I guess I'll watch the parade on television. I know Dr. Fitzpatrick isn't going to let me mingle with a million people."
"Not yet anyway, but someday. Someday, Jimmy. You'll see. Things are finally starting to turn for us, for you."

Halloran: All right, we've got time for one or two more calls. Bill's in Clinton. Make it quick, Bill.

Bill: What a year it's been, gentlemen. What we've witnessed in the past 12 months – three championships – is nothing short of a miracle.

Halloran: A miracle? That might be a little strong. I don't know if anybody's rising up from the dead.

Bill: No, but blind men now see. People who could never see that their faith could be rewarded now know that sometimes great things come to those who wait. And while, yes, 'miracle' may be a bit of an over-statement, it's pretty darn close to a miracle when the psyche of an entire region, and an entire generation has been altered forever.

Safreed: You're not talking about an identity crisis, are you? All that stuff about New England fans not knowing how to act or who they are now that everything's going so well. Because that's nothing but the blathering of idiots.

Halloran: You're not an idiot, are you Bill?

Bill: I don't think so. And no, I'm definitely not talking about an identity crisis. I'm talking about people having a new belief system. People changing at their core. Miserable bastards becoming happy, shiny people. It's all going to be different from now on.

Halloran: We'll see. And we'll see what Jesse in Jackson, New Hampshire can add to this conversation. Jesse?

Jesse: I think what Bill was talking about for New England fans is a new iden-tity, and a new serenity. He was talking about joyousness replacing contentious-ness. About life finally being fair, without so much despair. He was talking about a brighter future for our children. And I'm talking about being able to keep hope alive!

Halloran: Keep it coming, Jesse!

Jesse: It's a change that's coming. Can't you see it?

Safreed: Show it to me, Jesse!

"Show it to us, Jesse!" Glenn shouted.

Jesse: Once there were generations of fans who watched their favorite teams. They cared for and nurtured those teams like babies from the time they were babies themselves. And as they grew, they only knew heartache. The Red Sox came so close so often only to fall short each and every time. The Patriots were a laugh-ingstock throughout the NFL. And when they finally squished the fish, they were squished themselves in the Super Bowl. Then they sunk even lower, and they al-most moved to St. Louis and Connecticut. Those were hard, hard times. Those two teams put their fans through the ringer. But a new bell is ringing today, people. Can you hear me?

Halloran: We can hear you, Jesse!

"Can I get an Amen?" Jimmy whooped.

Jesse: Well, listen up! Now it's all different. Hope has been replaced by faith. And make no mistake, they are not the same thing. For instance, Red Sox fans hoped for good things. Yankee fans had faith those good things would happen. They believed while we hoped. Now, a new generation is about to grow up with a new found faith. Some kid who's 12-years-old has experienced four championships since he was eight, and he has every reason to believe he'll see four more by the time he's twenty. And many more before he goes underground.

Halloran: I don't know, Jesse. Some fans won't be able to let go of their negative memories. They'll keep waiting for when things will change and we become Loser-ville again. They'll expect it to happen, and they'll be waiting to say I told you so.

Jesse: But they'll be waiting a long time. And then they'll die away. And that 12-year-old and all his friends will dominate the local sports mood. The children are our future, gentlemen. And those children are optimistic. And our future is bright. We are witnessing a change.

Halloran: I'm not so sure about that. Do you seriously think that all the negativity that used to permeate these airwaves is just going to stop overnight? People can't change that quickly. The negativity is down deep in their bones. That negativity's not going anywhere. Keep in mind, Celtic fans were treated to an incredible run in the 60's, and…

Jesse: Something everybody over the age of 50 can remember.

Halloran: …and then they had Bobby Orr in the 70's, and the Celtics were champions again in the 80's. It wasn't all bad. Fans didn't have to be defeatist. There was a bright side, you know.

Safreed: That's true. But if you take it a step further, the Bruins broke up when they should have won several more Cups. And Larry Bird got old in a hurry. Then Lenny Bias and Reggie Lewis died. DIED! Can you even fathom that? Two great athletes in the same franchise dying! And you don't think fans had a right to look at things in a negative light? What about injuries to Bruins like Gord Kluzak and Cam

Neely? It was like, even when things were going well, good fortune was snatched away. If you were inclined to look at it this way, it was just more proof that life isn't fair. Cripes, we even had to sit there and accept it when Ray Bourque left the Bruins in order to win a Stanley Cup in Colorado. It's like we all knew there was no way he was ever going to win one here, so he might as well go out and win it somewhere else. And then when he brought the Cup to Boston, we celebrated! We actually celebrated! God, what a pathetic bunch of losers we were!

Jesse: But our time has come. Our time has come. Suffering breeds character. Character breeds faith. In the end, faith will not disappoint. Our time has come. Our faith, hope, and dreams will prevail.

Halloran and Safreed: Our time has come!

Jesse: Weeping has endured for nights, but now joy cometh in the morning.

"Our time has come," Glenn and Jimmy proclaimed in unison.

Jesse: We come from disgrace to amazing grace.

"Our time has come!"

Halloran: And our time has come to say good-bye. The Patriots will have their parade through Boston tomorrow, and on Friday the Red Sox equipment truck will be loaded up and then it will head for Fort Myers and the start of spring training.

Safreed: It's great that the Patriots' extended season drops us right off on the cusp of the baseball season. No down time.

Halloran: Literally. Nobody's down at any time these days. But we'll see how long it lasts. The Red Sox go into the new season without Pedro Martinez, without Derek Lowe, and without all those guys they got in the deadline deals last July who made such big contributions, Dave Roberts, Orlando Cabrera and Doug Mientkiewicz.

Safreed: A lot of turnover for a championship team.

Halloran: So, it's going to be very interesting to see what the Red Sox get out of their three new starters -- an aging David Wells, an underachieving Matt Clement, and an injured Wade Miller.

Safreed: Plus, Schilling's coming off ankle surgery.

Halloran: Sent that bloody sock to the Hall of Fame. So, we'll see. We'll just have to see how long the good feelings last. Maybe we should have an office pool predicting when the first Red Sox player will be booed, and who it will be.

Safreed: I'm in for Manny Ramirez right after the All-Star break.

Halloran: Uh-oh. Do you think we're being too negative anticipating problems like that?

Safreed: No, I just think that somewhere in between pessimistic and optimistic is realistic. And we'd be foolish to think we're not going to end up on a speeding train to disappointment somewhere down the line. It'll happen sometime, but in the meantime....

Halloran: You're miserable without misery, aren't you?

Safreed: I'm fine, Mr. Clever With Words. In fact, I'm better than fine. I'm feeling great today!

Halloran: And so is the rest of New England.............today.

EPILOGUE

Former Boston Celtic head coach Rick Pitino dubbed Boston's sports talk radio culture specifically, and by association, the fans of New England as the "fellowship of the miserable". With three championships to celebrate in twelve months, and more titles since then, those fans are a little less tormented today.

But in truth, the real fellowship of the miserable is the cancer patients and their families. They don't show it. Their misery is well hidden, but it's constantly infecting their lives. They smile in wonderment at the little miracles that occur every day. They thank God for the blessed moments that are too few and far between. And they show tremendous courage in everything they do. These are the people who have endured prolonged suffering, not disappointed sports fans. Their misery is incessant. It is unmerciful, and it is palpable every time a child or loved one dies prematurely in some incredibly weakened, tiny, and frail state. The misery of a sports fan is the stuff of hyperbole. It is self-induced, overstated, and easily remedied. They are the fellowship of the whiney and the self-indulgent. They are a group who feels a sense of entitlement simply because they choose to root. But they will live to root another day. They are not miserable. They are merely temporarily disappointed. They live to complain. But they live.

Thankfully, the fellowship of cancer families, always supportive and united by their pain and prayers is becoming less miserable as more and more miracles are happening. More children are being cured than ever before. Hope is greater than it's ever been.

And so, as Jimmy returned from Dana Farber and sat in his backyard, breathing fresh air and running his fingers through his full head of hair, he thought about the Red Sox and the Patriots. He recalled some of his own most dire moments from the past year. He exalted in those special moments of celebration and each little victory along the way. He acknowledged that his health was good right now, but there was no guarantee it would stay that way. He considered the possibilities, even likelihoods, that he would have long term liver and kidney problems, high blood pressure, cataracts, and a myriad of other complications, including secondary cancers. But he smiled anyway. He drew another long, deep breath, and dreamed of the day that the real fellowship would no longer be miserable.

ACKNOWLEDGMENTS

This was quite a large undertaking, and it never would have come to fruition without the help of a great many people. In no particular order, those wonderful people include Alan Rubel, a new friend whose vision, dedication and altruism helped keep this project moving forward. He just wanted to do something good, and he was great at it.

Lisa Scherber at the Dana Farber Cancer Institute was there for me at the very beginning and at the very end. In between, she probably wondered what happened to me. You see, it was in the summer of 2005 that I went to her and asked for a tour of the facilities, which she graciously provided. She also connected me with a doctor to help me write about the medical and technical aspects of leukemia, bone marrow transplants, and the recovery process. Then I disappeared for five years.

During that time, I wrote the book, and tried and failed to get it published the traditional way. I put it aside while I wrote two other books. It wasn't until I received a phone call from Alan Rubel that I returned to The Fellowship of the No Longer Miserable and ultimately also returned to Lisa Scherber.

This time I asked Lisa if she knew of a boy I could put on the book's cover to represent not only the fictional character Jimmy Macomber, but the Jimmy Fund as well. Oh, and I needed another doctor to read the book and make sure what I had written about Jimmy's ordeal was plausible and medically accurate. So, I give special thanks to Dr. Christine Duncan.

R.J. Agostinelli is the happy, smiling face you see on the cover of this book. Thanks to him and his family for agreeing to that. They fight leukemia so bravely, they inspire all of us to be better than we thought we could be.

Several Proforma owners, Kevin Montecalvo, Russell Howarth, Charles Janosick, Andy Kaye, Ross Levine, Mark Resnick and Alan Rubel put up the money for the printing of the first five thousand books, and they took care of all the business stuff that I don't have much aptitude for. Thank you. Other people associated with Proforma, most notably, Jennifer Hogg and Cris Nigro, were amazingly helpful in expediting and improving the quality of this book. Special thanks to them.

My wife, Eileen Curran, not only helped in the development of the idea for this book, she helped edit it, and she believed in it, and as always, she believed in me.

My son, Sean Halloran, designed the cover. By the way, he's starting up his own graphic and web design business known as EyeOnFireDesign.

My son, Liam Halloran, alphabetized the Index for me. He's 12-years-old and I'm pretty sure he did a much better job than I would have.

My brother-in-law, Fred Safreed originated the idea of a sports talk radio book, and who let me use his name as one of the show hosts, even though I know the opinions expressed by his character are not shared by him.

Rebecca Friedman is my point person at the Jimmy Fund who handled the fundraising aspects of this project.

Thanks everyone! We did it!

INDEX

Clemens, Roger
Clement, Matt
Coleridge, Samuel
colonoscopy
Color of Money
Connecticut School of Broadcasting
Contreras, Jose
Crespo, Cesar
Curt in the car
Cyclosporine
Cystoscopy
Cytomegalovirus, CMV
Cytoxan

Damon, Johnny
Dana Farber Cancer Institute
Dangerfield, Rodney
Darren from Dalton
Daunorubicin
David from Wells
Dean, Howard
Deion from Warwick
Delhomme, Jake
Dent, Bucky
Denver Broncos
D.H. from Lawrence
Diamond, Neil
Die Hard
diffuse alveolar hemorrhage, DAH
Dilaudid
Dilfer, Trent
Dillon, Corey
DiMaggio, Joe
Dirty Rotten Scoundrels
Dodgeball
Don from Adams
Don from Sutton
Douglas from Adams
Drago, Dick
Dumb and Dumber
Dusty from Springfield

Earl from Monroe
Earl from Warren

Ebert, Roger
Ebony and Ivory
Eddie from Belmont
Ed from Norton
Edmunds, Jim
Elway, John
Epstein, Theo
Ericson, Mark
Everybody Loves Raymond
Evil Empire

Fellowship of the Miserable
Fenway Park
Fisk, Carlton
Fitzpatrick, Dr.
FleetCenter
Fletch
Florida Marlins
Fly, The
Foulke, Keith
FOX
Francona, Terry
Frasier
Fred from Lynn
Fred from Marion
Friday the 13th

Garciaparra, Nomar
Gedman, Rich
George from Clinton
George from Foster
Ghost Busters
Gibson, Bob
Givens, David
Glaus, Troy
glomerular filtration rate test
Godfather, Part Three
Goodwill Hunting
Graft versus host disease, GVHD
Griffey, Ken
Grinch, The
Guerrero, Vladimir
Gutierrez, Ricky

Samuel from Jackson
San Francisco Forty-Niners
Schilling, Curt
Schiraldi, Calvin
Scioscia, Mike
Scrubs
Sean from Salisbury
Seinfeld
Septra
Seymour, Richard
Shawshank Redemption
Sheffield, Gary
Shrek
Sierra, Ruben
Simon from Bridgewater
Simpsons, The
Six West
Smart, Rod
Smith, Steve
Southeast Expressway
Sports Overtime
Springsteen, Bruce
Spy Who Shagged Me, The
Stanley, Bob
staphlyococcus epidermis
Steinbrenner, George
Steve from Lawrence
St. Louis Cardinals
St. Louis Rams
Super Bowl
Sveum, Dale
Sweet Caroline
Swingers

Teminator, The
Terry from Franconia Notch
thalidomide
Thrombocytopenia
Tim from Conway
Tim from Wakefield
Timlin, Mike
Titanic
Tom from Becket

Torre, Joe
total body irradiation, TBI
Trivial Pursuit
Tweeter
Ty from Warren

U.S. Olympic hockey team, 1980

Varitek, Jason
Vazquez, Javier

Vinatieri, Adam
Vincristine

Walt from Whitman
Wayne's World
Weis, Charlie
Wells, David
Whitey from South Boston
What About Bob
Williams, Bernie
Williams, Ted
Willie from Nelson
Willie from Sutton
Willy Wonka
World Series
WTED

Yastrzemski, Carl
Young, Cy
Young, Dmitri

Zimmer, Don